W9-AFG-196

WORLD CLASS SCHOOLS

WORLD CLASS SCHOOLS

SCHOOLS

NEW STANDARDS FOR EDUCATION

Donald M. Chalker
Western Carolina University

Richard M. Haynes
Western Carolina University

TECHNOMIC
PUBLISHING CO., INC.

LANCASTER · BASEL

World Class Schools
a TECHNOMIC® publication

Published in the Western Hemisphere by
Technomic Publishing Company, Inc.
851 New Holland Avenue, Box 3535
Lancaster, Pennsylvania 17604 U.S.A.

Distributed in the Rest of the World by
Technomic Publishing AG
Missionsstrasse 44
CH-4055 Basel, Switzerland

Printed in the United States of America
10 9 8 7 6 5 4 3 2

Main entry under title:
    World Class Schools: New Standards for Education

A Technomic Publishing Company book
Bibliography: p. 251
Includes index p. 257

Library of Congress Catalog Card No. 94-60606
ISBN No. 1-56676-144-1

To two world class families:
The Chalker family and the Haynes family.

Contents

Authors Donald M. Chalker and Richard M. Haynes, in their excellent *World Class Schools: New Standards for Education,* have tackled head-on the question most comparative education specialists shy away from—what features of ten national school systems are best and why? How do United States schools compare? Where do they fall short? United States schools are compared critically with those in Britain, Canada, France, the former Federal Republic of Germany, Japan, New Zealand, Republic of China (Taiwan), Korea, and Israel.

Specific factors the authors compare, factors that make the reader ponder beyond what is covered, include *educational expenditures* (which countries spend what amounts per pupil, how and why?), *time on task* (student instruction in classrooms per day and school year), *class size* (large, medium, small; does it make a difference, if so, how and why?), *teachers* (selection, professional preparation, placement, problems, conditions of service, and pay scale), *students* (family and other socio-economic-political background), *curriculum* (what knowledge is of most worth? what subjects are taught, how, and why?), *assessing student achievement* (student testing—when? at what stages? and how valid are the tests?), *school governance* (who makes educational policy, why, how, toward what ends, and how are these policies administered at each school level?), and *parents, home, and community* (expectations and degree of parental involvement and help).

The authors also use as a test case of significant recent national school reform the experience of British education before and since the precedent-breaking Education Reform Act of 1988. That act brings into being in the 1990s a national curriculum, national testing, parental school choice, links with business and industry, and other forward-looking changes. Finally, the authors try to define a world class school: its features, in what combination, and under what circumstances these features are promulgated in the ten countries studied. In short, this book, replete with charts and statistics from official sources, is a search for the best of all possible schools, that is, a World Class School, *world class* being a relatively new term to mean the very best.

The book is of wide interest to United States' educators and to educators in other countries. It is of special interest to teachers, school principals, superintendents, and other officials at all school levels; to comparative education students and professors; to educational policymakers at all school levels and at the local, state, and national government level; and to laypeople particularly interested in United States' education. Its essence is for those who want to see United States' education in comparative and international perspective — those who want to compare United States' schools with schools in other leading industrial countries. All readers will find this book readable and useful.

The finer points in this book came from many presentations the authors gave with charts and illustrations before such professional organizations as the American Association of School Administrators and the Association for Supervision, Curriculum and Development in 1992 — 94 and after extensive visits to schools in England and Scotland.

Donald M. Chalker has had lengthy teaching and administrative experience in Ohio and Michigan, culminating with successful tenure as a school superintendent in Ypsilanti Lincoln Schools, Michigan. He also taught at Eastern Michigan University, Ypsilanti, before coming to Western Carolina University in 1989 as associate professor and head of the Department of Administration, Curriculum, and Instruction. Richard M. Haynes was a North Carolina assistant superintendent and central office administrator for fifteen years prior to coming to Western Carolina University in 1988 as director of field experiences and teacher certification, Department of Administration, Curriculum and Instruction. He has written for young adult readers *Wright Brothers,* Silver Burdett, 1991; *Ida B. Wells,* Steck-Vaughn/Raintree, 1993, and five earlier books.

FRANKLIN PARKER
Distinguished Visiting Professor
School of Education and Psychology
Western Carolina University

This book is a compilation of research gathered by the authors on the subject of world class standards for schools. Many gracious people made this text possible by sharing time and expertise with the authors. The use of abundant research and literature on the subject of world education was equally important. The authors have appropriately credited the copyrighted materials reproduced in this book and appreciate the generous sharing of information by experts, authors, and publishing companies.

The Alliance of Business Leaders and Educators (ABLE), College of Education and Psychology, Western Carolina University, made possible the travel and correspondence necessary to conduct the world class school research. The authors express appreciation to Gurney Chambers, Dean of the College of Education and Psychology, and Margaret Studenc, ABLE Coordinator, for encouragement and support. We appreciate the support and encouragement of James Dooley, Assistant Vice Chancellor for Student Affairs at Western Carolina University. The authors express appreciation to the Office of Academic Affairs and the Center for the Improvement of Mountain Living, Western Carolina University, for providing the Great Britain study grant. We thank our colleagues in the Department of Administration and Curriculum at the university for providing research used in this study, but primarily for listening politely to talk about world class education standards for hours without exploding. Special thanks go to Franklin Parker, distinguished visiting scholar at Western Carolina University, whose encouragement and insight were of particular value. We thank William Clauss, Director of the Office of Rural Education, who provided materials and equipment essential to our research, and Malcolm Loughlin, Associate Director of the Office of Continuing Education, who was a one-man travel service arranging our study tour of British schools.

Without the excellent assistance of support staff at Western Carolina University, this study would have been tedious, rather than exhilarating. The authors express particular thanks to Merry Woodard and Mary Parsons for technical assistance and to our research assistants who were major contributors to the completion of this study: Todd Beaver, "Emma" Chwan-Huey, Chris Wilson, and Brian Shaw. Mrs. Chwan-Huey not only contributed essential research for the project, but she arranged to have materials faxed from Taipei when they were not available from local sources such as UNESCO. Early on, she learned that American slang for "teacher turnover" was not a pastry for American educators! We thank Karen Anderson and Libby Truill, Public Information at Western Carolina University, for media support that earned the project national recognition.

While conducting the world class research, many individuals in consulates and embassies graciously received us as guests. While the interviews were in progress with these dignitaries, other individuals within hearing range often joined the conversation. It is impossible to thank all participants, but we express our appreciation to the following staff members:

- Mr. Stephen Allen and Ms. Yukari Takeda, Japan Information Center, Consulate General's Office, Atlanta, Georgia
- Honorable Duck Haeng Hur, Consul General of the Republic of Korea, Atlanta, Georgia
- Mr. Sam S. Peng, Special Assistant, Coordination Council for North American Affairs, Republic of China Consulate, Atlanta, Georgia
- Consuls Shraga Karyan and David Akov, Consulate General of Israel, Atlanta, Georgia
- Ms. Leslie Jackman and Mr. Ian Roy of the Embassy of New Zealand, Washington, D.C.
- Mr. Murray E. Lawrence, Chair, International Assembly of National Council of Teachers of English and a New Zealand national
- Miss Jillian Cooper, British Consulate-General's Office, Atlanta, Georgia

- Ms. Bridgett Pierre, Education Specialist, French Embassy, Washington, D.C., with heartfelt thanks to Megan Alday who aided in locating a fallen American hero in France
- Mr. Horst Busek, German Consulate Offices, Atlanta, Georgia, assigned to the Georgia Department of Education
- Ms. Judith Costello, Political/Economic/Academic Relations Officer, Canadian Consulate General's Office, Atlanta, Georgia

As we began to understand the research data, we decided that Great Britain had much to offer American educators. Our travel to England and Scotland offered us a glimpse of America's educational future. The British were wonderful hosts, and we express appreciation to Jillian Cooper, British Consulate in Atlanta; Susan Fasken and Sandra Moore, Foreign and Commonwealth Office, London, England; and Robin Miller, Scottish Office, Edinburgh, Scotland, for arranging the visit. We thank the following persons in England for being gracious and helpful hosts: officials of the Department for Education; teachers, administrators, students, and parents at Rush Common Primary School, Fitzharrys Secondary School, and Denefields School; and staff members of the National Foundation for Education, the Educational Management Information Exchange, and Reading University. We thank the following persons in Scotland for being equally gracious and helpful: officials of The Scottish Office, Education Department; teachers, administrators, students, and parents at Balerno Community High School, Currie Hill Primary School, and Jordanhill School; and staff members at Moray House Teacher Training College and the University of Strathclyde, Jordanhill College.

A vital part of the research involved interviews with students from the ten countries studied. Their openness and willingness to explain their native school systems made this study unique and more meaningful. Among those participating were

- Mrs. Chwan-Huey Liao (Emma) and her husband Chi-Yuan Chiu (Kevin), Taiwan
- Mr. Li Ganlin from People's Republic of China
- Mr. Hyoung-Tae Kim from the Republic of Korea
- Mr. Katsuta Setsuo and Mr. Tommy Takahaski from Japan
- Mr. Tilman Gunther from Germany
- Miss Julie Senecal from Canada

- Mr. Graeme Dornan, Miss Nicolai Dobby, Miss Karly Champion, and Miss Claire Edmunds from England
- Mr. Jonathan Simpson and Miss Joanne Henderson from Scotland

Finally, we acknowledge the assistance and encouragement received from our students at Western Carolina University. We also express admiration and respect for public school educators throughout the United States for helping make the United States a great nation. About 182 American school administrators from twenty-two states completed the questionnaire about world class education that appears in the book. Also, both authors drew heavily on previous public school experiences when writing this book, and we acknowledge our many colleagues from the public schools we served in Florida, Michigan, North Carolina, and Ohio. Finally, we thank our families for patience, love, support, and encouragement.

Only through the support and teamwork of the above-mentioned individuals could something as important as *World Class Schools: New Standards for Education* take shape. The study reshaped our views of education, and we hope that you too learn a bit of information that will help American schools continue to be ''world class.''

Chapter 1

INTRODUCTION

World Class Schools! Americans want them, yet don't feel they have them. Presidents Bush and Clinton promised to provide them, but politicians still find them missing. When international test comparisons showed the United States lagging in area after area, a United States Office of Education official explained, "You will only have world class results when you have world class schools and world class students." In the heat of the moment, that almost made sense. When questioned about the term, *world class schools,* the official replied, "Oh, yeah. I use it in every other sentence." Then came the obvious question, "Exactly what are *world class standards,* anyway?" Following a pregnant pause, he replied, "Hell if I know!"

The objective of this book is to provide the first known uniform set of world class education standards and to compare those standards with the United States' education system. The *New Dictionary of American Slang* (Chapman, 1986) defines the term *world class* as an adjective, meaning "very superior; outstanding; super-excellent" (p. 473). Therefore, the concept of "world class education" means very superior or super-excellent education. Certainly both educators and parents want their children to be world-beaters.

INTRODUCING THE STUDY

What are "World Class School standards?" Defining this often-used term was as nebulous as nailing Jell-O to a wall. The authors expected

1

that there were some little-known, but available, standards on which the nations of the world could rank their schools. That was not the case—a definition had to be created. Literally hundreds of standards existed and sorting them was crucial, as was careful selection of nations to study and standards with which to compare the nations.

Parameters

In designing this study, great care was taken to use a ''level playing field,'' meaning that only comparable data were reported. The authors were aware of inconsistencies with which comparisons among nations were made. For example, two large international comparisons of student achievement in science and mathematics showed the United States faring poorly, yet the nation most educators might expect to have the best results, Japan, was not included in either study. Another major study of literacy did not include all of the same nations that were studied for science and mathematics achievement. Other reports on issues such as the length of the school year compared the United States to different, unrelated countries. Uniform, consistent comparisons of the United States to the nations selected for comparison did not exist.

Selecting the Research Nations

The first step in the study was to establish a set list of countries against which to compare the United States. The authors asked Dr. Franklin Parker, Distinguished Visiting Scholar in the College of Education and Psychology at Western Carolina University, to help in the selection of nations to which the United States could be compared. The nine nations and the reasons for selection are shown in Table 1.1.

Comparison Standards

With the nations selected, the next decision was what standards or measures of education would be used for comparison. The selection of standards required a critical decision about studying ''input'' standards vs. ''output'' standards. The term *output standard* was defined as a measurable *result* of education, such as a comparative international test score. The authors felt there were enough such comparative outputs, and studying them would do little to assist American educators in determin-

TABLE 1.1.

Nation	Reason for Selection
Canada	Close United States neighbor Population similar to the United States Largest expenditure on education
France	Intellectually and culturally oriented society World's most copied school system
Federal Republic of Germany (West)	Home of great educators Introduced compulsory education One of Europe's most dynamic economies
Great Britain	High literacy rate Major school reform in 1988 Model for American schools
New Zealand	Among the most literate societies on Earth Reputation for innovation and excellence
Republic of China (Taiwan)	A world leader in student achievement in science and mathematics Rapid economic development and "high tech" industry
State of Israel	Reputation for being resourceful and innovative Historic reputation of valuing education One of the newest education systems
Japan	Cited as better than the United States History of economic growth Historic reputation for valuing education
Republic of Korea (South)	World leader in student achievement in science and mathematics Rapid economic development and "high tech" industry

ing the cause of the discrepancies. The term *input standards* was defined as the education factors that establish a learning climate. Input standards are standards that determine what goes into education such as finances and curriculum. The study was designed around ten major categories of input standards that are closely related correlates of effective schools. The correlates are shown in Table 1.2.

Ultimately, the authors researched a total of thirty-five specific standards in the above ten categories. The questions were selected from dozens that educators could ask, with a careful eye on using only comparative data. Unless at least seven of the nations in the study provided such data, the authors removed the question from the study. The reader will find occasional blanks in the data, because reliable, comparative data were not available for a specific country. The authors experienced another limitation when it became evident that countries use different definitions of educational standards. When the authors examined literacy rates, for example, a single definition of literacy was chosen. When the authors researched economic data, they compared the data for common years only. In many cases, the authors chose to use United Nations data; and since the United Nations does not recognize Taiwan, comparisons including Taiwan were difficult.

Triangulated Research

The authors conducted the research in three phases:

(*1*) In order to establish a knowledge base, the authors combed the literature for reports on international comparisons of the ten nations.
(*2*) The authors contacted the embassies of each nation selected for study and requested available material about their schools. The authors then scheduled appointments in the consulates or embassies of each nation to conduct a structured interview with a cultural attaché or education officer.
(*3*) The authors interviewed students from the countries studied who were enrolled in American schools.

Establishing a "World Class Education Standard"

The result of the research is a matrix of world class standards. Since the nations selected are all highly regarded for their education system,

TABLE 1.2.

Category and Specific Standards	Reason for Selecting
(1) Educational expenditure Percent of GNP spent on all education Per capita GNP Percent of increase in GDP over five years Public per-pupil expenditure Per capita income	The amount of money spent should relate to the results.
(2) Instruction: time on task Average days in school year Average minutes of instruction in a school day Average hours of instruction in a school year Number of years and range of years in compulsory education Average minutes of math instruction per week at age thirteen Average minutes of science instruction per week at age thirteen	The amount of time spent on learning is directly related to how much is learned.
(3) Class size Average class size for age thirteen Primary school pupil-teacher ratio Secondary school pupil-teacher ratio	American educators cite class size as a positive influence on teaching and learning. Smaller class size is negotiated regularly by teacher unions.
(4) Teachers Number of years of higher education Classroom atmosphere Percent of time where teacher teaches thirteen year olds math most or all of the time Percent of time where teacher teaches thirteen year olds science most or all of the time	The amount of teacher education and working conditions affect student achievement.

(continued)

TABLE 1.2 (continued).

Category and Specific Standards	Reason for Selecting
(5) Student data Percent of students reaching final grade offered in school Percent of thirteen year olds who spend more than four hours on math homework a week Percent of thirteen year olds who spend more than four hours on science homework a week Percent of thirteen year olds who spend two or more hours on all homework daily Percent of thirteen year olds who watch five or more hours of TV daily	The number of students staying beyond compulsory attendance and students' use of nonschool time affect a nation's overall educational achievement.
(6) Curriculum Organization of primary curriculum Organization of secondary curriculum	The design and structure of the course of study affects what is learned. Methodology was not considered.
(7) Standardized test evaluation Purpose of standardized testing Who prepares tests Are results made public	The purpose and use of student evaluation affects the outcome of education and student effort.
(8) Governance of the schools National, state, or local control Percent of students in private vs. public schools	Locus of control affects student outcomes.
(9) Home and community National literacy rate Parent involvement Number of TV sets per 1,000 persons Number of daily newspapers per 1,000 persons Use of "cram schools" or other private education to raise test scores Student suicide rates, by gender and age ranges Rate of divorce per 1,000 persons	Social indicators affect the ability of the student to learn.

the authors felt an average of the ten nations was a better indicator of a world class standard than any single nation's standard. It became clear early in the study that no one nation was best in all thirty-five categories. Much of the data were numeric, so the authors derived the "world class standard" from the mean of the ten countries. The matrix also includes the range of the data for each standard from least to most. Finally, the authors compared the United States' data to the newly established mean, yielding the United States' deviation from the world class standard. The reader can easily determine the action needed by the United States to reach the world class standard. Each nation studied is a leader in some world class category but not in others; this implies that "world class education" only results from blending the best of all nations rather than any single country.

The authors had to consider cultural variables. For example, the highest class size figures exist in eastern Pacific Rim nations, yet Asian students score the best on international science and mathematics tests. This phenomenon is an excellent example of a cultural variable. In addition, the time spent teaching mathematics to South Korean thirteen-year-old students was about one-half of the time reportedly spent with the same age group in Taiwan; yet the South Korean test scores were slightly higher that the Taiwanese scores. Clearly, the input standards of class size and time on task do not explain the results reported. The data suggest a cultural variable.

Each nation views the purpose of schooling as an important vehicle for transmitting its culture and social mores—i.e., education does not simply involve filling the heads of students. Likewise, the authors view education as an important part of cultural continuity, whereby a nation passes the society's culture, knowledge, and ethics to the next generation. Given the variances among the world's nations, the authors expected variances among schools from one country to another. Variance is exactly what the authors encountered. Americans do not want their schools to turn out Japanese students any more than the Japanese want their schools to turn out Americans.

ORGANIZATION OF THE TEXT

This book is written for educators and others interested in understanding the world class standards existing in ten nations. Depending on the reader's needs, this book may (1) be skimmed and returned to for further reference, (2) be read in copious detail, or (3) be used as a springboard for extensive additional study. The text will assist the reader in locating specific information. Chapter 2 presents an overview of the ten world class countries selected for the research featured in this book.

Chapters 3 through 11 present the standards used for identifying a world class school. Chapter 12 features education in Britain, particularly the reforms instituted since 1988 and their usefulness for the United States. Chapter 13 presents the authors' blueprint for world class schooling in the United States.

Chapters 3 through 11 contain the following features:

- *Shaded Box:* A shaded box appears at the beginning of each chapter and contains a brief abstract about the topics and issues in the chapter to assist those who wish to skim.
- *Perception, Ranking the United States:* Each chapter reports the results of a survey of approximately 182 people from twenty-three states, two Canadian provinces, South Korea, and the United States Virgin Islands, who responded to a twenty item questionnaire about the rank of the United States versus the nine other countries on the subject of world class standards. One hundred eleven (approximately 66.5 percent) of the respondents were administrators, approximately 28.4 percent were teachers, and approximately 4.6 percent were other educators (school board members, consultants, students, etc.). The purpose of the questionnaire was to measure the group's perception of the relative rank of the United States to other nations on specific education issues such as class size, student suicide rates, etc. At the beginning of each Chapter 3 through 11 appear the question(s) and responses appropriate to the subject presented in the chapter.

  For example, the respondents answered the question: ''In your opinion, how would you rate United States' education globally?'' Table 1.3 displays the results in the format used in Chapters 3 through 11. A majority of the surveyed educators perceive that education in the United States is either average or below average when compared globally. The response speaks to the need for this book. Either respondents did not have a working definition of the term *world class schools,* or they truly

TABLE 1.3.

Rank United States schools as they compare to the following nine national school systems: Canada / France / Germany Britain / New Zealand / Taiwan Israel / South Korea / Japan	Above Average	Average	Below Average
	(Percentage of Total Responding)		
In your opinion, how would you rate United States' education globally? (*n* = 168)	14.0	48.0	38.0

feel that American education is average or worse when compared globally. Each chapter presenting standards begins with the perceptions of the survey group.

- *Reality, the World Class Standard:* This section reveals the reality of the world class standard in each area studied, in chart, graph, and narrative form. This section presents a world class standard for every subject presented. A symbol of a globe 🌐 in the left-hand margin marks the world class standard.

- *Implications:* The reality of world class standards frequently raises more questions than it answers. Some of the questions include: Are these comparisons really fair? What does this mean to American educators? This section answers these questions and sometimes includes common "folk wisdom" of American educators (i.e., increased test pressure raises suicide rates) that is often accepted without question. The authors present their suggestions for improving American education in this section.

- *Afterthoughts:* The afterthoughts are summary findings derived from the implications. The afterthoughts present salient issues to American educators interested in changing America's schools. The afterthoughts present leaders with the opportunity to act on each standard presented.

- *Worksheet:* The worksheet appears as a box at the end of several chapters. The worksheet allows the reader to compare his or her own school district to the world class standard. The authors repeat the world class standard, and the reader fills in the local data.

- *References:* The reference section appears at the end of each chapter to cite sources of information.

- *Recommended Further Study:* In some chapters, the authors recommend carefully selected additional readings for the reader wanting more specific information on a particular world class subject.

A reader who wants to skim the material should read the shaded box, the survey, the charts or graphics in the reality section, and the after-thoughts. The authors hope that each reader will read the entire book for a complete understanding of world class schools. The reader who wishes to use this text as the basis for extended study should make use of the references or selections recommended for further study.

REFERENCE

Chapman, R. 1986. *New Dictionary of American Slang.* New York: Harper & Row, Publishers, p. 473.

Chapter 2

THE WORLD CLASS COUNTRIES: THEIR EDUCATION SYSTEM AND THEIR CONTRIBUTION TO WORLD CLASS EDUCATION STANDARDS

Nearly 200 countries were eligible for inclusion in this study of world class education standards. Ten countries were chosen. Each country selected contributes to excellence in education. Together, they comprise a "world class education system." Demographic data appear as an introduction to each country, followed by a brief description of the educational system. The section on each country concludes with the contribution of each country to world class education.

BRITAIN (ENGLAND, NORTHERN IRELAND, SCOTLAND, WALES)

Parliament acts to provide education for all the youth of Great Britain; but the separate principalities of England, Northern Ireland, Scotland, and Wales interpret the legislation differently. Education in England and Wales is quite similar, but Scotland and Northern Ireland provide a more localized version of British education. School leaders in Scotland, for example, remind visitors that the laws of Parliament are merely guidelines.

Education in Britain has deep historical roots. Universal public education results from the English Education Act of 1872 and the Scottish Education Act of 1870. State secondary schools began in 1902 and connected with primary schools in 1918. Previous to these dates, education was private and usually a function of the Church of England. Even after the arrival of public education, church schools dominated British

11

TABLE 2.1 Britain.

Population (1991):	57,500,000
Area (1991):	94,247 sq. mi.
Density (1990):	102 per sq. km.
G.N.P. (1989):	$818.0 billion
Government:	Parliamentary democracy
Physical quality of life index:	96
Elementary enrollment (1988):	4,414,966
Secondary enrollment (1988):	4,365,912
Ethnic distribution (1992):	English 87.5%
	Scotch 9.6%
	Irish 2.4%
	Welsh 1.9%

education and state schools supplemented church schools. The transfer of education from church to state was more prolonged in Britain than other countries (Parker and Parker, 1991). Religion remains a required subject in British schools, with parents given the right to withdraw their child from religious instruction.

During the first half of the twentieth century, the governance of Britain's schools passed from local authorities to county authorities. Interestingly, the Reform Act of 1988 allows schools to reverse the process and return to the control of the local governing board. During the course of the twentieth century, British schools produced the leaders of the British Empire, one of the most literate societies on earth. English speaking countries throughout the world adopted some aspects of British education.

Following World War II, discontent grew over the education system. Citizens labeled schools elitist and blamed them for the economic decline of Britain. The government encouraged the development of comprehensive schools to equalize educational opportunity, but the movement from traditional grammar schools to comprehensive schools was never popular in a country where tradition reigns. There was no prescribed curriculum, vocational education drew criticism, and local autonomy prevailed. The structure of schooling in Britain became a political issue between the Labor Party and the Conservative Party. International comparisons of schools showed British students behind students in leading industrial nations such as Japan, Germany, and the United States (Parker and Parker, 1991).

Discontent with the present system produced the Education Reform Act of 1988. Five themes dominate the reform movement:

(*1*) *Quality:* Quality comprises a national curriculum, parental choice, and improved inspection of schools.

(*2*) *Diversity:* Education exists to provide for students' individual needs, and schools better provide for diversity by opting for local control.

(*3*) *Parental Choice:* Parents have greater involvement in school management and the opportunity to choose their student's school. The Parent's Charter is a guarantee that parents remain involved in their child's schooling.

(*4*) *Greater School Autonomy:* Local management of schools is encouraged and culminates in the opportunity for parents to opt for grant-maintained status.

(*5*) *Greater Accountability:* Accountability is provided by national testing, parental involvement, and improved inspection of schools (*Choice and Diversity: A New Framework for Schools,* 1992).

This massive reform effort makes Britain a world class contributor to excellence in education. Most nations encourage educational reform, but Britain's reform package is the most ambitious. The themes of reform in Britain are the same as reforms under consideration in America, and American leaders must learn from British experiences. Chapter 12 presents the themes in more detail along with suggestions for the states.

CANADA

Education in Canada evolves from a dual heritage—French and British. The French colonists in Canada patterned their educational system after the French system. Through direct teaching and strong direction from the central government, established schools fostered a distinctive, homogeneous, and cohesive French society that changed little until the middle of the twentieth century (Whitworth, 1993).

The British heritage began in the maritime provinces in 1867, and provincial legislatures accepted responsibility for education as they developed. The colonial movement produced a wide variety of schools including church schools, some Latin grammar schools, academies, community schools, and other special schools. The Constitution Act of

TABLE 2.2 Canada.

Population (1991):	26,832,000
Area (1991):	3,851,809 sq. mi.
Density (1990):	3 per sq. km.
G.N.P. (1989):	$513.6 billion
Government:	Parliamentary democracy
Physical quality of life index:	97
Elementary enrollment (1989):	2,345,000
Secondary enrollment:	2,254,654
Ethnic distribution (1992):	British 25%
	French 24%
	Other English 16%
	Mixed 28%

1982 reaffirmed the constitutional provision for provincial education. The Yukon and the Northwest Territory do not have provincial status, and each administers its schools through a territorial department of education. The federal government assumes responsibility for education outside provincial jurisdiction such as education for native peoples and armed forces personnel. Financial assistance to education is increasing and the federal government requests contributions to national education objectives (*Education in Canada,* 1989).

Each province has its own unique demographics and economy, and each province considers education its own responsibility. Each province has a department for education headed by a minister of education who is an elected member of the provincial legislature. Each province separately undertakes

(*1*) Training and certification of teachers
(*2*) Inspection of school standards
(*3*) Financial assistance
(*4*) Development of courses of study and school textbooks
(*5*) Rules for governance (*Education in Canada,* 1989)

During the 1960s, Canadian Schools had four purposes according to Reimer (1973): (1) custodial care, (2) sorting of students into social slots, (3) distribution of values, and (4) teaching cognitive skills. During recent decades, critics have charged that the schools have failed to develop these purposes.

Local boards of education legally preside over Canadian school districts. Local boards maintain schools, hire teachers, approve budgets, purchase supplies and equipment, and establish goals and objectives for the district. Most provinces levy taxes (*Education in Canada,* 1989).

A continuing crisis in Canadian education is the fear that American practices will dictate Canadian education. Byrne and Quortos (1972) contend that Canadians have been worrying about United States dominance ever since the Revolutionary War created a boundary between the two countries. The Canadians copied many elements of American education and continue to use ideas and materials from across the border.

The provinces today propose reform much as does each individual state in America. Quebec, nearly 85 percent French, established the following priorities for the 1990s:

(*1*) Reduce the school drop-out rate
(*2*) Consolidate vocational education reforms
(*3*) Consolidate general education reforms

The ministry of education determines the program of study and rules of organization. The ministry now administers compulsory examinations at the end of secondary school.

Ontario shares responsibility for education between the ministry of education and the local school board. The ministry establishes broad goals and the local board delivers programs and student services. The ministry does not administer a provincial-wide examination.

Alberta is a resource-rich province with a multicultural population living primarily in urban areas. Provincial examinations monitor the progress of students. Alberta citizens criticize the education system and seek reform.

New Brunswick is one of the smallest provinces but is typical of Canadian educational structures. It is Canada's only official bilingual province, where about two-thirds of the population classify themselves as English and one-third French. The provincial government finances all public schools and prescribes the curriculum, but local school boards still exist. New Brunswick is issuing a study on excellence in education to initiate future dialogue about education (Lapointe et al., 1992).

Canada presents a world class education system, because the educational system is traditionally admired and respected throughout the world. Canada also leads other nations in educational expenditure. Education in Canada mirrors education in the United States, and Americans can learn from the neighbor to the North.

FRANCE

Education in France is predictable and precise and is copied by more nations than any other system. Schools are uniform throughout the country and stress traditional intellectual development. The Ministry of Education in Paris is supreme in terms of governing education and few initiatives exist in local communities.

The French education system traces its roots to the philosophies prevalent in seventeenth and eighteenth century France: rationalism, universalism, and utility. Rationalism or the pursuit of knowledge through reasoning manifests itself in offerings such as philosophy, foreign language, math, and science. Subjects with strong logical structures take precedence over expressive subjects such as art and physical education.

Universalism translates into a standard curriculum with a similar timetable delivering similar content. Textbooks are similar and teacher methodology is similar.

French educators believe in the utility of rationalism and universalism. Using these approaches to education, French students can apply reason to the solution of everyday problems. French students today look to the great thinkers of French history for models. Voltaire, Rousseau, Descartes, and others are products of the school philosophy described above (McLean, 1993).

TABLE 2.3 France.

Population (1991):	56,700,000
Area (1991):	211,208 sq. mi.
Density (1990):	102 per sq. km.
G.N.P. (1989):	$819.6 billion
Government:	Parliamentary democracy
Physical quality of life index:	97
Elementary enrollment (1989):	4,163,161
Secondary enrollment (1989):	5,398,599
Ethnic distribution:	French 93%
	Other 7%

Public elementary schools in France developed from private and religious educational efforts in the early nineteenth century. Elementary schools became free, secular, and compulsory during the 1880s. France achieved secondary education for all French youth in 1959. During the second half of the twentieth century, students have pushed for a system more responsive to individual needs. Tradition has been difficult to overcome, however, for the traditional patterns of French education associate with quality education.

The educational system in France today remains traditional but driven toward ideas such as equality of opportunity. A majority of three-year-old youth and almost all four- and five-year-old youth attend *ecoles maternelles,* preschool education. France leads all European nations in percentage of youth attending preschool education, a world class standard. The presence of nearly all preschool youth in educational programs alleviates the day-care problem and, hopefully, increases achievement later in regular school.

The goal of the French elementary school is literacy, and nearly all youth attend primary school for five years. Fixed standards exist for each grade, and students pass from one level to the next by vote of a committee, including teachers, parents, and students.

Students pass from the elementary school to the lower secondary school. Since 1964, a four-year secondary school, the *college d'enseignement,* exists to serve French students through the compulsory education years. Teachers assign students to one of three tracks, with the lowest often terminal at the end of four years and the upper track leading to the Lycee.

Students completing the elementary years at age eleven compete for few openings in the Lycee or academic high school. The traditional French Lycee serves today as the upper secondary and technical school leading to the *baccalaureat* examination and hopefully higher education. The Lycee has two branches, the general Lycee and the professional Lycee. The general Lycee offers three years of academic instruction in specialized subject areas. Studies remain abstract and emphasize either philosophy or mathematics. At the conclusion of the experience, students take the *baccalaureat* according to their level of specialization (Pierre and Auvillain, 1991). The professional Lycee offers three different courses:

(1) A technical education for students in lower tracks of the college

(2) Part-time courses for young workers leading to a certificate

(3) Higher level courses in technical and vocational specialization

The technical courses lead to the *baccalaureat* and often higher education.

The French control education from a centralized department in Paris, and educators make very few decisions at the local level. About 65 percent of school funding comes from the national government with the remainder supplied locally and from industry and parents (McLean, 1993).

Local teachers exercise new freedom to vary instructional methods; and parents, once removed from the local school, involve themselves more with their children's education and help children more with homework and course selection (Lapointe et al., 1992).

The contribution of France to world class education is

(1) A centralized school system focused on basic education

(2) A system copied perhaps more than any other educational system

(3) Preschool experiences for a greater percentage of youth than other countries

(4) The use of essay testing for assessment from primary through school completion

GERMANY (FORMER FEDERAL REPUBLIC OF GERMANY)

Educators remember Germany as the home of the first kindergarten, and indeed, kindergarten started in Germany in 1837. The principles of this early kindergarten effort spread to all developed nations; and today, kindergarten prevails in the world class countries.

The German contribution to world class education is much greater than just the kindergarten experience. German schools are steeped in history. The universities spawned humanism and the reformation in the sixteenth century, movements that also helped shape Germany's public schools. Germany's schools helped foster political unity in the nineteenth century and helped make Germany a world power in the twentieth century. The economic growth of Germany during the twentieth century is largely a result of the outstanding quality of its vocational and technical schools.

TABLE 2.4 Germany.

Population (1991):	78,700,000
Area (1991):	137,838 sq. mi.
Density (1990):	244 per sq. km.
G.N.P. (1990):	$1,579 billion
Government:	Federation
Physical quality of life index:	96
Elementary enrollment (1989):	2,473,000
Secondary enrollment (1989):	3,905,600
Ethnic distribution (1992):	German 93%
	Other 7%

When the Nazi party assumed power in 1933, Germans were probably the best educated populace in the world. However, the schools became the means for disseminating Nazi ideology, and Germany rejected its humanistic tradition in favor of racism. Following Germany's defeat in World War II, German schools split into East and West. The German Federal Republic (West Germany) reestablished traditional, successful schools such as the Gymnasium; but the German Democratic Republic imposed a centralized system of education devoted to the principles of Marxism-Leninism. For forty years, the two Germanys competed and their educational systems supported the political, social, and economic beliefs of the respective countries (Fishman, 1993).

In the Federal Republic of Germany, the federal government is only responsible for establishing general educational policy. Accordingly, educational matters are the responsibility of the *Länder* (states). Agreements among the *Länder* produce uniformity in the length of the school year, facilities, organizational form, curriculum sequence, and student evaluation. Each *Land* (state) recognizes the *Abitur* test results earned by students in other *Länder.* Each *Land* recognizes a school-leaving certificate issued by other *Länder.*

The Federal Republic of Germany (West Germany) was the country used for educational comparisons in this book. The educational structure in the former Federal Republic of Germany is as follows:

- *Kindergartens:* Enrollment in Kindergarten is voluntary, but a majority of students attend the classes run by voluntary associates and local authorities.
- *Grundschule:* This primary school covers the first four years of

school. All students attend the Grundschule and consideration is given to individual needs and interests. The mission of the Grundschule, however, is to prepare students for secondary education.

- *Hauptschule:* Hauptschule is the secondary school attended by students who do not attend either the Realschule or Gymnasium. The school is compulsory through Class 9 and voluntary through Class 10. The mission of the Hauptschule is to offer a general secondary education and to facilitate transition to other types of secondary schools.
- *Realschule:* The Realschule has become favored over the Hauptschule as the vocational preparation school. Students attend from Class 5 to Class 10. The mission of the Realschule is to prepare students for further basic training in various vocational areas.
- *Gymnasium:* The Gymnasium is the grammar school leading to *Abitur* after nine years of attendance. Successful passage of the *Abitur* leads to university access. The mission of the Gymnasium is to prepare students for higher education. The Gymnasium offers a general education in the early years and specialization is encouraged in the later years.
- *Gesamtschule:* The mission of the Gesamtschule is to combine all educational programs into a comprehensive program similar to the comprehensive school in the United States. In 1990, the Gesamtschule enrolled only about 5.7 percent of the students in a given age group (*Report on the Development of Education in the Federal Republic of Germany, 1990–1992,* 1992).

Vocational training is world class in Germany. Students enter a variety of vocational schools at the end of compulsory education, and most of the vocational schools provide cooperative training with a firm or industry. Germany also provides advanced training for workers already on the job.

German Democratic Republic Schools (East Germany) committed schools to the propagation of Communist doctrine and organized under a strong centralized government. The mission of the schools was to educate youth to assume a socialist lifestyle. East Germany accomplished this goal by the establishment of a ten-year school, *Polytech- nische Oberschule,* for all pupils.

Reunification of the German schools occurred in 1990. East Germany created five new *Länder,* and each Land, along with the eleven in West Germany, assumed responsibility for providing education. East Germany abolished the polytechnic school and adopted the western model in all sixteen *Länder* (Fishman, 1993).

In spite of ideological differences, striking similarities already exist in the teaching patterns and curricula of the two educational systems. Germany continues to be a world class school system building on the following world class contributions:

(1) High achievement on international examinations
(2) Emphasis on kindergarten experiences
(3) Development of a cooperative state education system
(4) Development of exemplary vocational education system

JAPAN

Japan's education system has a long, consistent history. It began during the Edo period (1603 − 1867) when fief schools were established in the pattern of Confucian schools in Edo, which later became Tokyo. These schools taught Chinese scholarship in military arts, ethics, and *bushido,* or "way of the warrior" to the *samurai* (warrior) class. Other students received their education in temple children's schools, some 16,000 of them, that taught the three R's.

With the beginning of the Meiji ("enlightened rule") period

TABLE 2.5 Japan.

Population (1991):	124,017,000
Area (1991):	145,847 sq. mi.
Density (1990):	850 per sq. km.
G.N.P. (1991):	$2,920 billion
Government:	Parliamentary democracy
Physical quality of life index:	99
Elementary enrollment (1989):	9,606,627
Secondary enrollment (1989):	11,143,930
Ethnic distribution (1992):	Japanese 99%
	Other 1%

(1868–1912), there was a move away from traditional Confucian schooling. Patterned after existing western models, a centralized school system emerged. In 1871 the Ministry of Education was formed to oversee and standardize schools, beginning the first major education reform in Japanese history (Ishizaka, circa 1990). The following year, a *Gakusei* (educational ordinance) mandated national compulsory education. The French system of administration and the American curriculum were copied as national school districts were created. This trend was attacked as "morally degenerate" for turning away from Confucian values. So in 1890, an education edict established a national school system that taught conservative values. It remained largely unchanged until the end of World War II (Shirato, 1985).

Following World War II, the Japanese began the second major education reform in its history, and great strides were made within a decade following the end of the war. Unlike the United States Constitution, the Japanese Constitution includes specific reference to education. Article 26 states:

> All people shall have the right to receive an equal education correspondent to their ability, as provided by law. All people shall be obligated to have boys and girls under their protection receive ordinary education as provided for by law. Such compulsory education shall be free.

On May 3, 1947, the Fundamental Law of Education and School Law established a modern school system. It used the American model 6-3-3-4 structure with nine years of compulsory education (Shirato, 1985). The following year the law created a new upper secondary school system and mandated a special education program for blind or deaf children (many of whom were war victims). In 1950 a junior college system started. In 1952 a powerful group, the Central Council for Education, was established to manage basic policies regarding education in Japan (Ishizaka, circa 1990).

The decade of the 1970s saw further refinement and centralization of education. In 1971 the Ministry for Education, *Monbusho,* became the Ministry of Education, Science, and Culture. The grouping of education, science, and culture is not coincidental as the three are clearly linked in Japanese society. The same year, the Central Council issued a report, "Basic Guidelines for the Development of an Integrated Education System Suited for Contemporary Society," which recommended basic measures of education and fundamental improvement in schools.

In 1973 the government made special education compulsory for all students challenged physically or mentally. The National Center for University Entrance Examination started in 1977 to administer the standardized joint first-stage achievement test used by all national and public universities (Ishizaka, circa 1990).

The decade of the 1980s was one of major school reform in Japan. The third major reform movement began in 1983, the year the United States released *A Nation at Risk*. The *Monbusho* began working with the National Council on Educational Reform directly under the Prime Minister's Office. The council issued four sets of recommendations between 1985 and 1987. The *Monbusho* continues to implement the reforms in the 1990s, including a restructured curriculum that is less rigid and stresses independent thinking (*Monbusho,* 1992).

Japan contributes to world class education standards through a centralized, reform-oriented, education system that clearly views growth as essential to Japanese success. The education system is so fundamental to Japan that it is included in its constitution. The education system is largely credited with the post-war reformation of Japan. The standardized test scores of Japanese students are among the highest in the world, notably in science and mathematics. Japan is the most commonly referred to example of educational success when the United States is cited for educational failure.

NEW ZEALAND

New Zealand has two main islands, North and South, stretching northeast of Australia across the Pacific Ocean. The total area of islands roughly equals that of England. They have been populated for over 1,500 years, first by Polynesians who established the Maori culture, and later by Europeans whose culture is now dominant. The latter group was first Dutch (1642), then English (1769), from which the three million New Zealanders trace their history (Franklin, 1985). By 1841 the New Zealand Company was incorporated under the theories of Edward Gibbon Wakefield. Feeling Great Britain was in decline, this capitalist felt that new prosperity for the middle class was possible in New Zealand, if education reduced privilege-provided opportunity.

Education has been a matter of keen interest to New Zealanders. In 1877, school attendance became compulsory, and the government raised

TABLE 2.6 New Zealand.

Population (1991):	3,308,000
Area (1991):	103,736 sq. mi.
Density (1990):	31 per sq. km.
G.N.P. (1989):	$41 billion
Government:	One chamber parliamentary democracy
Physical quality of life index:	96
Elementary enrollment (1989):	312,773
Secondary enrollment (1989):	341,249
Ethnic distribution (1992):	European 87%
	Maori 9%

the school-leaving age to fifteen in 1944. In addition, school kindergartens and play centers are provided, and education through the secondary schools has no fees. While few private schools exist, the state subsidizes and sets standards for them as well as for all public schools. Because of the great distance some students travel to get to school, the state provides "radio schools" and boarding schools for students from remote rural areas (Sinclair, 1985).

Preprimary education is widely available in New Zealand, with nearly one-half of all two year olds enrolled in some form of schooling. The government subsidizes these schools, which are divided into two types: playcenters that are structured in a family-cooperative style and kindergartens that have a more formal education structure. Both reflect the New Zealander's belief in the importance of education. The government sets the curriculum and provides the textbooks but leaves control of these schools to local education boards.

In recent years the government consolidated schools with an emphasis on bussing students to larger schools. Called "area schools," these schools often include all compulsory grades. Students seldom drop out of school, a decision termed "wastage." Students take between fifteen and thirty months to move through the primers before advancing to intermediate grades (Sinclair, 1985).

Intermediate schools have two forms or years of study, and they separate the primers from secondary schools. Teaching is more specialized during these years, and there are no entrance examinations to keep students from attending.

Secondary schools are commonly comprehensive and called by a variety of names: grammar schools, high schools, colleges, or technical high schools. The curriculum varies less than the names given to the schools. A primary purpose of these schools is to prepare students for the national examinations that determine the education available to them following these years. A board of governors composed of parents, district education authorities, and other public groups runs each school. The curriculum comes from syllabi provided by the Ministry of Education, and it is regulated by school inspectors who monitor standards in New Zealand's schools (*New Zealand Official 1990 Year Book of Education,* 1990). Students in forms five through seven (grades eleven through thirteen) take rigorous examinations for certification at four levels:

(*1*) School certificates follow three years of secondary education. Students elect to "sit" examinations in one to six subjects, with English being the most common area examined. Students may pass single subjects, but the greater the number passed, the better the option for higher examinations later.

(*2*) Students receive Sixth Form Certificates after an additional year of study. As many as six subjects may be tested, but most commonly, students take five subjects.

(*3*) After five years of secondary study, students who have been accepted into form six and who have completed an advanced course of study for two years may be awarded a higher school certificate.

(*4*) Students take Bursary and scholarship examinations in form seven. They are competitive and offer awards for study at the university level. In 1988 nearly a quarter of all students earned a school certificate, and slightly more earned a sixth form certificate. During the 1980s, students leaving school without formal examination greatly decreased, and the performance of Maori students increased (Shuker and Adams, 1985).

New Zealand's schools are funded from a variety of sources. The national government provides most funds, but school-raised funds, and private-sector investments provide some variance in funding among the schools. Volunteering in the schools is also popular. In 1988 a much-touted report, *Administering for Excellence,* began a reform movement in New Zealand education. It reduced the centrality of education with enhanced local school control, but left the basic standards of education controlled by the Director-General for the Department of Education.

Experts know the New Zealand schools for a high level of literacy in the population, and for the creation of whole language reading programs. Attention also focuses on the reading recovery program for students who fall behind in reading level at grade one. Each television receiver is taxed annually, and New Zealanders boast the highest number of books read per capita in the world. There is a de-emphasis on competitive team sports in favor of Olympic competitions. The driving age is eighteen, that may account for greater attendance in school beyond the school-leaving age of sixteen. The fairly recent arrival of satellite and cable television access may have some effect on the literacy rates of this island nation (Shuker and Adams, 1985).

New Zealand contributes to world class education standards through the high level of literacy of its population and the consistently high level of reading proficiency by its students on international tests. Additionally, it contributes to world class standards through innovation and the use of site-based management of schools.

REPUBLIC OF CHINA (TAIWAN)

The Republic of China, or Taiwan, is one of the most densely populated nations on Earth. It is a nation that is both new and old, with a history of education dating to the Confucian era over 2500 years ago, and a government that is largely new since the end of the second world

TABLE 2.7 Taiwan.

Population (1991):	20,688,000	
Area (1991):	13,885 sq. mi.	
Density (1990):	1,478 per sq. km.	
G.N.P. (1990):	$161.7 billion	
Government:	One party system	
Physical quality of life index:	92 (est.)	
Elementary enrollment (1988):	2,400,619	
Secondary enrollment (1988):	1,707,270	
Ethnic distribution (1992):	Taiwanese	85%
	Chinese	14%

war. Sun Yat-sen recognized eight national moral virtues of Confucianism in education for all Chinese children: filial piety, loyalty, kindness, love, faith, righteousness, harmony, and peace (Epstein, 1985). There is a well established reverence for education in the culture.

Another Confucian effect on education was an examination system that rewarded rote memorization, reciting classical works, and strict order in the classroom. The modern era called for a reformation of education, starting in the twentieth century.

The current educational system is a blend of historic Chinese and foreign educational concepts. The Japanese controlled the area from 1895 to 1945, and their cultural impact included education. By 1949 the educational system fell under the control of the Republic of China, and much of the Japanese infrastructure was replaced. The riptides of native Taiwanese, Japanese, and mainland Chinese cultures coalesced into a nation that has one of the most aggressively growing economies in the world (Limley, 1985).

Taiwan essentially rebuilt its schools following the exodus from the mainland in 1949. The result is a system reflecting cultural history and modern educational thought. Under Japanese control, the native population was quite different from its mainland cousins, who comprise about 14 percent of the population. Even the language is different, but Mandarin Chinese from the mainland is the official language of the government and the schools.

The school system is basically autocratic and governed by a centralized education authority, the Ministry of Education, that is part of the powerful executive branch of government. The political structure of the nation is organized around provinces, although the two largest cities, Taipei and Kaohsiung, are treated as separate provinces. The system of education closely follows this political pattern.

Unlike the United States, the function and organization of education is specifically outlined in the constitution. There are primary, secondary, and vocational schools, as well as colleges and universities. Compulsory education covers nine years and is free for all eligible students. The schools use a 6-3-3 scheme with the end of the middle grades representing the school-leaving age. In addition, there is an extensive preprimary school with optional attendance. The school year runs from August 1 to July 31 and is divided into two semesters totaling 222 days of school (Ministry of Education, n.d.).

Taiwan, like other Asian countries, uses a rigorous examination system to limit the number of students who have access to education beyond the compulsory attendance level; and competition on the exams is excessive. High schools are either vocational or academic, and attendance at the best school is essential for success later in life. While each province has attendance zones for schools, and schools allot teachers based on the number of students in the attendance area, the extended Chinese family is used by parents to move students into the most prestigious attendance areas. This results in unusually large classes, most commonly in Taipei, in the so-called ''star schools.'' The top academic high schools do not offer competitive sports, but the so-called ''cow schools'' or less attractive schools do offer competitive sports. This fact explains why the Little League World Series so often comes down to the United States versus Taiwan, with the latter represented by a ''cow school'' (Liao, 1993).

Ministry of Education specialists establish the national curriculum, and the national curriculum dictates the writing of textbooks. Other teaching materials must be approved by the Ministry before they can be sold to schools. The average teacher would be ashamed if even one page of a textbook was not carefully taught during the year.

Many students supplement their education by attending a cram school, or *bushibon*. During elementary school, much of the teaching in the *bushibon* is cultural, including second language, arts, and music education. During the secondary school years, the *bushibon* becomes a high-pressure school where students cram for entrance examinations to star schools and admission to the best colleges. Cram schools employ the most famous teachers, and the most respected cram schools charge the highest tuition (Peng, 1993). In Taipei, where the most famous *bushibons* are located, some teachers may have classes with as many as 150 students (Liao, 1993). Similar forms of schools can be found in other eastern Pacific Rim nations.

Taiwan contributes to world class education with one of the world's most rapidly growing economies when measured in terms of five-year growth of GDP. It has a highly centralized school system and a nationalized testing program designed to limit educational opportunity for the less able after compulsory attendance ends. Taiwan has consistently ranked among the highest scoring nations on comparative tests of both science and mathematics skills.

REPUBLIC OF KOREA

The Republic of Korea has a long, well-established tradition of reverence for education. The influence of Confucianism is obvious in the organization of Korean education. Japanese colonialism challenged the system, as did the influence of Western missionaries. Both wanted to change it. The presence of Confucian ethics and the Korean civil-service system combined to resist those changes. By the dawn of the twentieth century, a wave of education reform resulted in the establishment of elementary and middle schools, as well as teacher preparation normal schools and a university system.

At the turn of the century, the influence of American missionaries resulted in the establishment of modern high schools, a decrease in commoners' illiteracy, and the spread of education to females (Kim, 1985).

Prior to World War II, colonial Japan tried to spread the Japanese language and culture in Korea. The Japanese established a dual education system with a high quality of education for the Japanese and an inferior education for the Koreans. By 1938, the Japanese outlawed the teaching of the Korean language, resulting in a large number of illiterate Koreans. The second world war brought further devastation to the people and the schools of Korea.

Following the war, less than two-thirds of Korea's children attended elementary school; and few had the opportunity to progress further. In the post-war years Korean education was reconstructed, resulting in the Education Law of 1949, which stated the rights of Korean students and

TABLE 2.8 Republic of Korea.

Population (1991):	43,134,000
Area (1991):	38,025 sq. mi.
Density (1990):	1134 per sq. km.
G.N.P. (1989):	$200 billion
Government:	Democratic republic
Physical quality of life index:	86
Elementary enrollment (1989):	4,894,261
Secondary enrollment (1989):	4,545,896
Ethnic distribution (1992):	Korean 99%

established the basis of Korean education. It included compulsory attendance for all Korean children and guaranteed an education for all individuals regardless of sex, race, or status. The law also established the goals and purpose of education for every school and called for lifelong learning.

During the early 1950s the Korean War plagued the education system as well as the people of Korea. Following the war, with American help, a 6-3-3 structure of schools was organized for elementary, middle grades, and high schools. In 1957, the Ministry drafted a remarkable "Children's Charter" (see Chapter 10) to codify the rights of children in Korean schools (*Education in Korea, 1991–1992,* 1992).

As is common among eastern Pacific Rim nations, the Ministry of Education wields a position of power and prestige. The Korean system is specifically designed to update the national curriculum in an orderly manner at five-year intervals. The Ministry sets both the curriculum and time allotments, and the Ministry writes and publishes textbooks or authorizes others to write or publish them. The academic year runs from March 1 through February 28 and includes 222 days per year.

School begins at age four for most Korean students. The two-year kindergarten program is privately funded, but the government sets the curriculum and provides some instructional materials. The percentage of the population in kindergarten has steadily increased during the 1980s. Primary education begins at age six and spans six years (Hur, 1992). The aims of education for this group are clearly understood:

(*1*) Improved language skills

(*2*) Development of morality, responsibility, and citizenship

(*3*) Nurturing scientific inquiry

(*4*) Fostering daily living skills

(*5*) Appreciation of art

(*6*) Creating harmony of mind and body

During the past decade, students in middle schools designed for students from ages thirteen to sixteen increased. Formerly, entrance examinations for middle schools existed, but they were abolished before 1970 to increase the amount of education for all students. The increased percentage of students electing to stay in school extended to high schools as well. The three-year high schools are either academic or vocational (Kim, 1985).

The Ministry uses a rigorous examination system, similar to that found in Taiwan, to limit educational access to students above the compulsory education age. A system of cram schools exists despite government opposition to them, and parents are known to have bankrupted themselves to provide ''star'' cram schools for their children. The only effective way to improve socioeconomic status in Korea is through improved educational attainment. While the examination system places great strain on the student, the suicide rate is considerably lower than the United States rate for the same sex and age groups. The reason for this is cultural — it is considered dishonorable for the child to die before the parent (Hur, 1992).

The Republic of Korea contributes to world class education standards by scoring the highest achievement test scores in science and mathematics in the most recent international testing. Korea spends the lowest percentage of GNP on education of the ten nations in this study. Korea contributes a highly centralized, autocratic, education system and a children's charter of rights that other nations should follow.

STATE OF ISRAEL

Education in the State of Israel is both old and new. The heritage upon which Israeli education rests is ancient, roughly paralleling the education standards of eastern Europe. The modern education system can be traced to Palestine in the late nineteenth century where Yiddish was the official language of instruction in Hebrew schools. Following World War I, the British controlled Palestine; and three separate school systems emerged:

TABLE 2.9 Israel.

Population (1989):	4,477,000
Area (1991):	7,847 sq. mi.
Density (1990):	570 per sq. km.
G.N.P. (1989):	$51.8 billion
Government:	Parliamentary democracy
Physical quality of life index:	92
Elementary enrollment (1989):	702,472
Secondary enrollment (1989):	291,754
Ethnic distribution (1992):	Jewish 83%
	Arab 16%

Jewish, Arab, and Christian. Due to the historic affinity Jews have for education, nearly all Jewish children attended elementary schools while far fewer Arab children attended. During the 1920s, the Jewish community assumed increasing financial control of their schools and the curriculum. The British did not contribute to the Jewish school system, which the British regarded as private education until nearly the end of the 1920s. The evolving school structure contained kindergartens, an eight-grade elementary school, and tuition-charging secondary schools with limited enrollment. Teacher training institutions were also developed (Safran, 1985).

By 1933, the country passed a historic education ordinance that recognized two separate systems: the Hebrew public system and the Arab public system. The ordinance also established a department of education to oversee school budgets and educational quality. Within the department, a small Jewish inspectors office was created to oversee Hebrew schools.

Following World War II and the establishment of the State of Israel, the government made school mandatory and free from age five (kindergarten) to age fourteen including all eight grades of elementary school. For students who had not completed all of their elementary education, compulsory attendance was extended to age seventeen. The federal Ministry of Education and Culture and local authorities shared control of the schools. A second education law established the curriculum and basic standards for the nation as a whole (Kurian, 1985).

Israel continued the dual system of Arab and Hebrew schools with each using its own language for instruction. Given the diversity of the Hebrew community in Israel, schools guaranteed parents the right to choose schools. The choice offered was attendance at a government Hebrew school or a religious school that is private but regulated by the Ministry of Education and Culture. The school year includes 215 days, with Friday being one-half day, in a school week that runs from Sunday to Friday. While students in Hebrew schools may elect to learn Arabic, Hebrew instruction is required in all Arab schools (Karyan, 1992).

The State of Israel reformed education toward the end of the 1960s and again during the 1980s. Both reform movements aimed at improving instruction and reducing the number of "unqualified" teachers in the schools. These efforts have been largely successful (Simmer and Simmer, 1992). In addition to the omnipresent military threat, Israel faces two challenges to its education system: (1) a high incidence of poverty among selected groups of Jews and (2) an increasing number of immigrants notably from former communist states in Europe. Both groups demand extra learning time at more expense to the government. Overall, student achievement in Arab schools is below that of Hebrew schools, although this study examines both systems as one. At the high school level, students select from a variety of special purpose schools (Kurian, 1985). No study of Israeli education would be complete without an awareness of the huge numbers of adults who continue their education. At any given time, as much as one-third of the population of Israel may be in school.

The State of Israel contributes to the development of world class education with one of the newest education systems in the world, and one of the most educationally oriented societies on Earth. The diversity and evolving nature of its population present unusual challenges, yet Israel tends to do well on a broad range of international student proficiency tests.

UNITED STATES

In colonial America, parents taught children in the home with a concentration on religious instruction. For pragmatic reasons, groups of settlers joined to create local schools controlled by leaders in the community. The Massachusetts Law of 1642 ordered local leaders to provide learning for each child, beginning the practice of compulsory education.

TABLE 2.10 United States.

Population (1991):	248,709,873
Area (1991):	3,540,939 sq. mi.
Density (1990):	26 per sq. km.
G.N.P. (1989):	$5,465.1 billion
Government:	Representative democracy
Physical quality of life index:	97
Elementary enrollment (1989):	29,147,000
Secondary enrollment (1989):	11,461,000
Ethnic distribution (1992):	Caucasian 70.4%
	African-American 16.1%
	Hispanic 9.9%
	Other 3.7%

American education today is a product of these roots. Home schooling has returned learning to some homes, and parents still claim ownership over schools. The local board of education continues to govern local school districts, and compulsory education prevails.

The United States Constitution is silent on the subject of education leaving control with each of the fifty states. Starting with Massachusetts in 1837, each state responded to the implied power by guaranteeing free public education. Each state has created a different governing structure for education, and cooperation is not nearly as prevalent as competition. Each state recognizes the importance of local governance and provides for local districts controlled by a local school board. Each local board of education hires a superintendent to serve as chief executive officer. In American education, the superintendent recommends policy, and the board of education determines whether or not to accept the recommendation. The process is not always smooth and for decades, the superintendent and board continued to compete for control in many local districts.

City school districts formed in the nineteenth century and rural consolidation began during the first quarter of the twentieth century. Schools formed during these years organized as comprehensive schools where all students remained together through completion. Prior to World War II, the most common structure was an elementary school housing grades one through six; a junior high school, housing grades seven through nine; and a senior high school housing grades ten through twelve. The completion rates, however, averaged around 50 percent, a comfortable figure because business and industry required an untrained work force.

Change has permeated the educational scene since World War II. Four major developments dominated the educational scene during the past fifty years.

(*1*) The federal government entered the educational arena during the 1960s and 1970s forcing the end of segregated schools and assuring equal opportunity for handicapped students, minority groups and women. Equal opportunity made huge strides during the past thirty years but remains an unfinished agenda item for the 1990s.

(*2*) Universal education became a goal in the 1960s and 1970s propagating the vision of education for all citizens and a diploma in every hand. Today, the completion rate stands at about 90 percent, including those who return to school after dropping out. American schools have not strayed from the idea of a comprehensive education for all students, so the task of keeping all students in school is formidable. Citizens criticize educators, however, for graduating students who are not literate. The struggle continues in the 1990s to graduate youth with the skills necessary to lead a productive and happy life.

(*3*) Control of schools shifted from the local board to the state government during the past three decades. Public dissatisfaction with the public schools led to a prolific number of reports during the 1980s pontificating on the improvement of education. The most famous report, *A Nation at Risk,* called for higher standards, increased graduation requirements, more homework, and greater parental involvement. Each state responded by developing an improvement plan that addresses the recommendations of the reports. State funding for education has increased and state control has stiffened.

(*4*) School restructuring became popular during the decades after the 1960s. The middle school movement changed the configuration of the grade structure as junior high schools gave way to middle schools stressing development of the total student. Methodology changed as a variety of new ideas, such as developmental learning, cooperative learning, and integrated learning caught the fancy of American educators. Outcome-based education is popular in selected schools and vocational education grew during the 1960s and 1970s with help from the federal government. Special education blossomed into several programs serving about 12 percent of the student population. In spite of restructuring, educational achievement today is not satisfactory to many citizens. At present, the nation engages in a concerted effort to raise the achievement level of students. The nation's fifty governors recently established seven education goals for the year 2000. Currently under discussion are significant changes leading to a more centralized educational system that includes voluntary national curricula and national testing. Adoption of these features would be a radical departure from state control and a major shift in the United States' educational policy (Lapointe et al., 1992).

The enviable position of the United States today as a world political leader, protector of democracy, and economic giant is a tribute to American education over the past few decades. America has overcome diversity in the past and has the future capacity to overcome perceived or real problems with the educational system. America's contributions to world class education are

(*1*) Equality of educational opportunity for all students
(*2*) Education for an ethnically and racially diverse population
(*3*) Education that has made the United States a world leader economically, politically, and socially

REFERENCES

Choice and Diversity: A New Framework for Schools. 1992. Presented to Parliament by the Secretaries of State for Education and Wales by Command of Her Majesty, London: HMSO.

Education in Canada. 1989. Ottawa, Canada: External Communications Division, External Affairs and International Trade Canada.

Epstein, I. 1985. *Taiwan.* New York: Facts on File Publishers.

Fishman, S. 1993. "Germany: Education," *Encyclopedia Americana, Vol.12.* Danbury, Connecticut: Grolier, Inc., pp. 621–625.

Franklin, S. H. 1985. "New Zealand," *Encyclopedia Americana, Vol. 20.* Danbury, Connecticut: Grolier Inc.

Ishizaka, K. 1990. *School Education in Japan.* Toyko: International Society for Educational Information, Inc., Reference Series 5.

Jonen, G. and H. Roche, eds. 1992. *The Educational System in the Federal Republic of Germany.* Bonn, Germany: Foreign Office of the Federal Republic of Germany.

Karyan, S. Interview (October 23, 1992).

Kim, J. E. 1985. *South Korea.* New York: Facts on File Publishers.

Kurian, G. 1985. *Israel.* New York: Facts on File Publishers.

Lapointe, A., N. Mead and J. Askew. 1992. *Learning Mathematics.* Princeton, New Jersey: Educational Testing Service.

Liao, C.-H. Interview (October 12, 1993).

Limley, H. 1985. "Taiwan," *Encyclopedia Americana, Vol. 26.* Danbury, Connecticut: Grolier Inc.

McLean, M. 1993. "France: Education," *Encyclopedia Americana, Vol. 11.* New York: Grolier, Inc., pp. 702–705.

Monbusho. 1992. Tokyo, Japan, photocopied monograph.

New Zealand Official 1990 Year Book of Education. 1990. New Zealand: Ministry of Education, Photocopied Monograph.

Parker, F. and B. Parker. 1991. *Education in England and Wales.* New York: Garland Publishing, Incorporated.

Peng, S. S. Interview (October 7, 1992).

Pierre, B. and S. Auvillain, eds. 1991. *Organization of the French Educational System*

Leading to the French Baccalaureat. Washington D.C.: Embassy of France, Office of Education.

Report on the Development of Education in the Federal Republic of Germany, 1990—1992. 1992. Report of the Federal Republic of Germany for the 43rd Session of the International Conference on Education, September 1992.

Safran, N. 1985. "Israel," *Encyclopedia Americana, Vol. 15.* Danbury, Connecticut: Grolier Incorporated.

Shirato, I. 1985. "Education in Japan," *Encyclopedia Americana, Vol. 15.* Danbury, Connecticut: Grolier Incorporated.

Shuker, R. and R. Adams. 1985. *New Zealand.* New York: Facts on File Publishers.

Simmer, S. and D. Simmer, eds. 1992. *Facts and Figures about Education & Culture in Israel.* Jerusalem, Israel: State of Israel Ministry of Education and Culture, Publications Department.

Sinclair, K. 1985. "Education and Cultural Life in New Zealand," *Encyclopedia Americana,* Vol. 20. Danbury, Conn: Grolier Incorporated.

Whitworth, F. E. 1993. "Canada: Education," *Encyclopedia Americana, Vol. 13.* New York: Grolier, Inc., pp. 402—406.

Chapter 3

DEFINING A WORLD CLASS STANDARD FOR EDUCATIONAL EXPENDITURE

The amount of money a country allocates to education is a highly visible indication of the importance attributed to education. This chapter explores the wealth of each country and the amount of that wealth allocated to education. The following educational expenditure standards are examined: (1) The per capita gross national product, 1989; (2) The per capita income, 1988; (3) The per-pupil expenditure for K – 12 education, 1988; and (4) The percent of gross national product spent on education 1988.

PERCEPTION: RANKING THE UNITED STATES ON EDUCATIONAL EXPENDITURE

How do educators rate the United States in terms of financial contribution to education? The conference sample of educators described in Chapter 1 responded to two questions (see Table 3.1).

The responses are evenly distributed across the five descriptors, indicating varying perceptions of the relative educational financial contribution of the United States compared to the nine world class countries. Equal numbers of educators believe that the United States ranks first or at least in the top third in terms of financial contribution to education and that the United States trails the other nine countries. A variance in perception could mean trouble. Large numbers of citizens already consider the United States' contribution to education quite generous, and citizens could refuse to vote additional educational funds if skeptics outnumber supporters of school funding.

TABLE 3.1.

Rank United States schools as they compare to the following national school systems:			First	Top Third	Middle Third	Bottom Third	Last
Canada	France	Germany					
Britain	New Zealand	Taiwan					
Israel	South Korea	Japan	(Percentage of Total Responding)				
1. Greatest percent of GNP spent on education? (*n* = 184)			7.6	25.0	27.2	33.2	7.1
2. Greatest K – 12 per pupil expenditure? (*n* = 178)			14.1	28.1	29.2	23.0	5.6

REALITY: THE WORLD CLASS STANDARD FOR EDUCATIONAL EXPENDITURE

National Wealth

How wealthy is the United States compared to the nine research countries? This chapter presents three indicators of a nation's wealth to provide the answer: (1) the gross national product of the ten countries in 1988, (2) the increase in gross domestic product from 1980 to 1985, and (3) the per capita income of the ten countries in 1988. Gross national product (GNP) is the total value of all goods and services produced by a country. GNP is probably the most commonly used indicator of a country's wealth, and therefore, the most commonly reported.

Figure 3.1 shows the per capita GNP during 1989 for the ten countries studied. Large differences in wealth exist among the ten countries reported. Since it has been established that all ten countries already excel at education, little correlation exists between educational accomplishment and per capita gross national product. Consider students in Korea and Taiwan, for example, where students rank first and second on international math and science tests given to nine- and thirteen-year-old students in 1991–92. The International Assessment of Educational Progress (IAEP) administered the tests, and the agency widely quotes the results as a measurement of education effectiveness. Korean and Taiwanese students performed well in spite of the fact that both countries are the poorest in the study, with a GNP under $5,000.00 per capita.

The world class standard for per capita GNP is the mean of $14,731.00. The United States ranks second in per capita GNP and is $6,369.00 above the mean.

The United States continues to produce a generous per capita GNP, second only to Japan. Citizens in the United States, however, must realize that the country is no longer the world leader in production of gross national product. Germany, which pushes the United States for runner-up status, continues to lead the European countries studied; and four countries, Canada, France, Britain, and New Zealand, fall in the range of $10,000.00 per capita GNP to $20,000.00 per capita GNP. New Zealand presents an interesting study of a country whose lifestyle is generally admired by outsiders, but whose per capita GNP is $3,000.00 below the world class standard.

Current GNP rankings take on more meaning when researchers examine the economic growth of each nation during the prosperous 1980s. Economic aggressiveness is a strong indication of the will of a people to improve living conditions. Education is usually the catalyst behind economic growth, so emphasis on education precedes growth. Figure 3.2 reports economic growth in terms of gross domestic product

Japan		$23,730.00
United States		21,100.00
Germany		20,750.00
Canada		19,020.00
France		17,831.00
Britain		14,570.00
New Zealand		11,800.00
Israel		9,750.00
Republic of Korea		4,400.00
Taiwan		4,355.00
	Mean	$14,731.00

Figure 3.1 The 1989 per capita GNP for ten nations identified as having world class education systems. Figures are stated in United States dollars. Note: From World Education Report *(1991).*

Republic of Korea	7.5%
Taiwan	6.0%
New Zealand	2.5%
Japan	2.4%
United States	2.4%
Israel	2.1%
Canada	2.0%
Britain	1.9%
Germany	1.3%
France	1.2%
Mean	3.0%

Figure 3.2 The percentage of increase in gross domestic product, 1980–1985, for ten countries providing world class education systems. Note: From The World in Figures *(1988).*

rather than GNP. Gross domestic product (GDP) differs from GNP in that GDP includes only the wealth of a country within the country's borders; while GNP includes a country's wealth internally as well as wealth in foreign countries. Figure 3.2 shows the growth in Gross Domestic Product from 1980 through 1985.

Notice that the countries reporting the lowest GNP in 1988, Korea, Taiwan, and Israel, had the fastest growth rate during the early 1980's. All three pursue the wealthier countries with impressive success. The emergence of each as an industrial nation could well be married to the emphasis placed on education in each country during the 1980s. European countries showed the smallest GDP growth rate, well below the standard, but each remains on the positive growth side. Japan and the United States grew at the same rate during the years measured, an indication of recent, intense economic competition between the two countries.

 The world class standard for national growth as measured by gross domestic product is 3.0%. The growth rate for the United States during this period is .6% lower than the standard.

The per capita income for each country is the amount of wealth on the average returned to each person in the form of income. The figure is an important indicator of an individual's ability to pay for education, since income determines taxes paid, and taxes pay the education bill. Figure 3.3 shows the 1988 per capita income for each research country.

 The mean or world class standard of $20,149.00 is $26.00 above the per capita income for individuals in the United States.

Per capita income presents a different measure of wealth than the measure presented by studies of GNP or GDP. In the United States, which ranks fifth in per capita income, residents do not reap the dollars in personal income that individuals do in several other world class countries. An unfavorable trade balance sends American dollars to foreign countries, and the distribution of wealth in the United States recently favors a smaller percentage of persons at higher income levels. Many American workers lost ground to inflation during the last two decades. Americans no longer appear to live in the wealthiest country in the world, and the percentage of persons living at the poverty level increased. Since income tax, sales tax, and property tax (taxes dependent on income) provide funding for a major portion of educational services, citizens in the United States are in a less enviable position in terms of ability to pay.

Japan		$23,356.00
Germany		20,311.00
France		16,842.00
Canada		16,760.00
United States		13,123.00
Great Britain		12,800.00
New Zealand		11,126.00
Israel		8,650.00
Taiwan		5,075.00
Republic of Korea		3,450.00
	Mean	$14,731.00

Figure 3.3 The 1988 per capita income for ten countries identified as having world class education systems. Figures are stated in United States dollars. Note: From Moody's International Manual *(1991).*

Wealth Allocated to Education

The second indicator of education expenditure is the amount of a nation's wealth allocated to education. Monetary allocation, no doubt, reflects the value a country places on education. Total world expenditure on education increased to just over a trillion dollars in 1988, equating to around 5.5 percent of world GNP (*World Education Report,* 1991). In 1988 four of the nations included in the world class study reported a contribution to education exceeding the 5.5 percent. Figure 3.4 shows in graphic form the percentage of GNP spent on education during 1988 in each of the ten world class countries.

Canada leads the world class countries with 7.1 percent of GNP spent on education. The United States appears a close second with 6.8 percent. New Zealand and Israel are the remaining two countries above the world class average.

The difference in the range of educational expenditure is the most interesting finding in Figure 3.4. Countries with the least expenditure

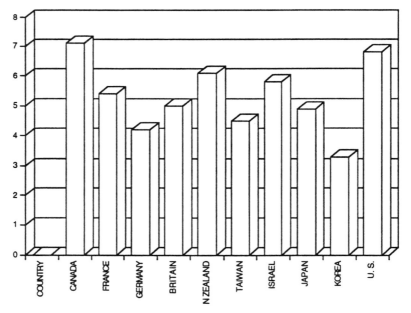

Figure 3.4 *Percent of gross national product spent on education in ten world class education countries, 1988. Note: From* World Education Report *(1991).*

produce excellent scholars. One must conclude that a large allocation of wealth to education does not necessarily produce excellence in education. A world class education system is dependent on other input factors. The formula for producing world class schools lies in the chapters ahead.

 The world class standard for percentage of gross national product spent on education is 5.31%. The contribution of the United States is 1.5% larger than the world class standard.

The United States appears generous in terms of wealth allocated to education. However, one must cautiously note that gross national product spent on education in all countries includes higher education expenditures as well as $K-12$ education expenditures. Many foreign nations consider the United States the world class leader in the provision of higher education, and a large percentage of students in the United States and other nations enroll in American universities. Higher education obviously takes a large share of the education dollar.

Figure 3.5 circumvents the higher education problem and creates a more level playing field by presenting expenditures for $K-12$ youth only. The main disadvantage of this approach is that $K-12$ per-pupil expenditure figures are difficult to find, and conflicting data exist from report to report. Figure 3.5 presents a study completed by the Centre for Educational Research and Innovation that functions within the International Organisation for Economic Cooperation and Development in Paris, France. Although only seven of the world class countries are members of the Centre, the study is considered dependable. Figure 3.5 does not present data for Taiwan, Israel, and Korea because data were not available from any source.

The per-pupil expenditure data correlate positively with the gross national product data. Even on the level playing field created by comparing $K-12$ expenditure, the United States spends generously on education. Canada again leads the ten countries in financial support for education with a 1988 expenditure of $4,745.00 per $K-12$ student. Canada, therefore, is the world class leader in educational expenditure, regardless of method of comparison. Second is the United States with a per-pupil expenditure of $4,301.00. The remaining five countries are

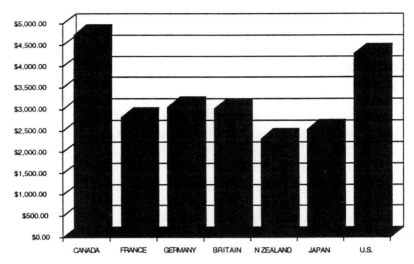

Figure 3.5 K – 12 per-pupil expenditure for seven countries having world class educational systems, 1988. Note: From Education at a Glance *(1992).*

closely grouped together between $2,311.00 per pupil (New Zealand) and $3,047.00 (Germany). Again the conclusion is that each of the five countries maintains an effective education system even though spending is close to average.

 The United States is $1,053.00 above the mean or world class standard for K – 12 per-pupil expenditure. The world class standard is $3,248.00.

Nelson (1991) reports data different from the data reported in Chapter 3 regarding gross national product spent on education. Chapter 3 data are primarily from the United States Department of Education and UNESCO. Nelson authored a study for the American Federation of Teachers (AFT) and gathered data from a report issued by the Economic Policy Institute. The AFT study reports the United States twelfth in educational expenditure when compared with fifteen economically advanced countries belonging to The Organization for Economic Development and Cooperation. The source of the data differs in two ways from the Chapter 3 data. First, Nelson reports data based on GDP rather than GNP; and second, different countries comprise the sample group. With two exceptions, countries in the study are European. The importance of the AFT study for the purpose of the world class research is to notify the reader that a second report exists that uses a different basis of comparison and reports different results.

IMPLICATIONS

Implications surface when examining the research related to world class standards for educational expenditure, and educational decision makers should consider all implications. The United States appropriates funds for education that exceed the world class standard defined in Chapter 3. However, a question arises that begs an answer. Should American education cost more than education in the comparison countries? If the answer is yes, then the ''why'' becomes important, so implications explaining the ''why'' follow.

Funding for education in the United States is at a crossroads. Educators ask for increased funding, but taxpayers rebel against new taxes for education. Politicians argue that throwing money at educational problems is not the answer. Perhaps each group is partially correct. Consider the following implications of educational funding. The implications do not always include answers or a recommendation for change. Educational funding is a complex issue.

As previously mentioned, the percentage of GNP spent on education includes higher education. Colleges and universities in the United States enroll many of the students entering higher education worldwide. Educators throughout the world admire the American higher education system, and foreign students seek enrollment in American universities, particularly for graduate work. The United States sets the world class standard for higher education. A large expenditure is necessary to maintain excellence in higher education. Legislators in each of the fifty states must allocate funds to public schools as generously as they allocate funds to higher education.

The K−12 expenditure for the United States stated in Figure 3.5 appears to be generous. Unique characteristics of American education require additional funding, however.

First, the goal of American schools to provide universal education carries a high price tag. Students in the United States attend comprehensive secondary schools and American schools do not sort students after the primary years, as is the practice in most other countries. The American dream, opportunity for all, costs more per-pupil.

Second, the United States identifies a large percentage of special education students. The Education for All Handicapped Children's Act, 1975, intended federal funds for all handicapped students in the United States; but funds never covered the cost of maintaining the costly programs. The United States also identifies more handicapped students by definition than other countries. The education of severely handicapped students costs as much as $50,000.00 a year in the United States, compared to $5,000.00 for regular students. States and local school boards fund special education programs often at the expense of the regular education initiative. Compensatory education in American schools also costs a great deal of money. Chapter 1 funding absorbs the largest portion of the federal dollar spent on education.

Third, the multicultural, multidimensional demands on American schools tend to expand the curriculum and, in turn, inflate costs. Otherwise, American educators teach more than just academics. Educators continue to answer the call for new programs that address the country's social and economic problems. Most American schools address career education, driver education, substance abuse education, sex education, personal development education, ethnic and race education, and a variety of educational programs dealing with social and personal problems. Chapter 8 concentrates on curriculum and provides expanded insight into the pregnant curriculum.

Fourth, the emphasis on the extracurricular, particularly interscholastic sports, inflates the cost of education in the United States. No other country researched emphasizes the extracurricular as much as the United States. It seems almost everyone finds extracurricular experiences valuable, and nobody wishes to interfere with the American love affair with Friday night high school football. In many school districts, the extracurricular programs steer the academic program. Extracurricular activities cost money.

Expensive support services such as transportation, food service, and custodial services operate in the United States. Parents demand transportation for their children; lunch and, many times breakfast; and clean schools. School construction in the United States costs dearly, for comprehensive schools require extensive facilities.

Other world class countries save money on support services. Japan, Korea, and Taiwan, for example, do not provide student transportation. German students often attend school for long half days, so food service is not always necessary. Students in Asian countries provide their own custodial services.

American citizens desire school services described above for their children. Common sense dictates acceptance of transportation, food service, and custodial care. However, citizens must consider the additional expense incurred by these services.

Data regarding per-pupil expenditure trigger the most serious implications about educational funding. The data show that the United States provides world class per-pupil expenditure when comparing averages. The range is quite another matter. Data showing the range of per-pupil expenditure from local district to local district are not included in the study, but it is common knowledge that per-pupil expenditure has a broad range and is extremely unequal. It is shameful that school districts must threaten legislators and initiate lawsuits against their own governing structure in order to correct unequal funding of schools. McAdams (1993) conducted an international comparison of schooling and observed the following:

> A major cause of the widening gulf in educational opportunities available to American students is our system of school finance. No other country surveyed allows such a degree of disparity in resources to exist among schools as is found in the United States. (p. 272)

Kozul (1991) presents a graphic comparison of inequalities in American school finance. Kozul found a range in per-pupil spending from $3,500.00 to $15,000.00 in districts in near proximity. State legislatures seem unable to deal with inequalities in per-pupil spending, causing legal action by educators and citizens. Kentucky initiated a new equality plan to solve the problem in that state. In the summer of 1993, Michigan legislators declared the property tax illegal for funding education, and in 1994, replaced a large majority of the property tax with an increase in sales tax and other excise taxes. Some states have the courage to address the problem, but others still engage in political gridlock. Little excuse exists for the wide range of per-pupil spending. States should not deny students a quality education because of their birthplace. Each state should act promptly to provide equal funding for students, or the federal government should attack the problem as it attacked the segregation

---

Worksheet

How does your educational agency compare to the world class standard on educational expenditure? Fill in the following information.

K – 12 Expenditure

$3,248

(World class standard)	(Your agency)	(Deviation)

Per Capita Income

$13,149.00

(Per capita income)	(Your agency)	(Deviation)

---

issue. If the states resist, Congress should consider federal funding of schools.

AFTERTHOUGHT

The United States appears generous in amounts spent on education given the fact that it is no longer the world's wealthiest country. The question remains, ''Does the United States spend wisely on education when compared to other world class countries?''

REFERENCES

Education at a Glance. 1992. Paris, France: Organisation for Economic Cooperation and Development.

Kozul, J. 1991. *Savage Inequalities: Children in America's Schools.* Copyright 1991 by Jonathan Kozul. Reprinted by permission of Crown Publishers, Inc., New York.

Lapointe, A. E., J. M. Askew and N. A. Mead. 1992. *Learning Mathematics.* Princeton, New Jersey: The International Assessment of Educational Progress, Educational Testing Service.

McAdams, R. P. 1993. *Lessons from Abroad: How Other Countries Educate Their Children.* Lancaster, Pennsylvania: Technomic Publishing Company, Inc.

Moody's International Manual. 1991. New York: Moody's Investors Service, Incorporated.

Nelson, F. H. 1991. *International Comparison of Public Spending on Education.* Washington D.C.: Research Department, American Federation of Teachers, AFL-CIO.

World Education Report. 1991. Paris, France: United National Educational, Scientific, and Cultural Organization.

The World in Figures. 1988. Boston: Editorial Information Gathered by Economist, G.K. Hall, Inc.

Chapter 4

DEFINING A WORLD CLASS STANDARD FOR TIME ON TASK

The amount of learning time a nation provides for student learning is a major indication of its commitment to education. The effective school research conducted during the last decade clearly demonstrates the relationship between the amount of learning time allotted per subject and the quality of student learning. The following time on task issues are examined:

(1) What is the world class standard for days in a school year?
(2) What is the world class standard for minutes of instruction in a school day?
(3) What is the world class standard for hours of instruction in a school year?
(4) What is the world class standard for number of years and the age span of compulsory attendance?
(5) What is the world class standard for weekly minutes of instruction in mathematics for thirteen year olds?
(6) What is the world class standard for weekly minutes of instruction in science for thirteen year olds?

PERCEPTION: RANKING THE UNITED STATES ON TIME ON TASK

How do educators rank the United States in terms of time provided for learning? The national sample of 182 educators ranked the United States with the nine other nations on two questions about time on task. The responses are reported in Table 4.1 by percentages rounded off to the nearest whole number.

TABLE 4.1.

Rank United States schools as they compare to the following nine national school systems:			First	Top Third	Middle Third	Bottom Third	Last
Canada	France	Germany					
Britain	New Zealand	Taiwan					
Israel	South Korea	Japan	(Percentage of Total Responding)				
3. Longest average school year? (n = 181)			0	5	20	40	35
4. Longest number of years of compulsory education? (n = 181)			2	4	21	39	34

The responses indicate a range of thinking. The respondents appeared to know that the United States did not rank well on the length of the school year, as 75 percent of the respondents ranked the United States in the bottom third or dead last. On the issue of compulsory attendance, the responses were quite similar. The respondents believe that the United States does not require a great number of compulsory school years. While this perception is not necessarily true, it does reflect America's concern with school drop-outs.

REALITY: THE WORLD CLASS STANDARD FOR TIME ON TASK

Average Days in School Year

For most Americans the education year is 180 days long. Since the end of World War II that has been the length of the school year in each state. Even schools experimenting with the "year-round concept" are usually configured on a 180-day school calendar. But is that the world class standard for a school year? Figure 4.1 shows the length of the school year in the ten nations studied.

The United States ranks ninth among the nations in length of school year when the longest school year is counted as number one. While Americans continue to reject the idea of a longer school year, students in other countries annually have more days to learn. Typically, reactions to a longer school year include rationalizations that the longer year adds too much stress to students and costs too much. The reader is referred to Chapter 7 for a presentation about students' out-of-school time and to Chapter 11 for a presentation on student suicide rates among the nations.

The issue of increased cost for a longer school year is real. A longer year would be a clear reason to raise teacher salaries, which also increases expense. Put into perspective, if just the amount of projected increase in medical costs from 1993 to 2001 were calculated, the *increase alone* would equal *the entire amount* America currently spends on education! Only when the American public takes the education of its next generation as seriously as it takes health care, can the cost of a longer school year be addressed in a meaningful way. Can the United States afford *not* to have a longer school year?

 The world class standard for length of the school year is 204 days. The United States has twenty-four fewer days or 11.7 percent less school per year than the world class standard. A longer school year is needed.

Canada[1]	188 days
France[1]	174 days
Federal Republic of Germany[1]	210 days
Great Britain[1]	192 days
New Zealand[2]	200 days (primary)
	190 days (secondary)
Taiwan[1]	222 days
Israel[3]	215 days (Friday 1/2 day)
Japan[1]	240 days* (Saturday is 1/2 day)
Republic of Korea[1]	222 days
United States[1]	180 days
Mean	204 days

[1]Note: From *Education at a Glance.*
[2]Note: From *New Zealand Official 1990 Yearbook Extracts.*
[3]Note: From Karyan, S. 1992. Interview.
*The length of the Japanese school year was dropped to 228 days (one Saturday a month there is no school, beginning in the 1992 – 93 school year).

Figure 4.1 *The number of school days in an education year in the ten world class nations for 1991 – 92.*

Average Minutes of Instruction in a School Day

The second gauge of time on task for learning is the length of the average school day (see Figure 4.2). The reader is cautioned to view these data carefully because the number of hours spent in a school building does not equate to actual hours of teaching and learning. For instance, in Japan, several school days are actually scheduled for festivals or other forms of play. Students learn during this time that school is fun, something Americans generally do not teach their students. Also, the Japanese count forty-five minutes of instruction in elementary school and fifty minutes of instruction in secondary schools as an hour (Ishizaka, circa 1990). The remaining time is scheduled for social purposes (Hess and Azuma, 1991). Japanese educators are often surprised how American school children come into school and immediately get to work and then only have a brief break in the morning, at lunch, and occasionally in the afternoon. The reader is referred to Chapter 6 for further insight into the use of classroom learning time.

The United States ranks second among the nations studied, which may surprise the reader. However, there is no certainty that teachers devote all of time spent in the school building to learning. Note that the Federal Republic of Germany and Great Britain do not provide lunch, and that

Canada	304
France	370
Federal Republic of Germany	300[2]
Great Britain	300[3]
New Zealand	n/a
Taiwan	318
Israel	278[4]
Japan[5]	330
Republic of Korea	264
United States	338
Mean	311

[1]Note: From Lapointe et al. (1992).
[2]Includes many half days and no lunch service.
[3]Includes some half days and a few Saturdays—lunch is not served.
[4]Has recently been lengthened (Karyan, S., 1992).
[5]Note: From Ishizaka (circa 1990).

Figure 4.2 The length of the school instructional day in minutes for the ten world class nations, 1991 – 92 school year.[1]

the Japanese eat in the classroom and clean the entire room at the end of the day. Also, the time reported here does not include time spent in "cram schools," the private schools that teach many of the arts and prepare students for elimination testing. Such schools are common along the eastern Pacific Rim. Cram schools may add two hours to the school day six days a week plus two additional hours of homework (Williford, 1992). American educators would be wise to view homework as a part of the instructional day and as a no-cost means of lengthening the instructional day.

 The world class standard for average minutes of instruction in the school day is 311. The United States exceeds this average by 27 minutes.

Average Hours of Instruction in the School Year

A more meaningful figure than days in the school year or minutes of instruction in the school day is the combination of the two that provides insight into the total amount of instructional time per school year (see Figure 4.3). The cumulative impact of more learning time is the same for a Japanese student after twelve years of instruction as the average American student at the end of sixteen years of instruction (Stevenson, 1992)!

Because these data do not include the effect of cram school education, the amount of homework, nor the different methods of instruction used in schools around the world, the reader is cautioned not to think that a longer school day and longer school year alone will cure the nation's education ills. For example, Stevenson reports that Taiwanese school children spend four times as long doing homework as do American school children. Homework expands the learning time for students.

Additionally, student attendance rates indicate the time that students are in school to learn. American students lose learning experiences when absent for a variety of reasons. Japanese mothers traditionally attend school and take notes if their child is absent, so the mother can teach the missed lesson at home. Additionally, the length of actual school attendance is longer in many nations, and many students attend beyond the compulsory years. McAdams (1993) reports that, beyond compulsory

Canada		952.5
France		1,073
Federal Republic of Germany		1,050
Great Britain		960
New Zealand		n/a
Taiwan		1,177
Israel		996
Japan		1,050
Republic of Korea		978
United States		1,014
	Mean	1,033.39

Note: Data derived by authors.

Figure 4.3 *Average hours of instruction in a school year in the ten world class nations, 1991 – 92.*

education levels in Germany, students are required to attend school at least on a part-time basis until the age of eighteen. Much valuable time is spent in extensive apprenticeships that blend actual work and class-room education.

 The world class standard for average hours of in-struction in the school year is 1,033.39. The United States is barely below the world class standard, not counting homework or extra schooling as part of the average. Regular use of homework should be part of the schooling experience for American students.

Compulsory Education

Another measure of time on task is the amount of time that a nation *compels* students to be in school. In the United States, compulsory attendance originated in Massachusetts in the 1850s, although parts of the South did not compel students to go to school until the first decade of this century. All ten countries in the study have established compulsory attendance, and there exists remarkable similarity among the ages for compulsory school attendance.

The reader is advised to read Figure 4.3 with care. It does not reflect the common practice in many nations of sending children to noncompulsory kindergarten or a "reception year" as it is called in Great Britain. Japan, for example, does not compel children to attend kindergarten, but attendance rates are similar to those in the United States. In addition, privately funded preschools are common in many nations. In New Zealand, for example, nearly half of all students attend a private school at age two (*New Zealand Official 1990 Yearbook Extracts*, 1990).

Consider the percentage of time that school is a part of a child's life. Using the total number of hours in eighteen years of life, the average American child is involved in school and directly related academic activities approximately 10 percent of the time, and this figure assumes no "snow days," illnesses, etc. Students spend one-third of their time sleeping (not counting naps in class), leaving a student awake and not involved in school 55 percent of the time between birth and high school graduation. In eastern Pacific Rim nations like Japan and Taiwan, where "cram schools" and additional private education increase the amount of time spent in school, the percentage of school life in the same eighteen years increases as much as 15 or 16 percent. Because they devote more

Nation	Age Span	Number of Years
Canada	6 to 16	Ten years
France	6 to 16	Ten years
Federal Republic of Germany	6 to 15	Nine years[2]
Great Britain	5 to 16	Eleven years
New Zealand	5 to 15	Ten years
Taiwan	6 to 15	Nine years
Israel	5 to 16	Eleven years
Japan	6 to 15	Nine years
Republic of Korea	6 to 12	Six years[3]
United States	6 to 16	Ten years[4]

[1]Note: Ministry or Department of Education publications for each nation studied.
[2]Students are required to continue in school, part-time, until age eighteen (McAdams, 1993).
[3]This figure is misleading since almost all students attended for nine years: since 1988 the Korean government has increased the compulsory education age to fifteen.
[4]This figure varies some state-by-state, although the *practice* includes the years shown. In North Carolina, for example, compulsory attendance covers ages seven to sixteen, yet the state funds programs from kindergarten (age five) up. In excess of 98 percent of the students in public school first grade attended public kindergarten (*North Carolina Statistical Profile*, 1992).

Figure 4.4 *Age span and number of years of compulsory attendance among the ten world class nations in 1988.*[1]

time to learning, it is no wonder students in other nations appear to achieve more.

 The world class standard for length and span of compulsory education is a 9.7-year span between the ages of five and sixteen. The United States meets this world class standard.

Average Minutes of Math Instruction per Week for Thirteen-Year-Old Students

Since this study began about the time several nations released the huge IAEP multinational comparison of mathematics and science achievement test scores for thirteen-year-old students, the authors include time on task data for teaching mathematics and science. Figure 4.5 presents the minutes per week of mathematics instruction, and Figure 4.6 presents the minutes per week of science instruction.

In Figure 4.5, the amount of time devoted to mathematics instruction varies from 175 minutes in the new Japanese curriculum to 230 minutes in France. The United States allocated 10 percent *more* time to mathe-

Nation	Weekly Minutes of Math Instruction
Canada	225
France	230
Federal Republic of Germany	n/a
Great Britain	190
New Zealand	set by teacher
Taiwan	204
Israel	205
Japan[2]	175
Republic of Korea	179
United States	228
Mean average	205

[1]Note: From Lapointe et al. (1992).
[2]Note: From *An Outline of Revision of the Courses of Study in Japan* (circa 1992).

Figure 4.5 *Average minutes of mathematics instruction per week for thirteen-year-old students, 1991 – 92.*[1]

Nation	Weekly Minutes of Science Instruction
Canada	156
France	174
Federal Republic of Germany	n/a
Great Britain	194
New Zealand	set by teacher
Taiwan	245
Israel	181
Japan[2]	247.5
Republic of Korea	144
United States	223
Mean average	205

[1]Note: From Lapointe et al. (1992).
[2]Note: From *An Outline of Revision of the Courses of Study in Japan* (circa 1992).

Figure 4.6 *Average minutes of science instruction per week for thirteen-year-old students, 1991−92.*[1]

matics instruction than the mean figure of 205 minutes yet did not score high on the test. When achievement test scores of other countries are reviewed, the Republic of Korea and Taiwan report the highest test scores. Along with Japan, teachers in both countries spend the least amount of time teaching mathematics compared to other nations reported. Japan was not included in the IAEP study, so figures come from another source, and implications are not made about the amount of time devoted to learning mathematics.

Figure 4.6 presents data for average minutes of science instruction per week for thirteen-year-old students in the IAEP survey.

 The world class standard for weekly time spent teaching thirteen-year-old students mathematics is 205 and science is 196. The United States exceeds the world class standard in both subjects.

IMPLICATIONS

The importance of time on task as a correlate in effective schools research and the importance of it as a world class standard are beyond question. However, given the variance in test proficiency among the world class nations, variables other than time on task must be considered. In a lengthy and enjoyable interview with Honorable Duck Haeng Hur, General Consul in the Republic of Korea, one author showed Consul Hur the test figures; and he was unable to explain the high test scores and low time on task reported from his nation. He did explain that, in the Republic of Korea, the only way for someone to improve their social class is by excelling in school. Given the previously reported fact that the Republic spends the least amount of gross national product on education among the ten nations in this study and that an enemy is always lurking on the northern border, Korean students perhaps are more motivated to learn than students in several of the other nations studied. Cultural variables involving work ethic, individual responsibility to learn, and pride in achievement must be considered along with the more simple concept of time on task. While time devoted to teaching and learning is important, cultural influence appears to be more important.

Caplan et al. (1992) shed some light on the education ethic. Researchers studied a group of slightly over 500 Indo-Chinese refugee students admitted to the United States on a quota basis, to determine how well they achieved in American schools over a three and one-half year period. These refugees knew little English when they arrived and had little or no formal schooling other than that available in the refugee camps. Unlike earlier refugees who had ties to the former South Vietnam government or American military, these people knew little about American culture. The refugees were scattered from coast to coast and involved with many different school systems.

In three and one-half years' time the researchers found that these students met world class achievement standards in both science and mathematics, and they were nearly at grade level in their understanding of English. If America's schools are as bad as they are often portrayed, how could this group do so well in American schools? The answer was the existence of an education ethic in the home that greatly exceeded the ethic found in the homes of American classmates.

Caplan et al. studied not only the time spent in school but time spent on learning at home. They found that the family ate dinner together without a television set competing for attention and then cleared the table and did homework collectively until everyone understood the homework. The children helped their parents with language and cultural issues; the older children taught the younger ones; and there was a family drive to learn. There is no doubt that the extra time provided by

American educators — 10 percent above the world class standard in time spent teaching mathematics and 12 percent above in science for thirteen year olds — was beneficial, but the drive to learn and learning time spent in the home clearly were factors accounting for better learning by the refugees.

The authors categorically reject explanations given by some educators that ''they are better at science and math than we are.'' The difference is the drive to learn.

Many eastern Pacific Rim nations use private, tuition-bearing education to further the learning of some students. Americans call these tuition schools ''cram schools,'' while the Japanese call them ''*juku*'' and the Taiwanese call them ''*bushibon.*'' ''Star teachers'' teach these classes and earn larger salaries in the cram schools than they earn in public schools. Teaching is provided late in the afternoon or evenings, and the school operates on Saturday in many eastern Pacific Rim countries. The teachers expect many hours of extra homework. *Bushibons* operate on some Sundays as well. Getting into the ''best'' cram school is very important in the competitive eastern Pacific Rim countries.

Many *bushibons* in Taipei may have a class size of 150 or more, and students concentrate on rote learning rather than trying to get individual attention from the teacher. The expectations are very high. When the authors interviewed Hyoung-Tae Kim (1992), a student from the Republic of Korea, one question asked was: ''Given the extreme expense of a *juku,* what happens if the student simply refuses to do all of the extra work?'' The reply was immediate and said with no air of surprise: ''Then we fire the student.'' The answer made sense to the authors!

The authors suspect two additional factors affect the relation of test results and time on task. First is the factor of student attendance. They found no comparative study of student attendance; but as was mentioned earlier, in Japan, if the child is sick, traditionally the mother substitutes in school for her ill child. Japanese parents also go to school several times during the school year to observe their child in school (Stevenson, 1992), and schools have been known to schedule Sunday as a routine school day so that working fathers can also observe the child. With so much parental support and involvement in school, is it surprising that Japanese school children learn more?

A second factor that may help to explain the relation of test results and time on task issue is the method of student learning. In the typical thirteen-year-old student's classroom in Japan, Hess and Azuma (1991) reported that the average school book may only contain 100 pages, yet the teacher might teach from the book for 300 hours. The difference between the Japanese classroom and the American classroom is an emphasis on understanding *process* rather than focusing on *content*. American students often provide a correct answer quickly and move to new material. The focus on *process mastery* could explain a great deal of the improved performance on international tests so familiar to American educators.

The American school year is simply too short. Only France reports a shorter year. The experiment with "year-round schools" is applauded by the authors even though year-round schools generally don't lengthen the school year. The Henderson County Public Schools in North Carolina offer four, nine-week sessions separated by breaks of three weeks. A student may opt to stay in school one or two weeks longer for remediation or enrichment, effectively lengthening the school year for those taking advantage of the opportunity. The year-round school appears to be heading in the correct direction.

The length of the instructional day in the United States exceeds the world class standard by nearly one-half hour per day. The increase is considerable and should increase student learning. But the United States loses this advantage because the school year is over one month sooner than the world class standard. Add to the shorter year the lack of parent involvement in education, and the lack of learning becomes more understandable. Perhaps American educators can take some solace in the fact that the number of two-earner families in Japan is increasing, and that the number of mothers taking notes for their sick children is greatly decreasing. The authors expect decreased family involvement to take a toll on Japan. However, reducing Japanese standards to American standards will not improve the outcomes of American education.

In summary, it appears that Americans generally don't want a longer school year, don't want a longer school day, and don't want greater amounts of student homework. Yet those same Americans want world class schools. Or do they?

AFTERTHOUGHTS

(*1*) The length of the American school year is too short. A longer year could be phased in, five days per year, until at least 205 days are involved.

Worksheet

How does your educational agency compare to the world class standard on time on task?

Days in the School Year

204

(World class standard)	(Your agency)	(Deviation)

Minutes of Instruction in the School Day

311

(World class standard)	(Your agency)	(Deviation)

Hours of Instruction

1,033.99

(World class standard)	(Your agency)	(Deviation)

Years of Compulsory Education

Ages six to fifteen
or 9.7 years

(World class standard)	(Your agency)	(Deviation)

Minutes of Math Instruction Weekly for Thirteen-Year-Old Students

205

(World class standard)	(Your agency)	(Deviation)

Minutes of Science Instruction Weekly for Thirteen-Year-Old Students

196

(World class standard)	(Your agency)	(Deviation)

(2) The lack of a general education ethic — the drive to learn — hurts American student achievement.

(3) American educators can work with parents to improve the amount and quality of homework as a no-cost means of extending time on task.

REFERENCES

Caplan, N., M. Choy and J. Whitmore. 1992. "Indochinese Refugee Families and Academic Achievement," *Scientific American.*

Education at a Glance. 1992. Paris: Organization for Economic Cooperation and Development.

Hess, R. D. and H. Azuma. 1991. "Cultural Support for Schooling. Contrasts between Japan and the United States," *Educational Researcher.*

Ishizaka, K. 1990. *School Education in Japan.* Tokyo: International Society for Educational Information, Inc.

Karyan, S. 1992. Interview (October 23).

Kim H.-T. 1992. Interview (October 14).

Lapointe, A. E., J. M. Askew and N. A. Mead. 1992. *Learning Science.* Princeton, New Jersey: The International Assessment of Educational Progress, Educational Testing Service.

Lapointe, A. E., N. A. Mead and J. M. Askew. 1992. *Learning Mathematics.* Princeton, New Jersey: The International Assessment of Educational Progress, Educational Testing Service.

McAdams, R. P. 1993. *Lessons from Abroad: How Other Countries Educate Their Children.* Lancaster, Pennsylvania: Technomic Publishing Company.

New Zealand Official 1990 Yearbook Extracts. 1990. Monograph Provided by the Embassy of New Zealand, Washington, D.C.

North Carolina Statistical Profile. 1992. Raleigh: State of North Carolina.

An Outline of Revision of the Courses of Study in Japan. 1992. Tokyo: Ministry of Education, Science and Culture.

Stevenson, H. W. 1992. "Learning from Asian Schools," *Scientific American.*

Williford, K. 1992. Interview (August 28).

DEFINING A WORLD CLASS STANDARD
FOR CLASS SIZE

Educators in the United States stress the importance of small class size as a factor in the improvement of learning. Do the nine world class countries consider small class size equally important? Chapter 5 explores the following world class standards for class size and pupil-teacher ratio in an attempt to answer the question.
(1) Primary and secondary pupil-teacher ratio for full-time and part-time teachers, 1988
(2) The average modal grade class size for 13-year-old students, 1991 – 92
Chapter 5 presents implications of class size research for the United States and suggestions for future decision making.

PERCEPTION: RANKING THE UNITED STATES
ON CLASS SIZE

Many educators and parents in America verbalize the need for smaller school class size. The subject surfaces at almost every teacher and board of education negotiation session. School improvement plans stress the need for smaller classes. Teachers rank smaller class size first on their wish list. One might assume that such a high priority for small classes indicates that the United States does not compare favorably with other nations. The assumption that class size in the United States does not compare favorably with other nations is not supported by either the perception of the conference sample group or the class size research shown in Table 5.1.

TABLE 5.1.

Rank United States schools as they compare to the following nine national school systems:			First	Top Third	Middle Third	Bottom Third	Last
Canada	France	Germany					
Britain	New Zealand	Taiwan					
Israel	South Korea	Japan	(Percentage of Total Responding)				
5. Smallest average class size? (*n* = 181)			8.8	34.8	34.3	18.8	3.3

The conference survey completed by educational leaders throughout the country did not reveal a perception that the United States provides small classes when compared with the other world class nations. Those surveyed spread responses across the five categories: first place, top, middle, and bottom third and last place. The response indicates that educators are not sure of the position of the United States pertaining to world class educational class size. Notice that an approximately equal number of respondents marked each of the thirds on the questionnaire.

REALITY: THE WORLD CLASS STANDARD
FOR CLASS SIZE

Pupil-Teacher Ratio

The pupil-teacher ratio indicates the amount available per student of the most important educational resource – the teacher. Figure 5.1 shows the pupil-teacher ratio for primary full-time and part-time teachers in column one and secondary teachers in column two. The countries with the smallest or most desired ratio are presented first.

Certainly the United States could try to emulate Israel, but the cost of reducing the pupil-teacher ratio by six students is excessive. Israel presents an unusual situation. Data show that Israel maintains the smallest pupil-teacher ratio of the ten world class countries; but later, Figure 5.2 shows their class size not nearly as favorable. Perhaps more Israeli teachers are part-time. Also, educational leaders not favoring an additional expenditure to reduce the per-pupil ratio can point to Japan,

Taiwan, and Korea as successful systems with an equal or much higher per-pupil ratio than the United States. The academic success of these countries, as measured by international tests, shows that the educational system of a country can be successful even if large classes are the rule.

> The world class standard for pupil-teacher ratio at the primary level is twenty-two students for each teacher. Primary class size in the United States equals the world class standard.

The secondary ratio found in Figure 5.1 places the United States third among the world class countries, a much more favorable position. Israel again occupies first place, but as with the primary ratio, the other countries would find this position hard and perhaps unnecessary to match. The favorable position of the United States at the secondary level as opposed to the primary level seems to give proponents of a smaller ratio in the early grades fuel to move teachers from the secondary to the primary level.

Primary		Secondary	
Israel	16:1	Israel	7:1
Canada	17:1	Germany	12:1
Germany	18:1	United States	13:1
France	19:1	France	14:1
Britain	20:1	Britain	14:1
New Zealand	21:1	Canada	16:1
Japan	22:1	Japan	18:1
United States	22:1	New Zealand	18:1
Taiwan	32:1	Taiwan	22:1
Republic of Korea	36:1	Republic of Korea	28:1
Mean	22:1	Mean	16:1

Note: From *World Education Report* (1991).

Figure 5.1 *Rank order of primary and secondary pupil-teacher ratio for the ten world class education nations, 1988. Figures include full-time and part-time teachers.*

The world class standard for pupil-teacher ratio at the secondary level is sixteen students for each teacher or three students per teacher more than schools in the United States.

Class Size

Pupil-teacher ratios are not indicators of class size. Countries can have equal pupil-teacher ratios but very different class sizes. The pupil-teacher ratio usually falls below class size because in most countries, students take six or seven classes a day while the teacher teaches four or five. Variance in teaching loads and the number of classes per teacher usually cause the difference. This seems to be the situation in Israel where the pupil-teacher ratio is by far the best of the countries, but class size is only at the average mark. An alternative method of arriving at a world class standard for numbers of students per teacher is the use of class size data.

The data in Figure 5.2 are primarily from the International Assessment of Educational Progress conducted in 1991. Twenty countries assessed the mathematics and science achievement of thirteen-year-old students and reported the average class size for the grade in which the most thirteen-year-old students were enrolled. Seven of the world class countries participated in this study. The data from those who did not participate, Germany, Japan, and New Zealand, are from different sources.

Figure 5.2 shows five countries with a range in average class size for thirteen-year-old students from twenty to twenty-five students. The United States with twenty-three is in the middle of this group. One observation of those who conducted the International Assessment of Educational Progress is that urban countries are more likely to have large schools and large classes (Lapointe et al., 1992). The countries studied have large urban areas. Very large classes of forty-nine are the norm in Korea, and Taiwan reports an average of forty-four students. These two extremes, along with the thirty-two per class reported by Israel and the 31.4 per class reported by Japan, raise the mean to twenty-nine students.

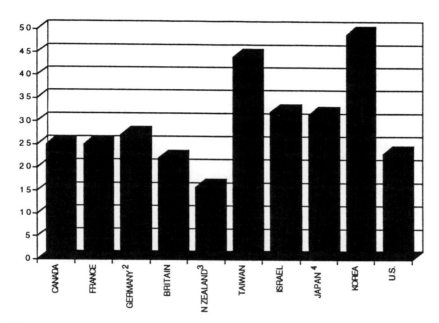

¹Lapointe et al. (1992).
²Busek, H. (1992).
³*New Zealand Official 1990 Yearbook Extracts* (1992).
⁴*An Outline of Revision of the Courses of Study in Japan* (1992).

Figure 5.2 Average size in the modal grade for thirteen-year-old students, of ten countries providing world class education, 1991 – 1992.[1]

The world class standard for class size is twenty-nine thirteen-year-old students per class, and the United States averages six students less than the world class standard.

Little relationship seems to exist between class size and student achievement. Countries with class size above the world class standard produce students who excel on international tests. Countries admired for the development and maintenance of world class education have classes larger than the world class standard. Important implications exist for educational decision makers.

IMPLICATIONS

Other things being equal, a smaller pupil-teacher ratio and smaller class size should make it possible for students to receive more attention from teachers. But does smaller per-pupil ratio and class size produce increased student achievement? The debate continues. Several factors complicate the relationship between pupil-teacher ratio or class size and the amount and quality of instruction received by each pupil. These complications are explored with emphasis on the implications for future class size development in the schools of the United States.

Data Consistency

The data concerning pupil-teacher ratio and class size are not fully consistent among countries. Countries differ on how or whether they even distinguish between classroom teachers and other personnel such as counselors, librarians, or administrators. The data determining the world class standard for pupil-teacher ratio and class size reflect inter-country variations in how broadly the ''teacher'' category is defined. The results of class size research also depend on the countries chosen for comparison. The research presented in this book includes data collected from ten countries chosen for educational excellence, and countries are included from Europe, Asia, and North America. Comparing different countries changes the results. The American Federation of Teachers, for example, conducted a study that finds class size in American schools higher than several other countries. The countries were not chosen because of their world class reputation but were selected from UNESCO data. All countries are European with the exception of Japan. The AFT-sponsored study authored by Nelson (1991) calls for lower class size if schools in the United States are to be world class. The implications in this chapter take issue with Nelson's conclusion.

Class Size and Student Achievement

Speaking individually and through their unions, teachers introduce favorable pupil-teacher ratios and smaller classes as desirable conditions for increasing student achievement. The National Education Association (1991) cites small class size as critical to the achievement of quality education. The association claims that elementary classes in the United

States have as many as thirty-two students and that city school classes are higher. The NEA stresses that *most* professionals believe class sizes should be no larger than fifteen students.

One author, with two decades of experience negotiating local contracts with NEA affiliates, believes that the NEA persists in raising the class size issue in order to enhance teacher comfort and reduce paperwork. These are worthy goals if affordable, but the NEA goal should not be interpreted as a goal to increase student achievement.

Stevenson and Lee (1990) compared student achievement in first and fifth grade classrooms in Japan, Taiwan, and the United States. During the process, the researchers asked teachers in the three countries to respond to a question about how each would spend new money given the school district. Teachers were to assume that their school had been given a large amount of money and that they could determine how the money would be spent. The answers available to teachers were categorized into five areas. The first category was the reduction of class size, and the remaining four categories covered the enhancement of programs, equipment, and activities for students.

Teachers in Japan and Taiwan made no mention of reduced class size in spite of their large classes. Over half of the American teachers chose to use the funds for class size reduction. The same teachers were asked to name the ideal class size. Chinese and Japanese teachers suggested twenty-nine per class. American teachers suggested twenty per class. The focus on small classes by the American teachers participating in the study probably reflects a similar focus among American teachers in general.

Serious implications surface about the class size issue and student achievement. The United States cannot likely afford to reduce class size substantially. Also, classes in Asian schools are large compared with classes in North American schools, with typically thirty-five to fifty students per class; yet teaching and learning in the Asian schools is effective (*International Comparisons in Education,* circa 1992, Copyright © Alberta Chamber of Resources). It is not the intent of this research to deny the benefits of teacher comfort, but to deny the contention that smaller class size increases student achievement.

Teacher Contacts with Students

Teachers in the world class countries seem to have fewer classes, or classes do not meet daily as they do in the United States. United States teachers probably spend more time with students each day than do teachers in other nations studied. Teachers in the other world class countries are also assigned fewer noninstructional duties. McAdams (1993) found that American teachers carry a heavy work load and a number of noninstructional responsibilities. McAdams offers a compelling alternative to American teachers seeking lower class size. He suggests raising class size! Minimal class size increases could save enough revenue to dramatically reduce teacher work loads. Increases in class size could increase the employment of paraprofessionals who would assume supervisory duties currently performed by teachers. The responsibility for supervising bus duty, cafeteria duty, and hall duty distinguishes American teachers from many of their counterparts in foreign countries. For example, American teachers still sit with their pupils during lunch in many local districts. Teachers find these non-professional duties demeaning and a distraction from the teacher's need to establish a caring, professional relationship with students. Paraprofessionals could perform these duties creating additional planning time for teachers. Teacher professionalism will be enhanced by the removal of non-instructional activities, and the trade-off is a small class size increase that still leaves American classrooms smaller than the world class average.

Instructional Organization

Teachers organize students using methods that might justify either larger or smaller class size. Smaller classes benefit teachers who individualize expectations and instruction for each student. Teachers who emphasize lecture and rote drill can appear before larger classes. Administrators in American schools shy away from judging teacher methodology, but the idea of varying class size according to methodology has merit. If teachers use individualized methods, give them smaller classes. If they use large group methods, give them large groups.

Ability grouping at the elementary level and tracking at the secondary level are excellent examples of practices analogous to larger classes. Ability grouping during the primary years is not world class, for teachers in many world class countries group students heterogeneously during the primary years. Many American educational experts also find ability grouping or tracking harmful. Herzog (1993) found that tracking during the middle years in school requires winners and losers. Teachers have low expectations for low track students, who come to feel inferior and like losers. Tracking and ability grouping remain common practices in American schools in spite of research condemning the practice. Teachers can group larger numbers of students, as well as smaller numbers. The thought might appeal to school leaders seeking an end to ability grouping and tracking, especially at younger ages.

Classroom Availability

Classrooms in the United States accommodate about thirty students, and room does not exist for smaller classes. Funding does not exist to build additional classrooms — American citizens struggle just to replace existing buildings that are outdated. It is unreasonable to think that most American citizens will vote to build additional classrooms or hire additional teachers in order to provide smaller classes. Unequal financing of education also means that rich districts can afford smaller classes, while poor districts have little chance to reduce class size (refer to Chapter 3). This is unfair.

Class Size and Classroom Atmosphere

Teachers themselves raise an issue about class size that should gather attention. A tolerable class size depends on student behavior. Countries with larger classes appear to have disciplined classrooms where students are motivated to learn and discipline problems are rare. Classrooms in the United States are too often notorious for violence, student indifference, and disruption; conditions that seem to be drifting from high school into the early grades. Teachers who lobby for smaller classes are often quick to admit that larger classes would be fine if all students came to school eager to learn. The argument presented against smaller class size should be contingent on efforts to improve classroom atmosphere. Teachers attempting to teach thirty students should not be required to perform police duties. If Americans cannot resolve the cultural problems that affect school-age youth, they may well have to pay the price for smaller classes in school and a smaller pupil-teacher ratio. The disruptive American student is examined in Chapter 9. Parent responsibility is examined in Chapter 11, but one thought about parent responsibility for learning seems appropriate at this point.

George Will (1993) writes in his syndicated column about the correla-

---

Worksheet

How does your educational agency compare to the world class standard on teacher ratio and class size?

Primary Pupil-Teacher Ratio

22:1

(World class standard)	(Your agency)	(Deviation)

Secondary Pupil-Teacher Ratio

16:1

(World class standard)	(Your agency)	(Deviation)

Class Size: Modal Grade for Thirteen-Year-Old Students

29

(World class standard)	(Your agency)	(Deviation)

---

tion between family and school success. Will quotes from Paul Barton's book, *America's Smallest Family,* who said that a more powerful measure of school quality than the pupil-teacher ratio is the parent-teacher ratio. He notes that the proportion of children living in single-parent families rose rapidly in recent decades, while standardized test scores declined. Will reports that states with the highest proportion of two-parent families rank the highest on SAT scores even though they often rank low in educational expenditure.

Parent-pupil ratio is an interesting term that has serious implications for American education. The importance of parents in the educational arena is a major theme throughout this book. Issues such as educational funding and class size grow insignificant when the importance of family involvement surfaces. The term, *parent-teacher ratio,* is worth remembering.

AFTERTHOUGHT

The United States presently offers a world class pupil-teacher ratio and class size. The quest for smaller classes can only be justified on the basis of teacher comfort and/or the presence of disruptive and unfocused students. Smaller classes will not improve America's world class status.

The answer is found in a society that sends students to school ready and eager to learn.

REFERENCES

An Outline of Revision of the Course of Study in Japan. 1992. Tokyo: Ministry of Education, Science and Culture.

Busek, H. 1992. Interview (October).

New Zealand Official 1990 Yearbook Extracts. 1992. New Zealand: Ministry of Education, New Zealand Council for Educational Research.

Herzog, M. J. 1993. "The Group," *Democracy and Education,* pp. 37–41.

International Comparisons in Education—Curriculum, Values and Lessons. 1992. Alberta, Canada: Alberta Chamber of Resources in Partnership with Alberta Department of Education.

Lapointe, A. E., J. M. Askew and N. A. Mead. 1992. *Learning Mathematics.* Princeton, New Jersey: The International Assessment of Educational Progress, Educational Testing Service.

McAdams, R. P. 1993. *Lessons from Abroad: How Other Countries Educate Their Children.* Lancaster, Pennsylvania: Technomic Publishing Company.

NEA. 1991. *NEA Mobilizes for Action: Advancing the National Education Agenda.* Washington, D.C.: National Education Association.

Nelson, F. H. 1991. *International Comparison of Public Spending on Education.* Washington, D.C.: Research Department, American Federation of Teachers, AFL-CIO.

Stevenson, H. W. and S. Lee. 1990. *Contexts of Achievement: A Study of American, Chinese, and Japanese Children.* Monographs of the Society for Research in Child Development, Serial no. 221, Vol. 55, Nos. 1–2.

Will, G. F. 1993. "Parent-Pupil Ratio Is Key to Success," *Cleveland Plain Dealer,* September 12, p. 3C.

World Education Report. 1991. Paris: United Nations Educational, Scientific, and Cultural Organization.

SUGGESTED READING

Nelson, F. H. and T. O'Brien. 1993. *How U.S. Teachers Measure Up Internationally: A Comparative Study of Teacher Pay, Training, and Conditions of Service.* A Survey Prepared by the Research Department of the American Federation of Teachers, AFL-CIO. Washington, D.C.: American Federation of Teachers, AFL-CIO.

DEFINING A WORLD CLASS STANDARD FOR TEACHERS

All nations in this study rely on training in pedagogy to prepare teachers for their nation's schools. Each nation requires some form of license to teach and some form of student teaching. Different educational standards for elementary and secondary teachers are common, as is a variable pay scale between elementary and secondary teachers. The different lengths of the school year make the length of the teacher's year differ by country. Trying to compare salaries between nations is, at best, difficult. Chapter 6 presents the best data available but not for all countries in the study. Working conditions for teachers vary among the nations as does teacher esteem. Generally, American teacher salaries appear to be near the norm for the nations reported, but the esteem of American teachers is lower than average. United States elementary teachers work longer weeks, have more student contact time, and are better trained than the world class average. United States secondary teachers work longer hours, have more student contact time, and are approximately as well-trained as the world class average except at the high school level. This is an area that needs considerably more study before definitive statements of teacher comparisons can be made.

PERCEPTION: RANKING UNITED STATES TEACHERS

In reviewing the 181 responses to question six, nearly one-half thought the United States ranked among the top one-third when teacher preparation is ranked among the ten nations (see Figure 6.1). Three-quarters of the respondents ranked the United States above average. The smallest percentage of respondents, barely over 1 percent, ranked the United

TABLE 6.1.

Rank United States schools as they compare to the following nine national school systems:			First	Top Third	Middle Third	Bottom Third	Last
Canada	France	Germany					
Britain	New Zealand	Taiwan					
Israel	South Korea	Japan	(Percentage of Total Responding)				
6. Best educated teachers? (n = 181)			15.8	46.4	28.7	8.8	1.1

States last. The overall high ranking of teacher preparation is significant, given the generally low self-esteem with which respondents ranked the United States on the overall questionnaire. It is uncertain whether the ranking of teacher preparation indicates that (1) the respondents think teacher preparation has little to do with learning outcomes or (2) the respondents feel the teachers in the United States are well-trained despite the overall low ranking of United States education. Actually, United States elementary teachers rank in the top one-third, while secondary teachers rank in the middle third in length of teacher training.

REALITY: WORLD CLASS STANDARDS FOR TEACHERS

Just as the fundamental purpose of school is common among the nations studied, so is the basic role and function of the teacher common among the nations. Universally, the teacher is expected (1) to be a role model for students, (2) to be knowledgeable of both content and teaching methods, (3) to meet a form of state sanction such as certification to assure minimum standards for teachers, and (4) to provide a safe and orderly environment in which students can learn. However the rewards for teachers and the work expected of teachers fluctuate considerably among the nations studied. This section is divided two ways: (1) into three grade spans – elementary, lower secondary or middle school – and higher secondary or high school and (2) an examination of teacher salaries, teacher work loads, and teacher training in each grade span.

When discussing international teacher comparisons with educators, the most common question is about teacher pay. This is the most difficult question in this chapter to report accurately, given the variations of currency exchange rates, comparative cost of living in each country, and the relative paucity of reliable comparisons of teacher remuneration among nations. At this writing the best available source is a recent American Federation of Teachers study, *How U.S. Teachers Measure Up Internationally—A Comparative Study of Teacher Pay, Training, and Conditions of Service* (Nelson and O'Brien, 1993). This study does not include all of the nations compared in this text and is limited to European, Canadian, and Japanese comparisons with American education. The charts shown in the salary area are adapted from the AFT study and report only the six countries compared in this study. Salary comparisons are less meaningful when other factors are considered. For example, teachers in Taiwan pay no income tax, making the effect of gross pay larger.

Elementary School Teachers

Salary

Overall the salary, training, and esteem with which nations reward elementary school teachers are significantly lower than that of secondary school teachers. The lower salary reflects the lower training expectations of elementary school teachers. The clear implication, unfortunately, is that many nations consider elementary school teachers worth less than secondary school teachers. Where countries require elementary school teachers to have training similar to secondary school teachers, salary parity exists. Figure 6.1 displays an index of teacher salaries to per capita GDP of each nation. The selection of a GDP index allows international comparisons based on relative ranking of the GDP of each nation. On this scale, 100 is the average salary per worker in the nation.

Nation	Minimum	Middle	Maximum
United States	97	150	165
France	90	148	172
Germany	135	165	178
Canada	108	186	197
England	106	192	200
Japan	93	168	228
Average	105	168	190

Note: From Nelson and O'Brien (1993).

Figure 6.1 Primary teacher salaries for 1992 indexed to per capita GDP (100 = per capita GDP).

Figure 6.1 must be read carefully. The United States has thousands of individual salary schedules; Canadian salaries vary from province to province; France recognizes several different salary grades; and Germany, England, and Japan have national salary schedules. These data represent the best calculations available, but considerable variance within countries exists. The United States and France rank below the six-nation average in all three categories of beginning, mid-career, and maximum salary grades. Only the United States, France, and Japan start teachers (who are more highly educated than the national average) below the GDP index of 100. Yet Japan has the highest maximum salary among these three nations, as it did when compared to the seventeen nations the AFT studied. While Germany offers by far the highest minimum salary, it also has by far the least minimum to maximum span of the six nations. Add a grain of salt to these data because variables like housing allowances, family allowances, and overtime pay cannot be adequately reflected in this comparison. It seems fair, however, to conclude that American elementary teachers rank poorly on the issue of pay relative to GDP.

 The world class standard for elementary school teacher pay based on per capita income is 105 for starting teachers, 168 for mid-career teachers, and 190 for teachers at the top of the scale. American elementary school teachers are below world class standards at all pay grades.

Work Schedule

Teachers are often chastised for not being full-time workers. When comparing teachers' work internationally, the amount of instructional time and weeks per year of work must be compared. Figure 6.2 compares the instructional hours per week and work weeks per year of elementary teachers in seven nations.

Educational leaders expect more work of elementary school teachers in the United States, compared to their counterparts in the other nations. While their salary is among the lowest of the six nations, their instruc-

Nation	Inst. Hours per Week[1]	Days per Year[2]
United States	30.0	180
France	27.0	174
Germany	21.0	210
Canada	27.5	188
England	26.0	192
Israel	30.0	215
Japan	20.0	228
Average	25.95	198.4

[1]Note: From Nelson and O'Brien (1993).
[2]Note: From Lapointe et al. (1992).

Figure 6.2 *A six-nation comparison of instructional hours per week, and days per year of elementary school teachers, 1992.*

tional week and overall work per year is substantially longer than average and the longest among the seven nations. These data do not include the amount of noninstructional time teachers spend planning, grading papers, and creating learning activities for their students. Given the greater amount of instructional time expected of American elementary teachers, more time must also be devoted to other facets of teaching.

American elementary school teachers have more noninstructional contact hours with students than many other nations' teachers. Teachers in other countries generally do not perform cafeteria duty, recess supervision, or bus duty. The data do not reflect the presence of teacher assistants, however; and the value of these paraprofessionals is not part of an international comparison. The United States data do not indicate how many noninstructional duties teacher assistants perform for classroom teachers. In summary, given the available data, it is obvious that more work is expected from American elementary school teachers than is the average in other nations studied.

 The world class standard for weeks of elementary instruction is 25.95 hours per week. American elementary school teachers teach longer weeks than the world class standard.

Training

Another means of comparing teachers internationally is by examining the number of years of teacher training required by each nation. The international standard for training elementary school teachers is two years of training above high school graduation. A normal school or teacher's college typically provides this training rather than a university, but the standard is increasing. For instance, as of 1992, Taiwan requires all elementary education graduates to have a four-year college degree. France promotes greater parity among teachers with a national salary schedule that reflects the years of teacher training, not the grade level taught. Figure 6.3 compares the amount of training each nation expects of elementary school teachers.

Nation	Teacher Training
Canada	Previously one year of professional training but currently four or five years are required.[1]
France	Three years training below university level or one year professional training after getting a university degree.[2]
Germany	Four years of teacher education.[2]
England	Three years of university study or a university degree and one year of teacher preparation.[2]
New Zealand	Three-year training at colleges of education.
South Korea	Two- or four-year teacher colleges.[4]
Taiwan	Two- or four-year teacher colleges.[5]
Israel	Teacher training college to university trained—a small percentage are "unqualified" teachers.[6]
Japan	From two-year college degree to master's degree; four years of teacher training is the norm.[7]
United States	Minimum four-year university degree; 45 percent earn a master's degree.[2]
Average	Less than a four-year degree in education.

[1]Note: From *Education in Canada* (1989).
[2]Note: From Nelson and O'Brien (1993).
[3]Note: From *New Zealand Official 1990 Yearbook Extracts* (1990).
[4]Note: From *Education in Korea, 1991 – 92* (1992).
[5]Note: From Liao (1992).
[6]Note: From Sprinzak et al. (1992).
[7]Note: From Shiina and Chonan (1991).

Figure 6.3 A comparison of the number of years of teacher training for elementary school teachers currently teaching in ten nations.

The variety of sources necessary to produce Figure 6.3 indicates (1) that all nations studied equate a number of years of teacher preparation to teacher qualifications and (2) that a variety of standards for elementary teachers exists. The large number of teachers comprising the pool includes those just entering the profession with one set of standards and also those exceeding thirty years of service credentialed using another set of standards.

All nations studied provide some form of continued training or in-service for practicing teachers, reflecting a belief that once formal training is completed, in-service training continues teacher growth.

Several nations require more rigorous standards of the most recently trained teachers:

(*1*) Taiwan and France both require four years of teacher training.

(*2*) Israel is working to reduce the number of ''unqualified'' teachers in Hebrew schools (data was not available on what effort is made in Arab schools).

(*3*) Japan has expected four years of teacher education for several years.

While the British reform movement of the late 1980s pushed for all new teachers to have five full years of training, the recession of the 1990s resulted in the Minister of Education, John Patten, suggesting a money-saving move — women with no teacher training or education beyond high school would teach five- to seven-year-old students. The press had a field day with the so-called ''Mums Army,'' and serious debate arose about the value of teacher education. Internationally, a ''Mums Army'' in a developed country would be unacceptable.

 The world class standard for elementary teacher training is less than four years of training at a normal school or teacher's college. Elementary teachers in the United States exceed that standard and are among the best trained in the world.

Internationally, most elementary school teachers are female. The Republic of Korea's Ministry of Education gave one reason for this that would not be accepted in the United States:

At teacher's colleges, some 67 percent of students are women. While this indicates that elementary school teachers are a preferred category of employment for women students, it also shows that bright male students find a lack of attraction and challenge. (*Education in Korea, 1991–92*, 1992)

One recent reform in American teacher education is a probationary period beyond student teaching, during which the novice teacher must demonstrate competence before receiving full certification. Some form of student, or cadet, teaching is common among the nations studied, and the idea of beginning teacher support is also becoming common. Japan provides a system of particular interest. The Ministry of Education, Science, and Culture requires a teacher in-service plan for novice teachers that each prefecture must implement. School leaders assign beginning teachers a mentor (usually a senior teacher) and reduce the mentor's load so there is time for involvement in detailed in-service training. The Ministry recommends an average of two days of in-service training per week for novices totaling about sixty days of training during the first year of teaching. This program came from Japan's well-established effort to improve the quality of teaching in their schools as part of a national effort to promote "life-long learning" for the entire population.

Shiina and Chonan reported in 1991 that many serious problems remain in Japanese teacher preparation. There are five regional groups whose title explains their efforts – Prefectual Contacting Discussion Group(s) to Improve the Quality of Teachers. Problems exist between what is taught in teacher education courses versus what is needed in teaching practice, and the quality of teaching at the university level has been criticized. Problems exist with senior teachers who mentor the novices and the conditions under which novices work. The Japanese also suspect the amount of time provided for both training and guidance may not be sufficient. Questions surface about the competency of the part-time teacher who replaces the novice during the in-service schedule and the impact on the students while the novice is away. While problems exist, the Japanese are making a concerted effort to improve their schools by improving their teachers – both future and current (Shiina and Chonan, 1991).

Lower Secondary (Middle School) Teachers

Salary

Like their elementary school counterparts, lower secondary school teachers have a lower level of esteem, are paid less, and are more poorly trained than their upper secondary school counterparts. The rising number of students who are not leaving school at the end of compulsory attendance has caused enrollment in the middle grade span to increase in many nations, most particularly Taiwan and the Republic of Korea.

Additional students cause some spot shortages of teachers and may help to explain the higher salaries paid to teachers at this level. Figure 6.4 displays the salaries of lower secondary teachers indexed to the per capita GDP.

American teachers rate poorly in all categories when compared to the six-nation average. American teachers' salaries fall in the bottom half as they start teaching and remain at the bottom, even at the maximum level. The American Federation of Teachers' study includes seventeen nations, and the beginning teacher in the United States ranked third from the bottom. The United States ranked fifth among the seventeen (below Norway, Denmark, Sweden, and Italy) for maximum salary. The United States, Canada, and Japan reported identical data for lower secondary school teachers. France, Germany, and England generally paid lower secondary school teachers more than elementary school teachers — in some cases, a great deal more. For example, France paid lower secondary teachers 5 percent more at the minimum and 9 percent more at the maximum than they paid elementary teachers. England started both groups at the same rate but paid lower secondary teachers 10 percent more at the maximum. Most amazing was the difference in Germany, where lower secondary teachers started at nearly 9 percent higher salary than elementary teachers, and teachers maintained the increase at the maximum level. A study of Figure 6.4 reveals how much Germany skewed both the minimum and maximum scales, but not the middle pay

Nation	Minimum	Middle	Maximum
United States	97	150	165
France	95	146	181
Germany	151	183	197
Canada	108	186	197
England	106	200	220
Japan	93	168	228
Average	108	172	198

Note: From Nelson and O'Brien (1993).

Figure 6.4 Lower secondary teacher salaries for 1992 indexed to per capita GDP *(100 = per capita GDP).*

scale. The message is clear—many nations pay lower secondary school teachers more than elementary school teachers.

As was the case with elementary school teacher data, the lower secondary data need to be viewed carefully, as they are intended only for international comparisons. When comparing elementary teacher salaries, Germany had the greatest difference between minimum and maximum salary, but in the lower secondary group, Germany had the smallest range between minimum and maximum. The United States had the next lowest increase, while England and Japan had by far the greatest increase in range. Issues about pay for part-time teachers, overtime pay, and salary enhancements, such as the German family allowance based on the number of children in the family, cannot be included in salary data, and this factor clouds the comparative picture. No matter how cloudy, America's teachers rank poorly on comparisons of international teacher salary.

 The world class standard for salaries of lower secondary school teachers, indexed by per capita GDP, is 108 for beginning teachers, 172 for mid-career teachers, and 198 for teachers at the top of the scale. Lower secondary teachers in the United States are below the world class standard at all three points.

Work Schedule

No reliable study was found that compared the instructional weeks of lower secondary school teachers with elementary teachers, but a general increase in the number of hours of school exists. The students at this age range have longer attention spans and should have the discipline necessary to accept greater academic rigor than younger children. For example, Israeli students in the first grade have twenty-four hours of weekly instruction that increases to thirty-five or thirty-six hours of weekly instruction by grades seven and eight (Sprinzak et al., 1992). The number of teaching hours per week is identical in elementary and middle level schools in the Republic of Korea. Elementary school student hours are forty minutes in length and increase to forty-five minutes in length by the middle school years (*Education in Korea,*

1991 – 1992, 1992). Teachers begin to teach by academic discipline during this time, and the training required of teachers changes.

Training

The training of lower secondary school teachers varies by country, as it did in the elementary teacher area. A trend toward longer periods of teacher training exists among the nations represented in Figure 6.5, which compares the training of teachers for lower secondary schools.

Internationally leaders expect teachers for lower secondary students to be more highly trained than teachers of elementary school students and expect recently certified lower secondary teachers to be more highly trained than their more experienced peers. France, Israel, and Taiwan recently increased the training requirements for teachers, although the use of separate teachers colleges rather than universities is still common. In New Zealand, for example, only colleges of education train teachers: Auckland, Wellington, Christchurch, Palmerston North, Hamilton, and Dunedin.

The type of teacher training provided in each nation varies slightly, but more similarities exist than differences. For example, to become a teacher in Japan, the individual must become certified by passing a teacher-appointment examination designed by a prefecture board of education. These tests are highly competitive and composed of written examinations of general, professional, and teaching subject content. There appears to be some correlation with the National Teacher's Examination required by many states in America. The prefecture requires a personal interview and may require additional tests. Teacher appointment depends primarily on university grades and the results of the examination. The teaching certificate, once granted, is lifelong. Once hired, the teacher expects to be moved several times within a given municipality or prefecture.

An example of Korean efforts to upgrade the skills of teachers is evident in two ways: (1) new night courses are offered to junior-college trained elementary teachers to upgrade them to four-year teacher training status and increase their certification grades, and (2) a number of graduate school programs are offered for working teachers. As is common in the United States, Korea offers courses either during evening hours or days when teachers are not working. The content of the courses includes research-based, in-depth study that sounds like teacher education courses in the United States.

Nation	Teacher Training
Canada	Four-year teacher training or a higher degree.
France	Three years of teacher education preparation— elementary teachers are additionally trained to teach lower secondary students at this grade span.[1]
Germany	Three years of teacher training, with those who do best preparing for teaching at the Gymnasium.[2]
England	Four-year preparation in teacher training except for a two-year exception for teachers in shortage areas.
New Zealand	Two options: one year of teacher training following degree completion or four years of teacher training.[3]
Rep. of Korea	Four years of study at a teacher's college or university.[4]
Taiwan	Four-year degree from teacher education.[5]
Israel	A university degree held by 60 percent of teachers—others are less trained and 7 percent are "unqualified."[6]
Japan	Majority of teachers hold a bachelor's degree. 35 percent are trained in a junior college.[7]
United States	Four years or more college training—California requires a master's degree. Over half of the states have alternative certification.[8]
Average	Slightly less than four years of teacher training, with a degree. The trend for new teachers is four years.

[1]Note: From McLean, M. (1993). "Education in France," *Encyclopedia Americana*.
[2]Note: From Neuber, M., ed. (1991).
[3]Note: From *New Zealand Official 1990 Yearbook Extracts* (1990).
[4]Note: From *Education in Korea, 1991 – 92* (1992).
[5]Note: From Liao (1992).
[6]Note: From Spirnzak et al. (1992). (Figures show Hebrew Education. The 3200 + Arab teacher training could not be found.)
[7]Note: From Shiina, M. and Chonan, M. (1993).
[8]Note: From Nelson and O'Brien (1993).

Figure 6.5 A comparison of the number of years of teacher training for lower secondary school teachers currently teaching in ten nations.

The world class standard for training lower second-ary teachers is slightly below the four-year university degree. The world class trend for new teachers for this grade span is a four-year degree. Lower secondary school teachers in the United States exceed this standard given the number of teachers with advanced degrees.

One other factor worth mentioning about teacher training for this grade span is the male-female ratio enrolled in teacher education. While data is limited, there is reference to the "increasing feminization" of teaching in several countries. For instance, in Japan, the percentage of female teachers falls from 56.5 percent at the elementary level to 34.7 percent at the lower secondary level and 19.2 percent at the upper secondary level. The number of female students increased at the elementary level as access to higher education became more available to women. While the pay schedules are the same between genders, males dominate the upper level. No data on the number of female administrators in Japan was found (Ishizaka, circa 1990). In Israel, women dominate Hebrew elementary schools where 89 percent of the teachers are female but not Arab schools, where only 43 percent are females. There is a drop in the percentage of women teaching in secondary schools, where 67 percent of Hebrew teachers are female and 24 percent of Arab teachers are female. Teachers in Israel are comparatively young, with a median age in the mid-thirties, compared to a median age of teachers in the United States of above forty (Sprinzak et al., 1992). The trend toward female domination of elementary schools was also found in New Zealand where over five times as many females as males were enrolled in elementary education programs. The numbers were more nearly equal for those training to become secondary teachers (*New Zealand Official 1990 Yearbook Extracts,* 1990).

Upper Secondary (High) School Teachers

Upper secondary school teachers generally enjoy greater esteem and greater salary and higher education levels. Most notably in Europe and particularly in Germany, higher status is afforded to those who teach the highest level of student. This increased status is somewhat like the

Nation	Minimum	Middle	Maximum
United States	97	150	165
France	95	146	181
Germany	151	183	197
Canada	108	186	197
England	106	200	220
Japan	93	168	228
Average	108	172	198

Note: From Nelson and O'Brien (1993).

Figure 6.6 *Upper secondary teacher salaries for 1992 indexed to per capita GDP (100 = per capita GDP).*

greater esteem offered advanced placement and college-bound teachers in American schools, except that salary and training differences exist for German teachers. At this level the United States no longer sets the world class standard for teacher preparation.

Salary

The United States leads only Japan in starting salary, and Japan has the greatest differential between minimum and maximum salary categories with a salary increase over two and one-half times. Germany, which had the highest salary span for elementary school teachers, has the lowest for upper secondary teachers with less than a one-half increase from minimum to maximum. France, England, and Japan have nearly the same salaries at the maximum end, and the United States has by far the lowest maximum. For all three grade spans, the United States ranks dead last for maximum salary, indicating a major problem for teachers. With the relatively low span between beginning and maximum salaries, the United States does not compare well to the five other nations in this study.

The world class standard for upper secondary teacher pay indexed on per capita GDP is 121 for beginning teachers, 185 for mid-career teachers, and 215 for teachers at the top. American upper secondary school teachers are below the world class standard at all three points.

The American Federation of Teachers studied seventeen nations; and among all seventeen, only Italy and Japan had lower starting salaries, and only Norway and Italy had lower maximum salaries than the United States. Switzerland paid both the highest starting salary at 178 and the highest maximum salary at 271. The maximum salary is one and one-half times as much as the maximum salary in the United States.

Work Schedule

The information in Figure 6.7 displays an upper secondary teacher's work schedule for seven nations.

When reviewed annually, the United States has the greatest number of teaching hours per teacher and is virtually tied with Japan, where the school year is considerably longer. England and Israel are close behind. The difference between the instructional year in the United States and both England and Israel is an artifact of their longer school years; but the difference between the United States year and the Japanese instructional year is much more difficult to rationalize because of the longer Japanese school year, much higher Japanese maximum teacher pay, and different working conditions of the Japanese and American high school teacher.

The Japanese teacher changes classes while students stay in the same room making hall duty unnecessary. While Japanese teachers eat with their students in their classroom, students display much better conduct than in the typical American cafeteria. Leaders expect Japanese teachers

Nation	Inst. Hours per Week[1]	Days per Year[2]
United States	23	180
France	17	174
Germany	18	210
Canada	20	188
England	22	192
Israel	24	215
Japan	20	228
Average	20.57	198.1

[1]Note: From Nelson and O'Brien (1993).
[2]Note: From Lapointe et al. (1992).

Figure 6.7 *A seven-nation comparison of instructional hours per week, and days per year of upper secondary school teachers, 1992.*

to plan together, then share and discuss plans. While the number of hours of instruction per week is similar for American and Japanese teachers, the latter has five and one-half days of work. The Japanese expect fewer hours of teaching in the longer week than Americans expect of teachers in five days.

 The world class standard for upper secondary school teachers is 20.57 hours of teaching weekly. American upper secondary teachers exceeded the world class standard by teaching more hours weekly.

Other differences are more subtle and speak to relative teacher professionalism. For instance, Germany does not expect teachers to stay on campus when they are not teaching. They are simply expected to be prepared once they begin teaching. And in France, teachers who work overtime—a concept that hardly exists in the United States—receive overtime pay. French teachers who assume supervisory duties and provide study time for students also receive overtime pay. As with elementary teachers, American upper secondary teachers do not have a good situation in terms of pay versus work expectations.

Training

Years of teacher preparation is one variable where United States upper secondary school teachers do not rank well (see Figure 6.8). In the United States, higher expectations for teacher training should result in higher pay.

Many countries pay upper secondary school teachers better than their counterparts in lower secondary or elementary schools unless there is a uniform pay scale, as is the case in the United States. Apparently, the amount of academic knowledge required of an upper secondary teacher causes many nations to require more education for upper secondary teachers. The type of training is commonly full university academic training, followed by teacher education. The overall trend toward increasing teacher training for all teachers seems tied to desire to increase the outcomes of schooling and it has widespread international support. The United States needs to recognize this trend in its own reform.

Nation	Teacher Training
Canada	Most are university graduates with a year of professional teacher training.[1]
France	Four years plus university training and teacher education, or an average of six years.
Germany	Gymnasium teachers complete eight semesters of university training, then eighteen months of teacher training.[1]
England	Four-year college required for an education degree; more education for teachers is unusual.[2]
New Zealand	Four years of teacher education taken toward a degree, or a university degree and one year of teacher education.[3]
Rep. of Korea	Must be four-year graduates of teacher education program. Alternate routes for noneducation students in areas of shortage, but requires teacher education.[4]
Taiwan	Minimum of four-year degree in teacher education.[5]
Israel	Data not available for upper secondary, but appears to vary based on school type: general, technological, or agricultural. Other levels require a university degree and four years of training.[1]
Japan	University degree plus four years of training.[1]
United States	Four years plus teacher education. California requires a master's degree.
Average	In excess of four years training; European standards are the highest.

[1]Note: From Nelson and O'Brien (1993).
[2]Note: From Peterson (1985).
[3]Note: From *New Zealand Official 1990 Yearbook Extracts* (1990).
[4]Note: From *Education in Korea, 1991–92* (1992).
[5]Note: From Liao (1992).

Figure 6.8 *A comparison of the number of years of teacher training for current upper secondary school teachers in ten nations.*

The world class standard for the training of upper secondary school teachers is more than a four-year college degree. American upper secondary school teachers are below this world class standard except in California where an advanced degree is required.

Upon completion of the executive summary of the AFT study, six recommendations were made. School districts should:

(*1*) Reduce interdistrict and interstate variations in teacher pay, standardize teacher training across state boundaries, and create a mechanism for converting pension plans across state lines; these changes would promote teacher mobility and reduce variations in the quality of teacher training.

(*2*) Reduce teaching time and give teachers more time to prepare and plan, especially primary teachers, while simultaneously adding a week or two to the school year.

(*3*) Increase training for senior high school subject teachers and improve pay commensurate with training.

(*4*) Eliminate the practice of placing experienced teachers new to a district lower on the salary schedule than warranted by their experience.

(*5*) Focus pay flexibility initiatives on the crucial issues of recruitment, teacher retention, and specific skills required rather than on more subjective efforts such as merit pay.

(*6*) Shorten the summer break and lengthen the fall and spring breaks to enhance the continuity of instruction and give both teaching and learning a year-round focus (Nelson and O'Brien, 1993).

IMPLICATIONS

This comparison of teachers and their training and work schedules provides a brief insight into the teacher's world. The teachers and schools examined in this study are among the most wealthy, best educated populations in the world. American teachers do not fare well when compared to that group.

Pay in any profession is a relative statement of a society's value of work produced. The AFT's use of the ratio to GDP provided an even, useful way to rank teachers to the production of the GDP. Teacher pay, when compared to annual hours of teaching, provides an insight into what is expected of teachers. Not seen in that ratio is the amount of time spent on noninstructional duties, out-of-school planning time, required in-service hours, or non-salary bonuses such as tax relief. American teachers are expected to work harder than other teachers and are rewarded with relatively low pay.

Because schools do not provide full-time work for students in all of the countries studied, teaching cannot be full-time work for teachers. This explains why the government of Israel views teachers as working 80 percent of the time. Pay schedules in most nations reflect the "part-time" nature of a teacher's work. The best way to raise teacher pay in the United States is to gradually lengthen the school year as recommended in Chapter 4. The authors agree with the AFT proposal that pay schedules among LEAs need to become more uniform, so the inequity of wealthy districts recruiting the best teachers can be discontinued. The "have nots" should recruit on a more level playing field with those that "have." If the school year were lengthened to the "world class standard" of 200 days, American teachers would likely work about 216 days, adding the equivalent of one month's income to their salary. The extra pay would go a long way toward salary parity on the international scene — both in learning time for students and pay for teachers.

The issue of working conditions and the enjoyment of work was not addressed in this chapter due to the nebulous nature of "enjoyment"; but Stevenson (1992), among others, indicates that Asian school children appear happier in school than do American school children. It is assumed that a school with happy children will also have happy teachers. Therefore, American educators may want to study the reasons for positive adjustment by Asian children and adopt those aspects that fit the American culture. While the American child works with few breaks from the time he/she enters school, Asian children may spend as much as one-quarter of their time in social activities that are not directly related to instruction but which impart powerful values.

In discussing American schools with experts from other nations who know the American system well, they almost universally indicated surprise at the level of violence found in American schools. The connection between a lack of enjoyment in school and organized violence is one thing to recognize and quite another to cure, but it is something American educators can and must control. American educators need to stop accepting the blame for violence that is beyond their control. Guns in schools, for example, obviously are not issued by school officials.

A theme common to all of the nations studied is the attempt to upgrade the teaching skill and preparation of teachers. The United States clearly sets the standard for elementary school teachers but does not do so with upper secondary teachers. The work of the Holmes Group and others pushing for increased teacher preparation is the route for the United

States to follow, but only as long as pay relative to length of work is considered. All nations in this study reward years of service with higher pay, but no discussion of merit pay surfaced among the other nations. During an interview with Her Majesty's Chief Inspector of Scotland's schools, Archie McGlynn (1993), the authors were asked to share America's knowledge of classroom observations and teacher evaluation. A similar interest was expressed during a New Zealand educator's interview (Malcolm, 1993). The interest in American practice indicates that the United States apparently does a better job of evaluating teaching. Other nations appear to be more dependent on test results as a form of teacher evaluation.

American educators might want to rethink the alternative certification now common in many states, as this is not a solution to teacher shortages used by many other nations. Those nations that reported shortages either hired teachers with less training but with a teacher education background or enticed disciplined, trained college students into teacher education.

American educators should be proud of their overall training and the direction in which the United States appears to be moving. However, the long teacher workweek, low teacher esteem, and poor teacher pay appear to be legitimate areas for American teachers' complaints.

AFTERTHOUGHT

American teachers are expected to work longer with more hours of instruction than their international counterparts. Both the pay level and pay range of American teachers is lower than the world class average. While American elementary teachers set the world class standard in preparation, their secondary counterparts do not. Before the United States addresses pay and preparation shortages, the equity issue among states and individual locales needs to be resolved. The best way to increase teacher pay is by increasing the length of the school year for teachers and students. The low self-esteem associated with American teachers will only be resolved when gifted athletes and musicians are put on a par with gifted teachers.

REFERENCES

Education in Canada. 1989. Ottawa, Canada: External Communications Division, External Affairs and International Trade Canada.

Education in Korea, 1991 – 92. 1992. Seoul, Korea: National Institute of Educational Research and Training, Ministry of Education.

Ishizaka, K. 1990. *School Education in Japan.* Tokyo: International Society for Educational Information.

Lapointe, A. E., J. M. Askew and N. A. Mead. 1992. *Learning Mathematics.* Princeton, New Jersey: The International Assessment of Educational Progress, Educational Testing Service.

Liao, C.-H. Interviews during the 1992 – 93 academic year as she worked as a research assistant on this project.

Malcolm, P. 1993. Interview (June 18).

McGlynn, A. 1993. Interview (June 18).

McLean, M. 1993. "Education in France," *Encyclopedia Americana,* Danbury, Connecticut: Grolier Inc.

Nelson and O'Brien. 1993. *How U.S. Teachers Measure Up Internationally; A Comparative Study of Teacher Pay, Training, and Conditions of Service.* Washington, D.C.: American Federation of Teachers.

Neuber, M., ed. 1991. *Inter Nationes Bonn.*

New Zealand Official 1990 Yearbook Extracts. 1990. Education monograph provided by the New Zealand Embassy, Washington, D.C.

Peterson, A. D. C. 1985. "Continuity and Change in British Education," *Encyclopedia Americana,* Danbury, Connecticut: Grolier Inc.

Shiina, M. and M. Chonan. 1991. Japan-U.S. Teacher Education Consortium, ERIC Document.

Sprinzak, D., E. Bar and D. Levi-Mazloum. 1992. *Facts and Figures about Education and Culture in Israel.* Jerusalem: Ministry of Education and Culture.

Stevenson, H. W. 1992. "Learning from Asian Schools," *Scientific American.*

Whitworth, F. E. 1993. "France: Education," *Encyclopedia Americana,* Danbury, Connecticut: Grolier Inc.

DEFINING A WORLD CLASS STANDARD FOR STUDENTS

The common denominator for schools internationally is students. Highly motivated and well-disciplined students perform well in school. Poorly motivated and undisciplined students struggle year after year, causing parents, educators, and themselves anguish and disappointment. Chapter 7 explores data identifying world class standards for students. Five standards are explored that pertain to students in the ten world class education countries:

(1) The percentage of thirteen-year-old students who spent four or more hours on mathematics homework per week, 1991 – 1992
(2) The percentage of thirteen-year-old students who spent four or more hours on science homework per week, 1991 – 1992
(3) The percentage of thirteen-year-old students who spent two or more hours on all homework every day, 1991 – 1992
(4) The percentage of thirteen-year-old students who watched five or more hours of television, 1991 – 1992
(5) The percentage of students reaching the final grade offered in the home school system

Reaction to the standards and implications for American education completes Chapter 7.

PERCEPTION: RANKING THE UNITED STATES ON THE CONTRIBUTION OF STUDENTS TO THE EDUCATION ENVIRONMENT

The sample of educators responded to three questions comparing students in the United States with students in the nine world class

TABLE 7.1.

Rank United States schools as they compare to the following nine national school systems: Canada France Germany Britain New Zealand Taiwan Israel South Korea Japan	First	Top Third	Middle Third	Bottom Third	Last
	(Percentage of Total Responding)				
7. Highest percent of pupils reaching final grade offered in school? (*n* = 180)	8.9	25.0	28.9	28.9	8.3
8. Most hours of homework by students? (*n* = 179)	1.1	1.7	11.7	46.9	38.6
9. Most hours of daily TV watching? (*n* = 184)	76.1	13.6	2.8	1.7	2.8

countries on the subject of student educational development. The answers to question seven reveal different opinions about the staying power of students in the United States (see Table 7.1). Equal numbers of respondents placed students in the top third, middle third, and bottom third. The response group appears uncertain about the staying power of students in the United States as compared to the other countries. Data are presented in this chapter to clear the muddy waters.

The responses to questions eight and nine show a rare display of agreement. Question eight asked, "Which nation's students do the most homework?" Eighty-six percent of the respondents replied that United States students would be in the lower third. Nearly half of that 86 percent place American students dead last on homework production. Question nine asked for the rank of American students regarding television watching. Ninety percent placed American students in the top third of the ten nations, with 76 percent awarding American students first place. The respondents perceive American students as world class television viewers but slackers at homework. On these two issues, the survey group is close to reality.

REALITY: DEFINING A WORLD CLASS STANDARD FOR STUDENTS

Defining a world class standard for students is difficult. The outside influences that shape a student's life cannot be ignored, but the outside influences are reserved for Chapter 11, leaving student behavior to be examined in this chapter. This chapter assumes that students have some control over their own lives. Abraham Maslow said that a person is capable of becoming whatever he or she chooses to be. Assume in the following paragraphs that a world class student controls his or her own behavior relating to school performance, homework, and television watching. Students do make decisions to overcome adversity.

Student's School Staying Power

A world class student is a student who reaches the final grade offered in school. Unfortunately, in the developing countries in 1990, there were approximately 130 million out-of-school youth aged six to eleven. Two hundred seventy-seven million out-of-school youths exist in the twelve- to seventeen-year-old age groups (*World Education Report,* 1991). Figure 7.1 reports the percentage of students reaching the final grade in each of the world class countries selected for this study.

Japan reports that 100 percent of all students enrolled in school reach the final grade offered in school. A student enrolls in either an academic high school or vocational high school long before he or she reaches the final grade. The staying power of Japanese students depends on the effort of the student rather than on the type of school in which he or she enrolls.

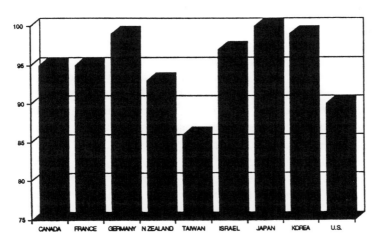

Note: From *World Education Report* (1991).

Figure 7.1 *The percentage of students reaching the final grade offered in each world class country, 1987.*

Germany reports that 99 percent of students reach the final grade offered; and like Japan, sorting students into vocational or academic schools following the primary experience prevails.

Korea, above the world class standard, follows the same sorting procedure for students entering high school. Data do not show that sorting keeps students in school longer, but countries that sort secondary students do show strong staying power. Israel is an exception, for Israeli educators track students in a comprehensive school, but Israel still remains above the world class standard. The common denominator in schools with the greatest staying power seems to be a belief that education is important regardless of a school's purpose.

 The world class standard for the percentage of students who reach the final grade offered in school is 95 percent. The United States reported that 90 percent of its students reached the final grade in 1987.

The United States reported that 90 percent of students reached grade twelve in 1987, an unimpressive figure. The emphasis on reducing the dropout rate in the United States, therefore, is certainly legitimate. Taiwan is the only country reporting a higher dropout percentage than the United States.

The dropout rate in America's cities is the major culprit. Urban educators face enormous social problems each school day that require solutions of the greatest magnitude. Federal intervention may be the only solution. However, urban schools are not the only schools coping with school leavers. Pittman (1993) found that the rural education environment impacts school leaving decisions. Rural school children (1) typically receive less funding than larger schools, (2) perceive school as less relevant when national accountability is imposed, and (3) often live in unstable home environments.

Statistics on student staying power deliver a clear message. Students stay in school if they see a purpose in school. Too many students in the United States find school boring and a dead end. Could this happen because less advantaged students compete with academically oriented students in American secondary schools? The data in Figure 7.1 lead to that conclusion. Increased staying power may mean adopting the successful practice of other countries, and secondary sorting of academic and vocational students is the successful practice of other countries. However, Americans must accept equality in both the vocational track and the academic track if the practice is to be successful. Germany accomplishes this practice of equality, and the German plan for educating vocational students is world class and an excellent model for American educational leaders.

Nontraditional approaches to education recently have attracted more interest internationally. Countries accept the idea that school need not always meet inside four walls or be conducted by a certified teacher. On-the-job training and experiential learning are more common in other countries, and the United States must consider similar alternatives if staying power is to increase.

A plan to increase staying power should account for children with learning disabilities. *World Education Report* (1991) concedes that systematic data on the extent of learning disabilities in children at the global level are not available, but estimates generally place about 10 percent of any age group into this category. Schools in the United States identify about 12 percent of a student body as learning disabled. Learning disabled students also must finish school in a program that meets their needs, if staying power is to become world class. Educators in the United States must also come to grips with the idea of mainstreaming, for educators currently disagree about the value of self-contained classrooms for handicapped youth as opposed to integrated classrooms. The argument distracts from the major issue of educating *all* youth through the final year of school and should be settled.

Homework Standards

Do students in most world class countries take homework more seriously than the typical student in the United States? The three graphic presentations that follow say yes. The 1991 – 1992 International Assessment of Educational Progress (IAEP) produced data for the presentations from seven of the world class countries. Figure 7.2 assesses the science homework practices of thirteen-year-old students, while Figure 7.3 reports similar data on mathematics homework. While analyzing both sets of data, the reader should assume that more homework means improved student performance. This should not be too difficult, for data

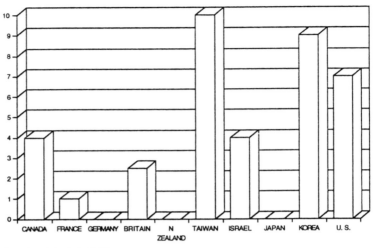

Note: From Lapointe et al. (1992).

Figure 7.2 *The percentage of thirteen-year-old students who spend four hours or more on science homework each week, 1991 – 1992.*

support the assumption. In fact, parents and teachers in the United States who continue to deny the benefits of homework are misled.

Nine percent of thirteen-year-old Korean students spend four hours or more per week on science homework This effort placed Korean students first on the 1991 – 92 IAEP international science test. In Taiwan, where 10 percent spend four hours or more per week on science homework, students ranked second. Students in the United States had the third highest percentage, with 7 percent spending four hours or more on science homework. Hopefully, the world class figure for the United States reflects the increased emphasis on elementary science instruction during the past few decades. The four remaining countries included in the study reported that less than 5 percent of their students spent four hours or more per week on science homework.

 The world class standard for thirteen-year-old students who spend four hours or more on science homework is 5 percent. Students in the United States are 2 percent above the world class standard.

Figure 7.3 is a companion study reporting the habits of the same students in completing mathematics homework. When compared with the science report, the larger emphasis placed on mathematics in the world class countries is evident. A much larger percentage of students spend four or more hours on mathematics homework than they did on science homework. Korean and Taiwanese students again significantly lead the pack. Canada, United States, France, and Israel show 15 to 17 percent of students spending four hours or more on mathematics homework, placing all four countries slightly below the world class standard. Students in Great Britain show the smallest percentage of students spending four or more hours weekly on mathematics homework.

Most educators and parents stress homework as a way of improving student achievement. Interestingly, IAEP results indicate that the majority of students in most populations *do not* spend a great deal of time doing either mathematics or science homework. Nevertheless, IAEP reports that, as time spent on mathematics and science homework increased, achievement increased. For example, Taiwan reported a moderate increase in performance for students spending two to three hours on science homework each week and a larger increase for students spending four hours or more (Lapointe et al., 1992).

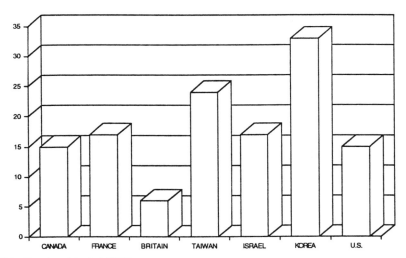

Note: From Lapointe et al. (1992).

Figure 7.3 *The percent of thirteen-year-old students who spend four hours or more on mathematics homework each week, 1991 – 1992.*

Jaeger (1992) analyzed the IAEP assessment results and noted that the data measuring the percentage of students who spend four hours or more per week on mathematics homework predicted success on the IAEP test better than all the instructional factors combined. Otherwise, homework production was more important for promoting student success than teaching methodology.

> The world class standard for thirteen-year-old students who spend four hours or more on mathematics homework is 18 percent. The United States reports 15 percent.

Figure 7.4 presents the third measure of homework performance assessed by IAEP officials. Officials asked students, age thirteen, who live in the seven world class countries, "How many hours daily do you spend on all homework regardless of subject?" Figure 7.4 presents the responses of students spending two hours or more per day on all homework. The chosen benchmark of two hours per day on homework

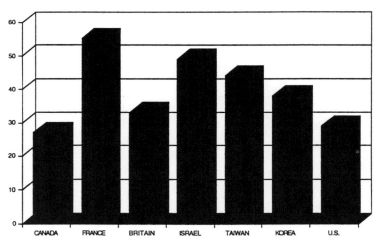

Note: From Lapointe et al. (1992).

Figure 7.4 The percentage of thirteen-year-old students who spend two hours or more on all homework every day, 1991 – 1992.

is a significant commitment. The commitment is more significant when one considers that the most common response of all IAEP populations was one hour or less per day on homework (Lapointe et al., 1992).

A new world class leader, France, emerges from the homework pack. In France, 55 percent of students reported doing two hours or more of homework daily. This factor, perhaps, compensates for the shorter school year in France. Students in Israel were a close second to the French, as 49 percent reported doing two hours or more homework daily. This figure becomes more interesting later when Israel is reported to be the co-leader in television watching. Students in Taiwan and Korea also exceed the world class standard perpetuating the reported strength of home environment in the Asian countries. Britain, Canada and the United States cluster close together at the bottom of the chart.

 The world class standard for thirteen-year-old students who do homework in all subjects two hours or more daily is 41 percent. Twenty-nine percent of students in United States schools reported doing homework two hours or more daily. The United States is twelve percentage points below the world class standard.

Several additional studies and interviews support the importance of homework. Two students at Denefields School, Reading, Berkshire, England, addressed the homework issue. During an interview with the authors, the students commented on the amount of homework each completed daily. Graeme Dornan (1993), a tenth level student, responded, ''I have much more homework this year. It depends — about two and one-half to three hours per day. On weekends, I go further.'' Nicolai Dobby (1993), Head Girl and a student at the A level or senior level, said, ''It depends. On most days I spend two and a half to three hours an evening. I'm doing much more this year. In an average week I spend fifteen to sixteen hours, but I spend a lot more when you count music homework.'' Neither student addressed their own homework habits at age thirteen, but currently both accept homework as a necessary ingredient for success at school.

The world class nations not participating in the IAEP study also stress homework. In Japan, homework time exceeds the world class standard, weekends included. The Japanese mother (dragon mother) supervises the homework (Yukari, 1992; Allen, 1992). Murray (1992) reports that one hour per day doing homework is typical for secondary students in New Zealand. In Germany, Borst (1992) estimated that 50 percent of thirteen-year-old students spend two hours or more on homework daily, except for weekends. This places German students at the world class standard for time spent on homework.

Since Asian-American students form a large population group in the United States, a noteworthy study exists claiming that Asian-American students retain their homework habits after arriving in this country and that the habit pays dividends. A university professor at Stanford, Sanford Dornbusch, surveyed 7,000 students in six San Francisco-area high schools about their achievement and homework activities. He found that Asian-Americans consistently get higher grades than any other group of students. He reported that Asian-Americans spend an average of 7.03 hours a week on homework, while non-Hispanic whites average 6.12 hours, blacks 4.23 hours, and Hispanics 3.98 hours (Butterfield, 1992). While the survey results show all groups below the world class standard, the fact that Asian-Americans spend more time on homework and achieve more than other groups in American schools is significant.

The Influence of Television

Television arrived on the international scene during the 1950s, and who can deny its effect on human behavior? In the worldwide education arena, some television targets the development of academics; but for many students, the content of television watching has little academic value and could actually be detrimental. There appears to be vast agreement among educators that television watching detracts from reading time, homework, and quality time among family members. The sex and violence portrayed on television may contribute to school behavior problems addressed in a later section of this chapter. To say the least, students *should* devote many of the hours spent in front of the television to activities more valuable to the development of their minds.

Figure 7.5 indicates the percentage of thirteen-year-old students who watch television 5 hours or more every day. Students who participated in the IAEP study again provided the data. Twenty percent of American students reported watching five hours or more of television every day, a figure larger than any other nation in the survey except Israel. This study

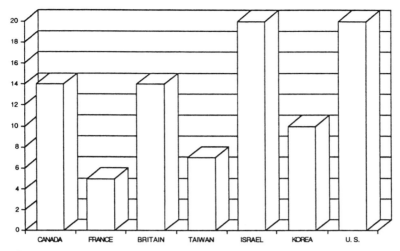

Note: From Lapointe et al. (1992).

Figure 7.5 *The percentage of thirteen-year-old students in seven world class nations who watch five hours or more of television every day, 1991 – 1992.*

supports the perception that American students are world class television watchers.

Why Israel ranks first in television watching is unclear; but, in addition to regular broadcasting channels, two cable channels exist that are common to all television viewers. Since Israel is a threatened nation, citizens may value television to keep abreast of the world news. Besides, recall the homework data that place Israeli students among the homework leaders; and it becomes clear that Israeli students balance television and homework.

It is helpful to look at the statistics for Canada regarding television watching, for Canada is a mirror for the United States educationally. Often, American educators look at Canada and see identical problems, but in this study, only 14 percent of Canadian students reported watching television five or more hours per week. This figure is close to the world class standard and considerably lower than the figure for the United States. Perhaps the presence of national television in Canada and the remote location of many Canadians in relation to television access explain the diminished influence of television.

The more interesting country is France where only 5 percent of students report watching television five or more hours per day. France is a country with numerous cable television stations, and programming is entertaining and attractive; yet school-age television watching is considerably less than in the United States. Remember, however, that French students are also world class leaders in homework production, so they apparently have the desired world class combination of little television and much homework. American students finding it difficult to turn off the set should learn the secrets of French students in terms of avoiding television.

 The world class standard for percentage of thirteen-year-old students watching five hours or more of television daily is 13 percent. Twenty percent of students in the United States report watching television more than five hours per day.

Considering data from all countries participating in the IAEP assessment, time spent watching television negatively relates to performance in school (Lapointe et al., 1992). This constitutes an important finding for American students and parents. Rhetoric in the United States often chastises the "couch potato" who specializes in television watching; but, in spite of the rhetoric, the country seems paralyzed in attempts to limit television watching. Until television watching diminishes as a student value, television will be suspect as a deterrent to student achievement.

Chapter 11 presents data concerning parental influences over television watching, because parents play an important role in forming the television habits of their children. If the message about television repeats itself, the importance of the message justifies the repeat performance. Americans must come to grips with a media that conflicts with school success.

IMPLICATIONS

The world class standards just presented for students are perhaps the most important standards researched. *In every country where students go to school motivated and ready to learn, schooling is effective.* Fortunately, many American students fit the above description. Every school in this country has bright, dedicated, motivated students. The unmotivated, however, are too numerous and drag down those eager to learn. Distracted students not only diminish their own chance for a quality education, they rob serious students of the teacher's time and establish an atmosphere of mediocrity that makes learning for the serious student difficult.

As the research that led to this book was in process during 1992, the authors conducted interviews with foreign diplomats in the Washington D.C. Embassy or the Atlanta Consulate serving each world class country. The authors also interviewed students and teachers from the world class countries who now attend school or work in the United States. When interviewing consultants or students for the world class research, the authors always asked the question, "How would you improve America's schools?" The response generally focused on students.

- *Remove the overemphasis on "fun" from the classroom and teach learning as a serious function of life* (Horst Busek, Teacher, Germany).
- *Establish control? Teachers must gain control for students will not learn as well without it. Student control has slipped in recent years* (Jillian Cooper, Public Relations Director, British Consulate).
- *Raise the driving age to eighteen, so students will work for an education and not a car. Remove the age of sixteen as a magic age for granting privilege. Increase student reading of books and newspapers* (Murray Lawrence, Educator, New Zealand).
- Bridgette Pierre (French Embassy) agreed with the suggestion *to raise the driving age to eighteen.*

A common response from persons who have experienced school in foreign countries was that American students are not serious about academic achievement.

- Shraga Karyan (Consul of Israel) agreed with Murray's suggestion that *students must read more newspapers.* He suggested, however, *that the strict regimentation in elementary school be abandoned. Primary students should learn in a relaxed atmosphere.*

- *Give students more homework. Test them more often to make sure they are learning. Apply more pressure to students* (Sam Peng, General Consul, Taiwan).
- *Change society to make education the number one priority in student's lives. End student violence in the schools* (Duck Haeng Hur, Consul, Republic of Korea).
- *Increase the teacher's ability to control students* (Stephen Allen, Consul of Japan).
- *When students in Korea fail tests in cram school, they fire the student* (Kim Hyoung-Tae, Western Carolina University student and former high school graduate, Korea).
- *In school, you can take two people who are equal, and their successes depend on how much they want to do. Some students are not academically interested and don't do as much homework* (Graeme Dornan, tenth year student at Denefields School, England).
- *Students in your country tell me they do not have homework. You must expect more of students. In the United States there are many dedicated, hard working teachers, but not enough is expected of students* (Li Gan Lin, visiting scholar from China).

The responses clearly indicate that school success depends largely on the attitude of students and that the attitudes of American students may be suspect. So restructuring schools is not the only answer to the improvement of education in the United States. Teachers cannot be expected to teach students who refuse to learn, although parents often expect them to do so. Parents must prepare children for school during the infant years; and once enrolled in school, the student's attitude about school must become and remain more positive and serious. This will not happen until societal values change, and people expect students to achieve as well as students in other world class nations. Educators can suggest how this might happen; but until American students become more motivated and serious, real success will be illusive. Following are implications about the development of world class students in the United States.

Competing Activities

Students lacking motivation will not come to school motivated and ready to learn if the peer culture places more value on competing activities. Think about the youth activities that compete with school for a student's attention. No doubt the list includes sports, a car, a job to pay for the car, dating, talking on the telephone, listening to rock music, watching television, cruising, hunting and fishing, mall watching, and more activities too numerous to mention. The list, unfortunately, might also include drinking and doing drugs, for the infusion of alcohol and drugs into the school culture over the past three decades has had a devastating effect on students and schooling. People living in urban areas, would probably add gang activities to the list. Students choose many of these behaviors rather than school related activities. Distractive and destructive student behavior is not nearly as prevalent in other world class countries as in the United States.

Although the decision would be unpopular in the beginning, many activities competing with school could be delayed until schooling is complete. States could issue the driver's license at age eighteen rather than sixteen. States could also change child labor laws that presently end at age sixteen, so that they discourage student employment until schooling is complete. The absence of a car and a job would probably remove several other competing activities. Laws exist in other world class countries limiting privileges for youth until age seventeen or eighteen, and youth do not seem to suffer.

Adult Priorities

American adults set standards for students that distract from school. For example, American adults would probably not favor a longer school year for students if a longer year were possible. The annual vacation would conflict, or child care would complicate life. Americans often oppose homework and express the belief that all schooling should conclude at the end of the school day. Parents often believe that homework, if favored at all, should not require much time or effort; nor should it interfere with the time that children devote to sports, part-time jobs, and recreation (McAdams, 1993). Adults often clearly show preference for sports, rather than academics. Few academic booster clubs exist, but football boosters work long hours to provide the best program for athletes. It is not suggested that Americans diminish their interest in high school sports, but it is strongly suggested that equal interest be developed for academics. Adults must lead the crusade for excellence rather than hinder if America really wishes its education system to be world class.

Parenting

The educational establishment recognizes the wisdom of promoting positive parenting before the child enters school. Society needs to act on that wisdom. Positive parenting must include the following activities in the home:

(*1*) Parents must discipline students so that they can accept discipline at school.
(*2*) Parents must instill in children a work ethic and the importance of goal setting.
(*3*) Students should be taught that school is a positive place where teachers help students grow and achieve.

Other institutions, such as social service agencies or day-care centers, must help if students are to enter school prepared to learn. Business and industry can be more pro-active instead of constantly criticizing schools. Adults who complain about the educational system in the United States are often blind to the meaningful key to educational change—sending a child to school ready to learn. Students will make better decisions when parents stress positive decision making.

Educators' Responsibility

Once a student enters school, the teacher becomes the significant change agent in the child's life. It is criminal for a student to face, for a full year, a teacher who does not believe that all children can learn, who does not set high expectations for children, and who does not establish a controlled and motivating classroom atmosphere. If developing world class students is an objective, educators must navigate the process. Most teachers in the United States positively mold student lives, but teachers who don't should be dismissed. States must reassess tenure laws, for they are often mentioned as a protector of poor teaching. Local districts must insist on effective administrative supervision and prepare to dismiss ineffective teachers. Teacher training institutions must do their share and improve preparation of all educators. The answer to effective teaching in a dysfunctional society is beyond the scope of this book, but the preceding suggestions would appear on any improvement list. The goal, however, is a teacher in every American classroom who believes that every student can learn and grow to be all that he or she can be.

Homework

Many teachers still foolishly debate the usefulness of homework. Most countries providing world class education require generous amounts of homework; research shows the value of homework; and a large percentage of students religiously completing homework seem successful. There appears to be no serious foundation for debate. However, teachers must follow acceptable guidelines for assigning homework. If homework provides a student with the opportunity to practice new information and if teachers check homework and give prompt student feedback, student learning will improve. Compared to most world class countries, the United States offers a short school year. Homework can help increase learning time for students.

Television Watching

Children become addicted to television even before entering school. The typical American elementary student clocks thirty-five hours of television watching per week. By age eighteen, a student has experienced about 12,000 hours of classroom instruction but has spent 25,000 hours in front of the television (McAdams, 1993). Parents will not destroy the television, so the next alternative is to insist that the set remain off until homework is complete. Television should be a privilege granted only for successful school performance.

Student Violence

Student violence, youth crime, and gang warfare provoke a serious implication for American schools. They dramatize a serious decay in the very fiber of American society that so far has defied correction. It is a miracle that educators perform as well as they do in a school atmosphere of such disruptive behavior. Nearly all schools — urban, suburban and rural — now experience teacher assaults, weapon searches, drug searches, and student assaults. Student death is not uncommon.

Educators in the United States warn that antisocial behavior appears in students at younger and younger ages. Elementary principals find themselves suspending students for infractions that previously were familiar only to the high school principal. The movement of violence to the elementary level sounds an alarm that is presently being addressed nationally and in many states. In North Carolina, a task force appointed by the governor is exploring crime in schools; and as of this writing, the task force reports serious, dangerous school conditions.

Officials must consider drastic steps to remove youthful criminals from schools. Military establishments, for example, have empty barracks that can house older youths who threaten students and teachers. Military personnel can train unruly students and teach them discipline and respect. At least this way, the weapons would be in the right hands.

Little information exists regarding violence in the schools of the world class countries, probably because printing such information deters from the establishment of positive public relations. However, visitors from foreign countries see the atmosphere in American schools as incomprehensible. In Japan private citizens cannot legally own a gun, but Americans defend the right to own and use a gun even if the gun is in the hands of a child.

A recent nationwide study found that 9 percent of secondary students in America had a gun. Eleven percent had been threatened by a gun, and over 50 percent of the sample group could place their hands on a gun in short notice. This is a crisis, and the importance of school restructuring pales in comparison to it. Americans must confront violence in a society that permits violence in the school.

Summary

The discussion about world class students continues in the chapters ahead that deal with teachers, testing, and home environment. The issue is important enough to visit a second time. But in bringing closure to this discussion primarily about students, it seems appropriate to return one more time to the premise that students can control their own destiny. Students can and do achieve under bad conditions. Home and cultural problems need not keep a student from becoming world class. Today's youths are tomorrow's leaders who must insure future generations that a world class education is available in America.

AFTERTHOUGHTS

Among the world class nations studied, those with the most successful education systems have students who are serious about learning and view learning as hard work. Successful students view the outcome of educa-

---

Worksheet

How does your educational agency compare to the world class standard for students? Fill in the following information.

Percent of Students Reaching the Last Grade Offered in School

95%

_____	_____	_____
(World class standard)	(Your agency)	(Deviation)

Percent of Thirteen-Year-Old Students Spending Four or More Hours on Science Homework

5%

_____	_____	_____
(World class standard)	(Your agency)	(Deviation)

Percent of Thirteen-Year-Old Students Spending Four or More Hours on Math Homework

18%

_____	_____	_____
(World class standard)	(Your agency)	(Deviation)

Percent of Thirteen-Year-Old Students Spending Two or More Hours Daily on All Homework

41%

_____	_____	_____
(World class standard)	(Your agency)	(Deviation)

Percent of Thirteen-Year-Old Students Who Watch Five Hours or More of Television Daily

13%

_____	_____	_____
(World class standard)	(Your agency)	(Deviation)

---

tion as preparation for life's work and believe that success in school establishes success in life.

REFERENCES

Allen, S. 1992. Interview (October 23).

Busek, H. 1992. Interview (December 2).

Butterfield, F. (1992). "Why They Excel," *Parade Magazine.*

Cooper, J. 1992. Interview (December 2).

Dobby, N. 1993. Interview (June 17).

Dornan, G. 1993. Interview (June 17).

Hur, D. H. 1992. Interview (December 2).

Jaeger, R. M. 1992. "World Class Standards, Choice, and Privatization: Weak Measurement Serving Presumptive Policy," *Phi Delta Kappan,* 74(2)118–128.

Karyan, S. 1992. Interview (October 23).

Kim, H.-T. 1992. Interview (October 14).

Lapointe, A. E., J. M. Askew and N. A. Mead. 1992. *Learning Science.* Princeton, New Jersey: The International Assessment of Educational Progress, Educational Testing Service.

Lapointe, A. E., N. A. Mead and J. M. Askew. 1992. *Learning Mathematics.* Princeton, New Jersey: The International Assessment of Educational Progress, Educational Testing Service.

Lawrence, M. 1993. Interview (October 12).

Li, G. L. 1993. Interview (June 15).

McAdams, R. P. 1993. *Lessons from Abroad: How Other Countries Educate Their Children.* Lancaster, PA: Technomic Publishing Company.

Peng, S. 1992. Interview (October 23).

Pierre, B. 1992. Interview (October 16).

Pittman, R. B. 1993. "The 21st Century and Secondary At-Risk Students: What's Ahead for Teachers in Rural America," a paper presented at the *ACRES National Rural Education Symposium,* Savannah, Georgia.

Setsuo, K. 1992. Interview (October 9).

World Education Report. 1991. Paris, France: United Nations Educational, Scientific, and Cultural Organization.

Chapter 8

DEFINING A WORLD CLASS STANDARD FOR CURRICULUM

The curricula in the nations studied are more similar than different. The course of study during compulsory attendance years is quite similar, and most governments recommend a specific amount of instructional time for each subject. One notable difference in the United States is moral and/or religious education found in the curricula of many of the other nations. High schools in other nations are most commonly special purpose schools rather than comprehensive schools. The most common curriculum is national in scope. Since it is impossible to list the curricula of each world class nation, interesting curriculum formats are listed in this chapter.

REALITY: THE WORLD CLASS STANDARD FOR CURRICULUM

Who Establishes the Curriculum?

Many of the nations in this study overhauled their curriculum as a major part of the reform movements in the 1980s. Most changed was Great Britain, which supported local curricula prior to the 1988 Reform Act that mandated national goals in education, a national curriculum, and national testing. See Chapter 12 for a discussion of this reform.

No country reforms its curriculum unless it feels dissatisfaction with the existing one. Even the Japanese redesigned their curriculum during the reform era. The United States is distinguished by its slow movement in that direction.

119

Association of Supervision and Curriculum Development (ASCD) writers (O'Neil, 1993) asked experts in the area: "Is the United States Headed toward a National Curriculum?" The experts responded:

> Over the past several years, groups representing all the subject areas have begun to develop "national standards" laying out the key content and performance targets. Eva Baker explained that the standards have become a code word for what we used to call curriculum. For political reasons, it's seen as inappropriate to call this entity curriculum in a national context. So those backing national standards have soft-pedaled the "national curriculum" connotation while insisting that adoption of the standards by local school districts will be voluntary." (p. 2)

When a New Zealand principal learned that the United States lacked a national curriculum and national testing, he asked how teachers in the United States know what to teach and what to test for mastery (Malcolm, 1993). ASCD (1993) quoted a second expert on the same subject, William Moloney, school superintendent in Easton, Pennsylvania, who answered, "The question is no longer *if* the United States will have a national curriculum, but *when* and *what kind*" (p. 2).

Figure 8.1 shows that the United States is far from the norm among the nations studied in terms of locus of control of the curriculum. The United States has, by far, the most fragmented system of curriculum

Nation	Locus of Control and Number of Agencies	
Canada	Province	12—10 provinces, 2 territories
France	National	1—Minister of Education
Germany	Länder[1]	16—Länder
Great Britain[2]	National	4—Department for Education
Israel	National	1—Minister of Education
Japan	National	1—Minister of Education
Korea	National	1—Minister of Education
New Zealand	National	1—Minister of Education
Taiwan	National	1—Minister of Education
United States	State/Territory	50+
World Class Standard	National	1—Minister of Education

[1]Since unification, Länder are somewhat like states.
[2]England and Wales coordinate; Scotland and Northern Ireland vary somewhat.

Figure 8.1 Locus of control of the curriculum in the world class nations.

development of any nation studied. The cause of this fragmentation is both historic and political. A similar pattern existed in Great Britain; but with the Reform Act of 1988, the British government established national goals for education, national curriculum, and national testing. The British national curriculum has three core subjects—English, mathematics, and science—and seven foundation subjects—technology, history, geography, music, art, physical education, and a foreign language. A great deal can be learned from this reform.

The world class nations appear to have reached general consensus about the core subjects taken while students are compelled to be in school. Among these subjects are a study of the national language, both written and spoken; mathematics; science; history and geography; and the fine arts. The particular teaching methods used by each nation are beyond the scope of this study, but the authors feel that cultural variables are more important to student understanding than teaching methods.

Following are sample curricula from Japan, Israel, and Korea.

Japanese Curriculum Revision

The Ministry of Education, Science, and Culture released *An Outline of Revision of the Courses of Study in Japan* (circa 1991) that defined its purpose as being ''to maintain a uniform standard of education throughout the country, and to secure substantially the equal opportunity of education guaranteed under the Constitution of Japan'' (p. 1). The Minister of Education, Science, and Culture sets the course of study as the national standards of school curricula that are to be prepared and taught by respective schools.

Since the end of World War II, revisions took place in Japan approximately every ten years. *An Outline of Revision of the Courses of Study in Japan* (circa 1991) explains the basic focus of the last revision: It fosters students who will be able to adapt to an emerging society in the future. Specifically, it focuses on both science and technology and the impact of them on the economy. The Monbusho acknowledged how Japan's past generation created the current affluent society in a time of major social, economic and international change. Based on that history, the aim of the reform movement was to develop that same skill in the next generation.

The revision was based on four principles.

First, there is a set, fundamental knowledge base everyone in Japan should know. That knowledge base should be designed to enlighten each person's character. Further, it called for alignment of the curriculum, and individual subjects, from the first day of school to the last.

Second, each student should develop the capacity to accept change and grow from it. To do so, the innate creativity of the individual should be expanded, with an emphasis on learning individually, rather than relying on a group.

Third, each student should revere Japanese culture and history, so that the world is better understood and appreciated as well. Japan's place in the world of nations will be improved through this approach to others.

Fourth, the result of the whole course of study should be development of a rigorous, intelligent student. This development will occur with each stage of school, from kindergarten to graduation.

The result was a curriculum with an increase in the number of teaching hours but with each hour defined as forty-five minutes in the elementary curriculum. The definition of several curriculum areas was expanded:

(*1*) Social studies were expanded to include particular businesses in Japan's expanding economy.

(*2*) History was expanded to include forty-two representative personalities.

(*3*) Social studies were to include an understanding of the significance of the national flag and the national anthem of Japan and understanding the need to pay respect to them (*An Outline of Revision of the Courses of Study in Japan,* circa 1991, p. 5).

The curriculum defines a total of eleven subjects. Figure 8.2 displays these subjects and the hours allocated to each.

The curriculum in the Japanese Lower Secondary School has rapidly expanded in the post-war years. In 1950 the number of students passing from lower secondary school to upper secondary school (what the United States calls high school) grew from 42.3 percent to more than 94 percent in the 1990s (Ishizaka circa, 1990). While there is an exam to qualify for the middle school years, all students pass it and are placed in the lower upper school. The fierce competition for placement in the "best" high schools fuels the determination of both lower and upper school students and their parents. Enrollment in a *juku,* or "cram school" is practically a requirement. Later, this chapter examines the role and function of the *juku* (cram school) separately.

	Grade and Teaching Hours					
Subject	1	2	3	4	5	6
Japanese language	306	315	280	280	210	210
Social studies	—	—	105	105	105	105
Arithmetic	136	175	175	175	175	175
Science	—	—	105	105	105	105
Life environment[1]	192	105	—	—	—	—
Music	68	70	70	70	70	70
Arts and handicraft	68	70	70	70	70	70
Homemaking[2]	—	—	—	—	70	70
Physical education	102	105	105	105	105	105
Total teaching hours	850	910	980	1,015	1,015	1,015

[1]Replaces social studies at these two grades. The purpose of this curriculum is to develop an individual who relies on him/her self.

[2]This is not the equivalent of home economics. It is a course of study for both sexes. Its purpose is to develop the innate ability to cope with change and to be intelligent consumers.

Note: From *An Outline of Revision of the Courses of Study* in Japan, Ministry of Education.

Figure 8.2 Subjects currently taught in the elementary school curriculum in Japan and the grade and hours taught for each subject.

Curriculum in the Republic of Korea

In the Korean primary system, students study nine areas: moral education, Korean language, social studies, arithmetic, science, physical education, music, fine arts, and crafts. Students are additionally engaged in extracurricular activities many hours each week. The school year is thirty-four weeks in length. Like the Japanese and Taiwanese, an "hour" of teaching is less than sixty minutes; and in the primary school it is forty minutes in length. This is due to a cultural variable where time in school is regarded as both social time and a time for learning. Americans, on the contrary, approach school as work from the beginning bell, with few breaks until the school day ends. Stevenson (1992) found that Asian students are happier in school than are American students, and the combination of work and social activities may be part of the reason.

Despite a long history of geographic closeness and historic conflict, some interesting differences exist between the middle schools of Japan and the Republic of Korea. In the Korean Middle School, an "hour" of teaching expands to forty-five minutes, but the allotted hours are minimums and may be expanded. The length of the school year remains the same. The principal has considerable authority over the teaching day, including the content of electives. The middle school curriculum is shown in Figure 8.3.

The Republic of Korea's middle grades curriculum is noteworthy for the emphasis on second language with both classical Chinese and English taught. The middle school separates males and females, which may seem strange to American educators. The high regard for moral education, which begins during the third year of schooling and continues through the tenth grade year, is linked to an emphasis on military training at the tenth grade level.

As the reader reviews the curriculum and the variance in teaching hours per week, the great latitude in types of schools should be kept in mind. The Taiwanese and Koreans label and rank schools and teachers.

Subject	Grade and Minimum Hours per Week		
	7	8	9
Moral education	2	2	2
Korean language	4	5	5
Korean history	—	2	2
Social studies	3	2	2
Mathematics	4	3 – 4	4 – 5
Science	4	3 – 4	4 – 5
Physical education	3	3	3
Music	2	2	1 – 2
Fine arts	2	2	1 – 2
Classical Chinese	1	1 – 2	1 – 2
English	4	3 – 5	3 – 5
Vocational/home ec.[1]	3	4 – 6	—
Agricultural/technical/com-merce/fisheries[2]	—	—	4 – 6
Elective	0 – 2	0 – 2	0 – 2
Extracurricular	2	2	2
Total teaching hours	68 +	68 +	68 +

[1]Males take vocational education subjects: females take home economics.
[2]Students select one subject. Depends on type of school.
Note: From *Education in Korea, 1991 – 1992.*

Figure 8.3 *Current Republic of Korea middle school curriculum, grades seven to nine shown by subject and minimum hours of weekly training.*

The best teachers and, presumably, the most strict curriculum are assigned to "Star Schools" that prepare the academically gifted. Lesser regarded teachers teach less academically inclined students in so-called "Cow Schools."

State of Israel Curriculum

The State of Israel revised the curriculum beginning in 1968 despite having the newest school system among the developed nations of the world. Free compulsory education extends from age five through sixteen, with free education provided through age eighteen. The aims of the reform movement were:

(*1*) To reach a higher level of scholastic achievement

(*2*) To advance the social integration of the various sectors of society

A school system of state schools, Arabic schools, and state religious schools were to carry out the reforms. The Pedagogic Council in each school recommended guidelines for primary education (grade one), but the Council allows each school to change the allocation of hours by grade. Figure 8.4 presents the subjects offered in the Israel primary curriculum for grades two through eight with teaching hours per week listed for each subject.

Approximately 71.4 percent of students in primary Hebrew education attend state education schools. The state religious education schools parallel the state education curriculum in the number of teaching hours per week. There is a greater stress on the Bible, prophets, Talmud, Mishna, and Jewish law in the state religious schools, with eight to nine hours per week in each grade spent on this. Schools schedule fewer hours on science and social studies as a result. Nationwide, approximately 83 percent of students attend Hebrew sector schools and 17 percent attend Arab sector schools (Sprinzak et al., 1992). The greatly increasing number of immigrants causes a strain on the mandated curriculum.

Secondary School Curriculum

Secondary school curriculum deserves separate mention because the

Subject	Grade						
	2	3	4	5	6	7	8
Bible/oral tradition	4	4	4	4	4	4	—
Hebrew	—	4	4	4	4	4	4
Mathematics	—	4	4	4	4	4	4
Science	—	2	2	4	4	3	3
Geography/soc. science	—	2	2	2	2	2	2
History/civics	—	—	—	0 – 2	0 – 2	2 – 3	2 – 3
English	—	—	—	2 – 3	2 – 3	3	3
Arts/crafts	1 – 2	1 – 2	2	2	3	3	—
Fine arts	—	2	2	2	2	2	2
Physical education	—	2	2	2	2	2	2
Education	1	1	1	1	1	1	—
Electives (Judaism, etc.)	—	—	2	2	3	2	—
Optional study	4	5	4	2	3	2	—
Weekly hours, total	24	26	28	33	34	35	36

Figure 8.4 State of Israel curriculum for primary schools grades two through eight in *state schools. Curriculum is shown in teaching hours per week.*

world class nations vary noticeably from the American approach to high school curriculum. Albert Shanker (1993) admitted, ''I am not sure about the answer to my own question about the importance of content standards vs. performance standards and which one should be the basis of setting world-class standards.'' He explained,

> Starting around secondary school, our competitors' content and perfor-mance standards and assessments vary according to whether their stu-dents are aiming for an apprenticeship in a technical school or hoping to go to a university; sometimes these standards and tests vary by what kind of technical education or university major students intend to pursue. (p. 14)

Many eastern Pacific Rim nations view their high schools as either ''star schools'' for the academically able or ''cow schools'' for the less academically inclined. The better teachers, more rigorous curriculum, and most attention are focused on the star schools. Teachers who are not highly regarded are sent to the cow schools to teach students who couldn't attain star status. Curiously, in Taiwan, the world class Little League baseball teams, which perennially play in the last game of the world series, come from the ''cow schools.'' The star schools do not include competitive athletics. One reason why the Republic of Korea actively discourages parents from going to school and becoming involved with their children's teachers stems from the tracking program. In the Republic of Korea, the teacher and the test results alone determine school placement. The only means of growth in social status comes from educational accomplishment. There is also a well known and perhaps illegal system of bribery among government workers that could explain why the government does not want close contact between parents and the authorities who determine their child's future.

It is not surprising that high schools routinely track or group students based on past performance, test scores, and future plans and that many nations do not offer a comprehensive high school in which students self-select a course of study. In Germany, for example, the Gesamtschule (comprehensive secondary school) didn't even exist until the reforms of 1969. To assist in the acceptance of such schools, the West German government nationally mandated the establishment of the schools. After twenty years, fewer than 5 percent of West German high school students attend comprehensive high schools (Fishman, 1993.)

Worldwide students commonly take competitive placement examinations as they complete middle school and the compulsory attendance years. These tests determine which type of further education the student will find beneficial. One result is rigorous tracking of students. Society benefits from this system as the cost and purpose of noncompelled education is more focused and not wasted on a nonreceptive audience. The individual, of course, can suffer, based solely on poor test performance. Because of this separation in most of the world class nations, world class high schools are examined in two categories: (1) vocational high schools and (2) academic high schools.

Vocational High Schools

The type and structure of vocational and special purpose high schools are closely related to the economy of the nation. Three examples of this relationship are

(*1*) In the Republic of Korea, there are several types of vocational high schools: agricultural, technical, commercial, fishery, and maritime.

(*2*) In Israel, there are general, technological, and agricultural tracks in high school. The technological track has recently expanded beyond the twelfth grade by creating a technological reserve in the Israel Defense Forces, and students remain enrolled until they receive their technician or practical engineer certificate. About 47 percent of Israel's high school students study in the technological track in one of these areas: information technology, machinery, woodworking, chemistry and biotechnology, construction and architecture, or electricity and electronics.

(*3*) In Japan there are three types of upper secondary schools: full-time, part-time (usually evening), and correspondence schools, the latter leading to a certificate somewhat equivalent to the American G.E.D. Japan has "general" or academic curricula and specialized curricula. The latter include agricultural, industrial, commercial, fishery, home economics, nursing, science-mathematics, etc. Japan also offers another option to those who have completed lower secondary (middle) school. Students may study in a College of Technology if they prefer preparation for engineering or mercantile marine studies. After five years or more, graduates earn the title of "associate."

The authors believe the German vocational education system is one to emulate, because German workers are among the most productive in the world. The workforce is highly regimented. Students must have a vocational certification to become a journeyman, helper, or skilled worker at a standardized rate of pay. After several years of work and another examination, the most skilled worker may earn the rank of master. Students in vocational education typically continue in school until they reach age eighteen.

The mission of German vocational education is to teach the basic skills needed in a specific field to be competent and career-oriented. The school-to-work transition is an integral part of German education. The system coalesces with industry, so entry into employment begins in school as the student attends part-time (usually) at a vocational high school, and works with a firm in an apprentice capacity. The firm provides a site-based craftsman with some training in pedagogy, so learning occurs in school and the firm.

The structure of vocational education combines the general academic education provided by the government with specific vocational training provided and paid for by the industry the student wishes to join. Federal legislation sets standards for cooperative education. The German view of such training is different from the vocational concept in the United

States. The German government recognizes and oversees ''in-plant,'' ''interplant,'' and ''non-plant'' vocational education at the work site. Both training regulations and in-school curricula are coordinated by federal and Länder government authorities. This assures cooperation and support from the work site and the school in the education of the student. There are currently 382 specialties requiring training. Industry trainers must meet certain select criteria, including having completed their own vocational training and gained several years of experience. The minimum age for trainers is twenty-four. The trainers must also have some background in teaching about work and vocational education. This bridges the gap between teachers and practitioners that plagues American vocational education efforts.

Trade associations, industrial and commercial associations, or non-education ministries administer final examinations in the various fields. These are self-regulating, mandatory, membership bodies that set industry standards. The final examination may be taken only twice and includes practical oral and written demonstration of skill. The certificate shows the results of the examination. Many American educators argue whether education is part of life or preparation for it. No such distinction is necessary in the German system because the system sets both educational and industry standards.

German students have a variety of school options, including six different types of vocational schools:

(*1*) *Berufsschule:* The Berufsschule is a part-time vocational school for students in grades nine and ten who have a job and are still under school-leaving age. These schools provide both general education and professional vocational knowledge. The curriculum is approximately 40 percent general academics and 60 percent vocational specific to particular industries. The school issues a certificate of completion, allowing the holder to enter higher vocational training. This is the most common school among the vocational schools.

(*2*) *Berufsfachschule:* The Berufsfachschule is a full-time vocational school that includes general academic training and specific vocational skill development. The course of study is at least one year in length and ends with a final examination. The school week is thirty hours or more.

(*3*) *Berufsaufbauschule:* The Berufsaufbauschule is a subject-area vocational school for students already attending a vocational school or who have completed compulsory vocational education. Subjects include such areas as economics, engineering, agriculture, or home economics. The school may be full-time or part-time with hours of study set by subject. Fifty percent of the instruction includes German, a foreign language, math, and science. Additional general academic education and specific vocational education are included. Completion occurs when the student passes a final examination showing mastery of the school's objectives. Completion yields a vocational training certificate that allows admission into higher vocational training schools.

(4) *Fachoberschule:* The Fachoberschule is a two-year vocational school for students in the equivalent of grades eleven and twelve. The curriculum includes general academic skills and specific vocational skills. Subject areas typically include engineering, business administration, home economics, design, etc. The first-year students spend four days a week in practical training or apprenticeship and one day a week in class. Second-year students spend thirty hours a week in class, 60 percent of which is academic training in German, social studies, mathematics, science, foreign language, etc. Graduation entitles the student to movement into higher vocational training schools.

(5) *Berufliches Gymnasium:* The Berufliches Gymnasium prepares students to qualify for entrance to an institution of higher education. There is a vocational emphasis usually in economics or a technical science area that is basic and intensified.

(6) *Fachschule:* The Fachschule is an advanced vocational training school, and students must have a certificate of completion from a lower vocational school to enter. The school requires most students to have actual work experience in their specialized vocational field to enter the program. The school trains middle-level managers and those with higher responsibility in a vocational field. The course of study is two years in length, usually ending with a required state examination. Passing the exam allows the graduate to be called a ''state-examined'' engineer or other appropriate title from among the sixty or more certification areas.

Academic High Schools

Most societies want their most able students to have the very best education possible so that the leaders of the next generation are well prepared. Many nations structure their education to serve the academic elite. In American schools the issue of academically gifted education takes the form of tracking or grouping the most able students.

Frequently, the argument against this American practice centers on spending priorities. Part of the American culture is equal treatment of all. Because of this, the most academically able should not be treated differently but, in reality, they are. In most of the other countries studied, testing eliminates students who do not test at a high level. Those who do test well are placed in carefully tracked academic schools, and there is no effort made to hide the fact that the best students are receiving a higher level of education. How do other countries provide for their most gifted students? Three examples follow:

(*1*) *Taiwan:* The star schools are most commonly located in Taipei, and gifted students are expected to get to the school. While there are attendance districts in Taiwan, the Chinese extended families will find a family member who lives in Taipei and have the student move to attend the star school. This makes class size quite large in many cases, but students expect excellence and class size is not a concern.

(2) *England:* Beyond the school-leaving age, the British use a selective system of tests to track students who wish to continue their academic training. Chapter 9 explains the tests. The best students remain in school, however, and small classes prevail. Students at this level generally seek university admission.

(*3*) *Japan:* The Japanese school system offers the academically oriented high school student an excellent opportunity to excel. After World War II, as the Japanese government was rebuilding the nation, the occupation forces strongly encouraged the development of comprehensive high schools. The Japanese were accustomed to ranking academic high schools as most important and vocational schools as least important. The same attitude toward ranking schools and universities pervades much of Japanese society today. During the elementary school years, there is no tracking or provision for ''gifted'' education. By the time students are ready to attend lower secondary schools, some schools are selective about the students who are admitted. By upper secondary school years, the schools in the attendance area are strictly ranked from most academic on down. Competition for admission to the ''best'' schools is keen. While less than 1 percent of the lower secondary schools in Japan is private, the number jumps to over 28 percent for upper secondary schools

(Ishizaka, circa 1990). The increase in private schooling is largely the result of enrollment of students unable to gain entrance to the public high school. Each prefecture (area government) designs an entrance examination, and the score on that exam and the transcripts from the lower secondary school determine attendance at the upper secondary school. The better rated the secondary school, the more likely the student will be admitted to a highly ranked university.

McAdams (1993) reports that three or four hours of homework for the average upper secondary school student is typical, but the most academically competitive students do five or six hours of homework and the highest ranked schools expect the most homework. The main difference in education for the Japanese gifted student is in the system of private education called *juku* or "cram school." This system, largely unknown in the West, is discussed below.

Cram Schools

Japan, Taiwan, and Korea use a system of private education that supplements the public schools. They are called *juku* or *yobiko* in Japan, *bushibon* in Taiwan, and "cram schools" in America. In primary school, the *juku* provides enrichment in swimming, fine arts, and foreign languages. Some *juku* provide remediation for students. By the time students reach lower secondary school, the purpose of the *juku* changes to "cramming" for the entrance examinations. *Juku* can be small, single-person schools or large, highly competitive schools. The most typical offerings for elementary school students are Japanese, mathematics, or science tutoring programs. The schools make it their business to know as much as possible about the lower secondary school entrance examinations for selective schools. Their tuition is directly dependent on the performance of their alumni on the selection tests. It is estimated that about one-third of Japanese year five and six students attend a *juku* (Her Majesty's Inspectorate, 1992). Classes tend to be large, often exceeding fifty students. In Japan, the government does not allow public school teachers to work in the *juku* because of the strain put on young scholars. Some parents report that ten- or eleven-year-old students rise at 6 A.M. for school, then attend the *juku,* and then do homework until 10 P.M. Students attend classes on Saturday and sometimes on Sunday.

The pressure to excel increases in the lower secondary school years, and over 80 percent of these students attend a *juku* at some time (McAdams, 1993). The cost of a *juku* may exceed $2,000 per year, and parents in the Republic of Korea sometimes bankrupt themselves paying the cost of a prestigious *juku*. When the authors interviewed a student from Korea regarding the cost of a *juku*, the question was asked: ''What happens if the parents pay all of this money and then the student simply will not do the work?'' Without hesitation, the reply came: ''Fire the student!'' with no refund of tuition (Kim, 1993). In Japan the salaries of *juku* teachers are similar to those of public school teachers (McAdams, 1993), but in Taipei the most famous teachers work in *bushibons* at salaries much higher than public school teachers (Liao, 1993).

By upper secondary school the pressure to excel again increases, and as many as 90 percent of Japan's upper secondary students attend a *juku*. As McAdams (1993) explained, ''Many Japanese are unhappy with the stress on students known as *examination hell*'' and with the time, energy, and resources families give to the *juku*. Nevertheless, parents continue to send children to *juku*, fearful that without this extra schooling, their students will fail the entrance exam to their chosen schools and seriously jeopardize the chances for later career and economic success. This fact is all the more remarkable in light of Ishizaka's (circa 1990) comment: ''While juku flourish as more and more parents want to send their children to good higher institutions, there are no definite research findings on the real effects of juku attendance. Some observers are very critical of the juku, while others praise their educational effectiveness'' (p. 43). In the competitive environment of many eastern Pacific Rim nations, perhaps the feeling that these schools help students succeed is enough reason to support them.

The Effect of Work Ethic on Curriculum

As indicated in Chapter 6, the school day involves more work and greater intensity in the United States than in other nations in the study. This has an obvious impact on the international curriculum and the way it is taught. Many American educators think of eastern Pacific Rim schools as sweat shops, but they are not. The Asian approach to teaching and learning is simply more intensive. Another major difference is the absence of grouping or tracking in most eastern Pacific Rim countries during the compulsory attendance years.

Stevenson (1992) provided a view of Asian schools that enhances student learning. Students in Asian schools are not *forced* to learn: they are *expected and allowed* to learn. Because the school day involves many social activities (what American educators would call "time off task"), teachers and students view school as a happy setting; and academic learning is approached with confidence and pleasure. Stevenson finds the impact of this approach obvious. While American school children tested near their Asian counterparts in the early years of school, by fifth grade American children fell far behind their Asian counterparts. Are Asian children more gifted, or is the impact of the curriculum and the way students and teachers approach learning the cause for this separation?

Stevenson (1992) also reported that American parents were more satisfied with their children's academic performance than were Asian parents, and that the American students were more positive about their abilities. Perhaps the lack of a specific, defined, understood curriculum in American schools leads to a false sense of accomplishment by students and their parents. Asian parents have a well-defined and measurable curriculum against which to gauge their children's progress. The Asian parents, usually the mother, stress the importance of doing well in school more than do their American counterparts.

The motivation to learn was notably different between Asian and American students. Asian students yearned for success as students, while American students sought rewards such as sweets or money. An educator from the People's Republic of China (Li, 1993) indicated that teachers give rewards to students who do well in class just as do many American teachers. The difference, however, is in the reward given. Many American teachers keep jars of candy on their desks and show the class who has done well by giving out candy. In China, the teachers give small rewards that encourage successful students to learn more. Evidently, both cultures respond well to rewards, but the *purpose* of the reward varies greatly. Most American educators know parents who pay their children for good grades. Yet Asian children expect no pay and prize effort as much as they do ability. Stevenson (1992) concludes,

> The idea that increased effort will lead to improved performance is an important factor in accounting for the willingness of Chinese and Japanese children, teachers, and parents to spend so much more time and effort on the children's academic work." (p. 74)

When students are more willing to put forth the effort to learn, the structure of the curriculum becomes less significant. American educators will not be surprised to learn that Asian students spend much more time on homework than do Americans (see Chapter 4 and Chapter 7). Nor will Americans be surprised to learn that New Zealand boasts the greatest number of books read per capita of any nation in the world (Lawrence, 1992), while American middle school children spend only a few minutes per day in pursuit of pleasure reading. Stevenson's finding that Japanese children in grades kindergarten through high school actually watch *more* television than do American students should amaze American educators. Even the research contained in this book presents American youth as world class television watchers. The difference is that Japanese students watch television more commonly *after* mastery of their homework, while American students watch television *instead* of doing homework (Stevenson, 1992).

American citizens commonly respond to the stress caused by rigorous curriculum and high-stakes testing in other countries by assuming that the result is a higher suicide rate for students. That simply is not the case, however. Chapter 11 explores comparative suicide rates and finds the rate in Japan is actually one-half that of American youth of the same age and sex. It is estimated that the suicide rate in the Republic of Korea, which stresses academic testing even more than does Japan, is one-half the Japanese rate. According to Stevenson (1992), the reason for academic success in Japanese schools, despite television viewing, is satisfaction with school, which may partly explain the lower suicide rates. Stevenson (1992) explains

> Our data do not support the Western assumption that Asian children must experience extraordinary stress from their more demanding curriculum. The clear academic goals and the enthusiastic support given by the family, teachers and peers may reduce the strain from working so hard. (p. 74)

Hess and Azuma (1991) report another difference between Asian and American approaches to the teaching-learning continuum. They compared the cultural support of education between America and Japan in an extensive study of 500 Japanese and 500 American mothers and the attributes they prized most in their children. When given a thirteen-item list and asked to pick out the characteristics they desired most in their children, the Japanese mothers selected basic habits, compliance and patience, most often. The American mothers ranked compliance and patience lower than most other items on the list. The smallest deviation between the two groups dealt with skills needed in school. Hess and Azuma concluded Japanese mothers prized ''diligence'' while American mothers preferred ''independence'' and ''acceptance of diversity'' (p. 3). Parents teach Japanese children to work hard and to try to learn. American parents encourage children to be independent and quick in giving answers, rather than working hard.

As Chapter 6 reported, the method of teaching in Japan and the United States reflects the expectations of the parent and child. While the Japanese teacher focuses on teaching an understanding of *process* and *reasoning,* the American teacher frequently feeds the expectations of parents and children by giving worksheets that students finish quickly so the child can be given another worksheet. The American teacher rewards with candy; the Asian teacher rewards with something to stimulate additional learning. The American student prepares for a test with memorization and short-term cramming; the Asian child prepares to demonstrate an understanding of the process, not just the answer (Hess and Azuma, 1991).

In Japan the typical middle grades textbook may be 100 pages long, and the teacher may be expected to teach with it for 300 hours so that process can be taught. A Japanese teacher would feel like a failure if so much as one page of the book went unstudied. The textbooks in Japan are small and not heavy, so all books are taken home each evening, and many schools will not allow students to leave books at the school (Ishizaka, circa 1990).

Work ethic often reflects a student's decision at the school-leaving age. Americans call students who do not complete the highest level of public education ''dropouts.'' In England and New Zealand such students are merely viewed as ''school-leavers.'' This distinction is more than polite semantics; it is an indication of the way society views the student between the end of compulsory attendance and the beginning of higher education. The idea of ''dropouts'' is a relatively new American phenomenon. Neither of the Wright Brothers graduated from high school although they had the credits to do so, yet they were never considered ''dropouts'' whose lives were over and who had no chance to succeed.

IMPLICATIONS

When viewed in the light of world class standards, the United States clearly needs a national curriculum based on national standards for education. It is possible for the United States to develop a national curriculum, but the process won't be easy because of the presence of strong states rights advocates.

Many efforts to nationalize education are already under way in the United States. A few follow here:

(*1*) The National Council of Teachers of Mathematics (NCTM) leads other professional organizations in science, geography, and history in the development of standards for their teaching disciplines. NCTM's work includes curriculum standards, teaching standards, and standards of assessment. Proliferation of this type of work is expected before the end of the decade (Hirsch, 1992).

(*2*) The National Board for Professional Teaching Standards designed national teaching certification standards in thirty-five fields. The Chair, Governor James B. Hunt, North Carolina and Vice Chair, Claire L. Pelton, called for "envisioning a renewed system of education and working to make it a reality" (*Preparing for Our Future,* 1992, p. 1). Hunt's reference was to a single system.

(*3*) The National Governors' Association and President Clinton have endorsed national goals in education in *America 2000.* The report calls for students to leave grades four, eight, and twelve demonstrating competence on standardized tests in English, mathematics, science, history, and geography, plus demonstrating thinking and citizenship skills. President Clinton called for individual states to voluntarily meet these standards. Who can say no?

(*4*) The entire concept of the National Assessment of Educational Progress (NAEP) explained earlier in this book is predicated on some understood educational minimum standards of student performance. Textbook companies design textbooks based on a presumed national curriculum. The proliferation of nationally normed, comparative standardized tests forces schools and teachers closer to a single curriculum under the omnipresent pressure to raise test scores.

There should be a single, national school system for America if the best education is to be provided. How can people consider the United States educationally united when the average per capita expenditure of local and state funds was $546.16 in Tennessee and $1,660.74 in Alaska in 1992? Yet Tennessee actually spent a greater percentage of its total state and local resources (21.0 percent) on education than did Alaska (17.2 percent). And both states spent a lower percentage of their available funds than the United States national average of $812.23 per capita (National Center of Education Statistics, 1992).

The United States clearly sanctions *de facto* economic segregation of education both among states and within states, among poor rural areas, and among inner-city areas and what the British call the "leafy suburbs." The problem of economic segregation of educational opportunity is not unique to the United States. Israel copes with inequality but uses its national education system to address the inequity. Special resources are made available for preschool children aged three and four who live in settlement towns, immigrant areas, and economically disadvantaged areas, designated "Tunnei Tipuach," or "those in need of nurturing." Once designated an economically disadvantaged area, the national government funds the schools at a rate of 130 percent of funding for other schools. Only a true national school system can care for "those in need of nurturing" so well. Had Thurgood Marshall argued the *Brown* case on the grounds of "separate cannot be equal" because of economic segregation of education, the application of the general welfare clause in the Constitution and the equal protection clause of the 14th Amendment might have allowed an even more sweeping decision than the original case provided. National curriculum depends on equal funding.

Those who lead the United States toward a national curriculum should be aware of several other large potholes in the road. Based on the British experience of developing a national curriculum, the following areas represent foreseeable pitfalls:

(*1*) The national goals of education need to coalesce with the standards of the national professional organizations that are developing their own standards. While the national government shapes standards into a simple guide for the states to follow, the temptation to be too complete can ruin the good intentions of national curriculum. North Carolina is an example of what to avoid. The first standard course of study was in a book less than an inch thick. Once performance testing was tied to the course of study, the state curriculum exploded to a voluminous 7,600 pages!

(*2*) Any national teaching standards need to be drawn from the national goals and curriculum rather than imposed on them.

(*3*) Educators will naturally seize on issues of educational access turning national curriculum standards into a debate on national access to education standards. While both need to be addressed, they must be separated. Once national curriculum standards are in place, then the issue of access is appropriate to address.

(4) It is inevitable that national curriculum will be nationally tested— first voluntarily, then mandatorily. The development of the tests must be done while the curriculum standards are being written and by the same group. Only through such a procedure can alignment exist.

(5) The debate on national curriculum will be lengthy and noisy. Falling into the trap of euphemisms such as calling national curriculum ''national standards'' will make the debate less honest and more confusing. The process should be clear, open, and honest.

The world class standard for curriculum leadership is a single national curriculum developed by the national government's education authority. The United States is farthest from this world class standard of any nation studied.

The basic curriculum in the nations studied is more alike than it is dissimilar. All nations teach the basics of language education, including reading and writing. They all teach some form of mathematics, science, social studies, physical education, and fine arts. Nations establish time allotments for teaching each subject with the exception of New Zealand, which leaves the time per subject ratio up to the individual teacher. The major difference in curricular offerings is when the offering is introduced to the student. The United States must study international curriculum and determine why countries can teach curricular objectives to students earlier in the school experience.

Culture has an obvious impact on the curriculum of each country. While most of the other nations in the study include religious education or some form of ethics/moral education, the United States culture does not support such a curriculum. Particularly in nations where an immediate military threat is a major concern (Republic of Korea, Taiwan, and Israel), an emphasis on nationalism affects the content of the curriculum. Schools in the United States must find an acceptable method of teaching moral education or ''right from wrong.''

The primary difference among the nations studied is a cultural variable, coming from the home in terms of an attitude toward school and learning and the definition of success. The lack of a measurable, clear, and publicly articulated curriculum keeps American parents from having a basis of comparison they can use to understand how well their child is doing in school. If American educators expect parents to send children to school ready to learn, they must clearly identify what is to be learned and how it is to be learned.

The authors have concluded that there are three world class standards for curriculum. The first standard involves curriculum during the compulsory school years.

 The world class standard for curriculum during the compulsory education years includes moral/ethical/religious teaching and teaching time per subject. Not all time in school is devoted to teaching per se. The United States deviates from the world class standard in the amount of learning time expected of students (greater than the standard) and in the lack of a curriculum for teaching religion/morals/values.

Based on the organization of high schools internationally, there are several types of high school curricula. The world class standard for high school curricula depends on the type of high school.

 The world class standard for high school curriculum is a division of schools into separate vocational or special-purpose technical high schools and academic high schools for the college- or university-bound student. Comprehensive high schools do not appear to be a world class standard, but they are the standard in the United States.

The authors set a world class standard for vocational education based on their own judgment rather than using a formula, as has been the case with other world class standards.

 The world class standard in vocational education is found in Germany. The United States should adopt a similar format for vocational education.

The authors set a world class standard for academic high schools as they did for vocational high schools.

 The world class standard for academic high schools is set by Japan, although world class high schools and high school academic tracks are found in most countries including the United States. The system employed in Japan would not be accepted in the United States, but standards of high expectations and academic rigor should be borrowed from the Japanese.

AFTERTHOUGHT

Cultural variables among the nations studied appeared to explain more about the variable performance of students than does an analysis of the curriculum. Those cultures that stress the work the education requires had better performance records than the systems that did not stress the relationship between effort and learning. The United States lags in this relationship. The norm for compulsory school years curriculum was heterogeneous grouping and an emphasis on teaching all children. The United States uses tracking and in-class grouping more frequently than do other nations in the study.

At the end of compulsory school attendance, the norm was special-purpose rather than comprehensive high schools; and students were rigorously tracked. School-leaving was an accepted practice for some students. Apparently, the best vocational training system exists in Germany with several different formats for teaching industry-related skills.

The academic and in-plant aspects of the curriculum are closely related. Trade organizations oversee the exit examinations that lead to certification.

The business-education communication is excellent. The most productive academic high schools supplement education with cram school attendance. Great pressure is exerted on students, and this system is not seen as one the United States would want to emulate.

REFERENCES

Education in Korea, 1992−92. 1992. Seoul, Korea: National Institute of Educational Research and Training, Ministry of Education.

Fishman, S. 1993. *Encyclopedia Americana, Vol, 12.* New York: Grolier, Inc., pp. 621−625.

Hirsch, C. R., ed. 1992. *Curriculum and Evaluation Standards for School Mathematics.* Reston, Virginia: National Council of Teachers of Mathematics.

Her Majesty's Inspectorate. 1992. *Teaching and Learning in Japanese Elementary Schools.* Edinburgh: The Scottish Office, Education Department.

Hess, R. D. and H. Azuma. 1991. "Cultural Support or Schooling−Contrasts between Japan and the United States," *Educational Researcher,* December.

Ishizaka, K. Circa 1990. *School Education in Japan.* Tokyo: International Society for Educational Information, Inc.

Kim, H.-T. 1992. Interview (October 14).

Lawrence, M. 1992. Interview (November 7).

Li, G. L. 1993. Interview (March 15).

Liao, C.-H. 1992−1993. Interviews as graduate research assistant.

McAdams, R. P. 1993. *Lessons from Abroad: How Other Countries Educate Their Children.* Lancaster, Pennsylvania: Technomic Publishing, Inc.

Monikes, W., ed. 1992. *Inter Nations Bonn,* pp. 9−22.

National Center of Education Statistics. 1992. Washington, D.C.: U.S. Government Printing Office.

O'Neil, J. 1993. "Is U.S. Headed Toward a National Curriculum?" *ASCD Update,* p. 2. Reprinted with permission of the Association for Supervision and Curriculum Development. Copyright 1993 by ASCD. All rights reserved.

An Outline of Revision of the Courses of Study in Japan. Circa 1991. Monograph provided by the Japanese Consulate in Atlanta.

Preparing for Our Future. 1992. Detroit, Michigan: National Board for Professional Teaching Standards, 1992 Annual Report.

Shankar, A. 1993. "Coming to Terms on World-Class Standards," *Education Week.*

Sprinzak, D., E. Bar and D. Levi-Mazloum. 1992. *Facts and Figures about Education and Culture in Israel.* Jerusalem: Ministry of Education and Culture.

Stevenson, H. W. 1992. "Learning from Asian Schools," *Scientific American,* December.

DEFINING A WORLD CLASS STANDARD FOR ASSESSING STUDENT ACHIEVEMENT

Regular and systematic assessment of student achievement is a correlate of effective school research. Chapter 9 examines the student assessment procedures for the ten world class education systems and concludes with suggestions for improving testing practices in the United States. The world class standard for student assessment is the most common practice of the combined nations.

PERCEPTION: RANKING THE UNITED STATES ON THE USE OF STANDARDIZED TESTING TO LIMIT ADMISSION TO HIGHER LEVELS OF EDUCATION

The sample group of 181 educators differed on America's use of standardized testing to limit admission to higher education. Table 9.1 shows the results of question ten on the questionnaire administered at three national educational conferences.

Nearly one-fifth of the respondents awarded the United States first place, indicating that one out of five respondents thinks the United States uses testing more than the other nine countries to limit admission to higher education. Another 31.5 percent decided that the United States belonged in the top third of the ten countries, adding to the perception that the United States relies on testing. The image of the SAT and/or the ACT as a discriminating factor in determining university admission probably accounts for the perception, but neither test really means as much as national tests do in most other world class countries. In fact,

143

TABLE 9.1.

Rank United States schools as they compare to the following nine national school systems: Canada France Germany Britain New Zealand Taiwan Israel South Korea Japan	First	Top Third	Middle Third	Bottom Third	Last
		(Percentage of Total Responding)			
10. Greatest use of standardized testing to limit admission to higher levels of education? (n = 181)	19.0	31.5	25.0	19.0	5.5

Canada is the only other country studied besides the United States that does not have a national test.

The reality section dispels the perception that the United States leads the world class countries in the use of standardized tests to limit admission to higher education. The other world class countries thrive on national testing to sort students before the secondary experience, and Britain has even adopted a program of national testing at four different levels of schooling. The reality section presents data describing the purpose and use of standardized tests in each world class country. The data support the 50 percent of respondents who placed the United States in the middle third or lower third on question ten.

REALITY: DEFINING A WORLD CLASS STANDARD FOR ASSESSING STUDENT ACHIEVEMENT

The individual or group responsible for developing curriculum in an educational setting should also be responsible for developing the testing program. For example, countries with a national curriculum developed by the education department should hold the same department responsible for developing a testing program. Seven of the world class countries follow this suggestion and have developed national examinations that measure national curriculum objectives. One of the three countries without national testing, Germany, delegates responsibility for testing to the sixteen *Länder* or states; but close cooperation among the *Länder* has, in reality, produced a national examination. Only Canada and the

United States lack a national examination prepared by the educational establishment to assess student growth.

Figure 9.1 summarizes the status in each country of assessment as a tool to limit admission to higher education. Figure 9.1 lists each country first, the name of the test second, and the agency responsible for test preparation third. The next sections describe testing data for each of the ten countries.

Figure 9.1 shows that the common practice in most countries is a national examination(s) prepared by the National Ministry of Education. Each of the ten countries developed a much more comprehensive assess-

Country	Exam	Origin
Britain	General certificate of education: advanced (A)	National Dept. for Education
Canada	None (Three provinces now administer examinations.)	Provincial Dept of Education[1]
France	*Baccalaureat*	National Ministry of Education
Germany	*Abitur*	*Länder* (Design is cooperative.)
Israel	Matriculation exams	National Ministry of Education
Japan	Test of the National Center for University Entrance Examination (INCUEE)	National Ministry of Education
Korea	Student Achievement Examination for College Entrance (SAECE)	National Ministry of Education
New Zealand	University Bursaries Examination	National Ministry of Education
Taiwan	Higher Education Entrance Examination	National Ministry of Education
United States	None (Scholastic Aptitude Test and/or American College Test usually required)	Private companies

[1]Exams are administered in Newfoundland, Quebec, and Saskatchewan.

Figure 9.1 *The examination administered in the ten world class education countries for the purpose of determining admission to higher education.*

ment program than can be shown in Figure 9.1. Two dimensions of testing practice are presented for each country. First, if appropriate, testing practice at the primary level is presented. Of the ten countries presented, only Britain and Israel test during the primary years. The Asian countries, however, test at the end of the primary experience, and the scores determine placement in a secondary school. The tests are extremely competitive, for placement in an academic high school generally means later placement in a university. The higher the score, the more prestigious the secondary school that a student enters. The more prestigious the high school, the more prestigious the university open to the student.

The second dimension presented is test usage at the secondary level. Secondary level tests determine placement in higher education. As Figure 9.1 discloses, all countries have some structure for national testing at the secondary level.

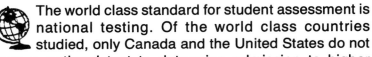 The world class standard for student assessment is national testing. Of the world class countries studied, only Canada and the United States do not have a national test to determine admission to higher education.

Following is a brief description of the testing practices in each world class country.

Britain

The Education Reform Act of 1988, which established national curriculum, also established national testing in England, Wales, Scotland, and Northern Ireland. A few differences exist among the countries, but the similarities prevail. The following description applies to similar testing practices in England and Wales. Reference is made, when appropriate, to practices in Scotland and Northern Ireland.

The Reform Act of 1988 requires student tests in England and Wales covering ten subject areas at the student ages of seven, eleven, fourteen, and sixteen. Scotland selects ages eight, eleven, and sixteen for mandatory testing. Demonstrations, portfolios, and essay questions assess attainment goals described in the national curriculum. The British avoid multiple choice questions (McAdams, 1993). National testing during the early grades is a new phenomenon in Britain, and the United States or other countries contemplating national testing should learn from the experience. The tests for seven-year-old students, Key Stage 1, started in 1991 and cover the core subjects of English, science, and mathematics. Assessment in history, geography, and technology is slowly being introduced, but recent events could cause delay or elimination of the assessment in these areas. A report from the Office of Her Majesty's Chief Inspector of Schools (*Assessment, Recording and Reporting,* 1993), calls Key Stage 1 assessment firmly established and claims that the quality of teaching and learning has benefited from the results of the tests.

British educators piloted Key Stage 2 testing for eleven-year-old students in 1993, and the tests are mandatory as of summer 1994. Teachers were scheduled to test Key Stage 3 students in June 1993 in the areas of English, mathematics, science, and technology (*Assessment, Recording and Reporting,* 1993). Assessments in art, music, or PE will probably not be developed as originally anticipated.

The testing at Key Stage 3 is controversial. Teachers in England, Wales, and Scotland refused to administer the examinations during June 1993. The boycott received some support from parents in England and Wales and strong support from parents in Scotland. Four principal reasons for the boycott surfaced:

- The tests in English literature are flawed and too narrow.
- The tests do not result in improved student learning.
- Local teachers administer and grade the tests, which requires excessive time.
- The purpose of the tests is to provide statistics for the construction of league tables used to compare schools.

The battle over testing appears to be a much larger conflict – a conflict over local control of curriculum and testing as opposed to national control of these crucial areas. The English media described the boycott against national testing, often citing the four reasons for the boycott listed above. The media also presented an argument for testing. The tabloids had a field day with the position taken by the National Association of Head Teachers, claiming the Heads would not tolerate actions such as boycotts by their own students. Several of the tabloids sided with the government, encouraging it to stand firm and ignore the teachers who wanted to boycott the new tests. At the same time, several boards of governors began debating whether teachers who boycotted should be paid if they refused to test. The controversy places the national government in an awkward position. In England, the Department for Education responded to the furor by placing the future of national testing in the hands of a study group appointed to calm the waters. The group, headed by Sir Ron Dearing, was scheduled to report sometime in the latter months of 1993. Dearing has the reputation of turning disaster into progress.

Key Stage 4 testing is not nearly so controversial in England, for the General Certificate of Education (GCSE) is a more established method of assessing the national curriculum. The GCSE also limits the number of students who continue with advanced study. England, Wales, and Northern Ireland administer the GCSE at age sixteen. Scottish pupils take the Scottish Certificate of Education (SCE) at age seventeen (*Education in Britain*, 1991). All students completing mandatory schooling take the examinations. All students sit exams in English, mathematics, and science; and students choose tests in history, geography, technology, foreign language, or other electives.

Students achieving grades of A, B, or C on five or more examinations generally begin two years of specialized college preparatory work. In 1991, about one-third of the sixteen-year-old students qualified. The two-year experience culminates with the administration of the General Certificate of Education (GCE), Advanced (A) level examinations (*National Tests: What Other Countries Expect Their Students to Know*, 1991). Decisions, regarding college or university acceptance depend heavily on the results of these examinations.

Chapter 12 presents additional commentary on the subject of British testing.

Canada

During the past few decades, each Canadian province discontinued school leaving examinations. The school record now determines university placement in most provinces, with heavy emphasis placed on a student's marks and the student's subject selection (*Education in Canada*, 1989). Recently, Manitoba, Saskatchewan, and Ontario reintroduced school-leaving examinations (McAdams, 1993). Students in Quebec complete a two-year program at a *college d' enseignement general et professional* and then pass an examination (*Education in Canada,* 1989).

Some Canadian citizens criticize the educational establishment as ineffective, and a cry for accountability is regularly heard. Parents and special interest groups, led by the business establishment, compare Canadian schools with educational systems in other countries and have determined that the schools are not meeting world class standards. The Canadian Council of Ministers proposes reform including additional accountability. A procedure developed by the council proposes national assessment of reading, writing, and mathematics for students at ages thirteen and sixteen. All provinces except Ontario volunteered to participate in 1993 (McAdams, 1993).

Canadians mirror the United States in proposed reforms leading to a more rigid curriculum measured by comprehensive testing. Canadians are returning to national assessment.

France

The French *baccalaureat,* established during the age of Napoleon, is the national examination for French students. Students recommended by their teachers for future study prepare for the *baccalaureat* while attending the Lycee, the French academic secondary school. At age fifteen or sixteen, each student begins three years of specialized study and chooses from three specialized areas of study: (1) philosophy and liberal arts; (2) economics and social sciences; and (3) mathematics, physics, and chemistry (*National Tests: What Other Countries Expect Their Students to Know,* 1991).

The French Ministry of Education requires all French Lycee to follow the national curriculum. Preparation for the *baccalaureat* really begins in kindergarten, for the latter part of the kindergarten experience requires children to master the physical skills needed for writing and to work with numbers and operations. The primary school provides a basic education for all students from age six to age ten or eleven. National test results no longer determine promotion from one level to another during the primary years. The Conseil de Classe, whose membership includes school administrators, teachers, parents, and students, determines promotion or failure. Students usually reach a predetermined level before a recommendation for promotion is forthcoming. The Lycee admits approximately 67 percent of students who enter the primary school at age six. The remainder of the students attend vocational training (Pierre, 1991).

Essay testing begins at the primary level and remains through the school years, the most common form of testing in France. The French *baccalaureat* contains questions requiring analysis that the student must answer in essay form. The written section lasts two to three days. Students take two to four mandatory oral examinations, and a student may elect up to two optional examinations (Pierre, 1991). The student's specialization determines the grade received on the examination. In order to pass, a student must obtain an average grade of 10/20. In 1990, 50 percent of students enrolled in the Lycee took the *baccalaureat,* and 75.2 percent were successful.

A future objective of the French educational system is to have 80 percent of students reach the *baccalaureat* level by the year 2000. To reach the goal, students will take a new *baccalaureat,* testing knowledge of professions such as sales and computers (*National Tests: What Other Countries Expect Their Students to Know,* 1991).

Germany

Germany does not have national testing. Educators in the sixteen *Lander* (states) prepare tests including the *Abitur,* the test most comparable to national tests in the other world class countries. *Länder* educators cooperate on the development and acceptance of the *Abitur,* so that the procedure appears nationalized. Universities in each *Länder* accept the *Abitur* results from each Länd as if they resulted from a single test.

The *Abitur* is the final examination offered to all students who complete thirteen years of study in the Gymnasium, the academic high school in Germany. The *Abitur* results, along with a student's grades during the final two years in the Gymnasium, determine entrance into the university (*National Tests: What Other Country Expects Their Students to Know,* 1991).

The general form of the *Abitur* is the same throughout the sixteen *Länder.* Students sit four examinations, and their choice must cover three of the following categories of knowledge: (1) languages; (2) literature and the arts; (3) social sciences; and (4) mathematics, science, and technology. Examinations are essay and include both oral and written questions.

Of the four subjects examined, students choose one general exam and two specialized exams. The fourth subject exam is oral. A 1986 study showed that an average of 23.7 percent of the students examined did qualify for the university (*National Tests: What Other Countries Expect Their Students to Know*, 1992).

Vocational students in Germany who wish to qualify for a technical or vocational occupation must pass one of about 400 occupational tests. If the test results are satisfactory, a student completing the Hauptschule or vocational school receives a school leaver's certificate.

Student evaluation in Germany is a serious venture for students, and students prepare seriously for tests whether they lead to university study or a vocational occupation. Preparation for the *Abitur* dominates the Gymnasium experience even though statistics show that slightly over 25 percent of the students successfully matriculate to the university. German educators think that the rigors of testing help establish the German educational system as a high-performance system.

Israel

Matriculation examinations form a capstone experience for Israeli students and have existed since the formation of the educational system soon after World War II. The Ministry of Education modified the exam structure in 1975; and since 1979, all students seeking a certificate of completion matriculate by examination. The reform obligates the student to write compulsory exams in several subjects and to elect exams in remaining areas. The student selects from four levels of exam difficulty named units (two, three, four, or five units), and the student selects enough units to earn twenty total units. A certificate requires twenty units.

The Ministry of Education implemented a modified examination schedule for grade twelve students in 1990–91. Students now write matriculation exams in three components: (1) compulsory core, (2) compulsory selection, and (3) additional selection. An explanation of each component follows:

(*1*) The "compulsory core" includes Hebrew, Bible, history and geography of Israel, mathematics (level of at least three units), and English (level of at least four units).

(2) The student selects one exam from the ''compulsory selection'' and the exam can be chosen from the General or Technology track.

(3) The student has an option to choose ''additional selections.'' Since students select eighteen units from the first two categories, the student must select an additional two units. Each subject in the curriculum tests at a low level (two or three units) or a high level (four or five units) (Simmer and Simmer, 1990).

Public outcry in Israel brought about recent testing changes amid charges that the exams were too easy and not used equally to select students for post-secondary education. The matriculation exams now have equal value for all students, but disadvantaged students gain advanced consideration when results are interpreted (Simmer and Simmer, 1990). It is not clear how this works, but apparently subjective judgment prevails.

In 1987 – 1988, approximately 74 percent of the appropriate age group enrolled in grade twelve, the final school year offered. Two-thirds of this group wrote at least one matriculation exam, and 31 percent earned the matriculation certificate. Noteworthy is the fact that, each year, over 20,000 grade twelve graduates write supplementary exams to improve their marks or complete matriculation. Educators encourage students to keep trying until successful (Simmer and Simmer, 1990).

Republic of Korea

Since 1974 standardized admission to Korean High Schools has depended on a qualifying examination. The middle school level offers two different examinations, one to determine placement at the vocational high school and a second to determine placement at the academic high school. The vocational high school examination comes first in the sequence.

Candidates for vocational school vie for early entrance to eight types of vocational high schools. Student achievement in middle school and the test results determine eligibility. Once students complete vocational testing, students who opt for academic high schools, and vocational students who failed to obtain entrance to vocational high schools, take a preliminary examination. (It is interesting that both vocational students and academic students take the preliminary examination.) A computer assigns students who pass the preliminary examination to a high school in their residential district. In 1989, 96 percent of middle school graduates entered high school.

Students in the top 3 percent of their school class may apply for entrance into one of seven science high schools for gifted students. Students must then pass an entrance examination composed of a written test and a physical fitness test. Students who pass these tests then must take an aptitude test and pass an interview (*Education in Korea, 1991 – 1992*, 1992). Korean success on the national IAEP examinations reflects the emphasis on science education.

Successful completion of the scholastic achievement examination for the college entrance (SAECE) determines entrance to higher education. A unique procedure requires Korean students to select a university before taking the examination. This procedure permits the university to administer essay tests to students in addition to reviewing scores on the SAECE. Recently grades have been awarded more weight in the selection process in order to diminish the importance of the SAECE. Since 1990, candidates for teachers' colleges or colleges of education have taken an additional aptitude test and a personality test. Gifted students interested in teaching may apply to the Korea Science and Technology College established in 1989. Passing a special test of scientific aptitude determines entrance (*Education in Korea, 1991 – 1992*, 1992).

Testmakers devote 30 percent of the test questions on the SAECE to questions calling for subjective thinking. The purpose is reduction of the teacher's emphasis on teaching to the test and using rote drill to prepare students for the test.

The Korean education system obviously focuses on the preparation of students for entrance examinations. Once the student completes the middle school years, achievement and success on the entrance examination determine entrance to the next level. Students take the examinations seriously, and attendance at a cram school is a necessity. Students compete to gain admittance to the most prestigious universities, and intense competition exists (Kim, 1992).

Japan

"Examination Hell" in Japan describes a testing process that captures the attention of nearly all Japanese citizens and a good portion of the outside world as well. "Examination Hell" is the process a Japanese student endures while preparing for and taking the national exam.

Through the eighth grade, students prepare seriously for high school entrance examinations administered in the ninth grade. Students not only prepare during the regular school day, but 86 percent also attend "cram schools" known as *juku*.

Success on the high school entrance exam means attendance at an academic high school; but more importantly, a superior score grants admittance to one of Japan's most prestigious high schools. In Japan, parents and students prefer public high schools to private schools (McAdams, 1993).

Once admitted to an academic high school, student competition becomes fierce for admittance to the university. Students must take the Test of the National Center for University Entrance Examination (INCUEE). The INCUEE contains tests in five areas: (1) Japanese, (2) humanities and social sciences, (3) mathematics, (4) science, and (5) foreign language. The questions are multiple choice, making them similar in construction to exams in the United States, but different from most other world class systems where essay testing is the norm. Universities, however, often require the student to take a second examination that is essay (*National Tests: What Other Countries Expect Their Students to Know,* 1992).

Attendance at *juku* provides a student important preparation for the INCUEE. Students who do not score well during the first administration of the test may take the test a second time, but most students return for a second sitting only after study at the *juku*.

Outsiders criticize the INCUEE for creating a stressful atmosphere for students and for promoting teaching to the test. However, the test appears to encourage academic achievement and focus student attention on preparation for life. The Japanese believe in the test and accept accountability as a cultural expectation. Testing is firmly established in the educational system.

New Zealand

Since New Zealand has a national curriculum, national tests evaluate the achievement of students on the curriculum. Students who reach the third year of secondary education take the school certificate examination. The third year of secondary school equals grade ten in the United States or Canada. A student chooses up to six subjects for examination and receives a grade from A1 (highest) to D (lowest). Successful students enter Form Six, an additional year of secondary school, where students take one or more subjects to a maximum of six. Students earn a Sixth Form Certificate upon successful completion of the Form Six curriculum. Students who complete the advanced course receive the Higher School Certificate that broadly equals completion of grade twelve in the United States or Canada. Students who obtain an A or B Bursary qualification from the University Bursaries Examination also receive the Higher School Certificate (*Education in New Zealand,* 1991).

Entrance to the university in New Zealand requires a satisfactory score on The University Bursaries Entrance Scholarships Examination, usually taken by students in Form Seven. High achievers also receive scholarships, and all-around excellence leads to the award of the New Zealand Qualifications Authority medal. In 1990, approximately 19 percent of students attained the University Bursary level (*Education in New Zealand,* 1991).

The New Zealand Ministry of Education assumes responsibility for all aspects of education and sets policy for the Minister of Education. Recently, New Zealand appointed an Education Assessment Secretariat to advise the Minister of Education on assessment policy. The administration of all national tests and the establishment of standards and qualifications are the responsibilities of the New Zealand Qualifications Authority, reporting directly to the Minister of Education (*New Zealand Official 1990 Yearbook Extracts,* 1990).

New Zealand has a committee studying the improvement of assessment, which has made recommendations to monitor the effectiveness of New Zealand education and to assess the effectiveness of individual schools (*New Zealand Official 1990 Yearbook Extracts,* 1990). New Zealanders value educational achievement and recent emphasis on national assessment reflects concern over proper measurement of achievement.

Taiwan

The role of student assessment in Taiwan follows the example established in the other Pacific Rim countries. National testing strongly influences a student's future life. The looming specter of testing motivates students from the first level of education through university matriculation.

As Taiwanese students complete the primary years, three choices exist for secondary school entrance: (1) general high school, (2) senior vocational school, or (3) a five-year junior college (Kurian, 1988). Entrance into each school requires an entrance examination. Secondary schools in Taiwan vary in the prestige accorded the school, and the reward for scoring well on the entrance examination is acceptance into a more prestigious secondary school. The reputation of the secondary school attended by the student will later earn the student entrance into a more prestigious university. Taiwanese label the schools with better reputations "star schools" (Liao, 1992). The competition for entrance into this pyramid of prestigious schools causes a great deal of pressure on students in their early teens and secondary school years.

The general high school is the academic high school in Taiwan. Once enrolled in the general high school, a student spends most of the time preparing for college and university study. Nearly all students seek extra tutoring usually through attendance at a "cram school." The secondary experience focuses on the test, making "teaching to the test" a necessity in Taiwan. The pressure peaks during the senior year, when students spend every minute of school time preparing for the college entrance examination. Over 50 percent of general high school students seek admission to the university.

At the end of the senior year, students elect to take the Higher Education Entrance Examination. The examinations are achievement oriented, and students test in four areas: (1) engineering and natural science, (2) humanities, (3) medical science and agriculture, and (4) law and social science (Kurian, 1988). A student's score and the reputation of the secondary school attended strongly influence the decision of the university regarding admittance. A job offer usually accompanies entrance to the university, once the degree is complete. In Taiwan, the public university remains more prestigious than the private university. In Taiwan, prestige obviously counts.

United States

Each separate state evaluates student achievement in the United States, but voluntary national testing is in the developmental stage. The Department of Education in Washington commissioned councils representing subject areas to prepare national tests; but at this date, only a mathematics test exists in preliminary form. Debate continues over national testing, however, for local school boards and state education departments are reluctant to pass power to the federal government. The fifty States cling to a legal right guaranteeing control over nearly all educational decisions, and many local educators and many parents oppose national testing.

Some states administer mandatory achievement tests, but the value is questionable. State educational leaders too often cause distrust by using test results to compare schools, and many local educators tend to ignore the results anyway. One might wonder how often educators in the United States use test results to develop appropriate programs for students, for such is the real value of testing.

Michigan, a pioneer in state testing development, introduced the competency test called the Michigan Assessment of Educational Progress (MEAP) in the early 1980s. First tested were reading and mathematics, with science, social studies, and writing recently joining the agenda. The MEAP tests only minimum competency, however, leaving the local school to select nationally normed tests to determine comprehensive achievement.

North Carolina implemented statewide competency testing in 1993 for all students in grades three through twelve. Teachers administer tests at the end of each primary year, starting with grade three and at the end of each course at the secondary level. The tests continue to use a multiple choice format but also require the application of higher order thinking skills and some essay writing. The state no longer requires the use of nationally normed tests.

The norm in all states is the administration of achievement tests produced by private companies that establish comparison tables based on national samples. Because testing companies established the norms on many tests years ago, almost all local schools find it possible to report student scores above the national average. Parents, on the other hand, find it nearly impossible to understand student progress or to compare their student's progress with that of other students.

The Scholastic Aptitude Test (SAT) and/or the American College Tests (ACT) measure a student's aptitude for higher education in the United States. Neither exam tests knowledge learned in the classroom, however, and usually only students interested in higher education take the examinations. The content of the exams seldom changes, although the Educational Testing Service introduced a new version of the SAT in 1994. Educators also label some questions on the SAT culturally biased, and educators criticize both the SAT and ACT because profit-making companies produce the exams. The tests encourage most students to study and achieve, however; and they remain the key to university acceptance. The tests appear firmly entrenched in the American design for education, and institutions of higher learning are not likely to replace them as a college entrance requirement.

IMPLICATIONS

Assessment practices in the world class countries raise several issues and implications for future assessment in the United States. For example, controversy currently exists over student assessment in four countries: Canada, Israel, Britain, and the United States. Canada and the United States flounder on the issue of testing, primarily over the issue of national testing versus state (dominion) testing. British teachers refused to administer national mandatory tests in 1993, and Israel struggles with equity issues in an educational system assessing two distinct populations. On the other hand, the Pacific Rim nations seemingly accept national testing as a form of student accountability at the end of the educational tunnel and as a proper sorting instrument for students entering secondary education and later higher education.

Educational researchers properly ask, ''Why is student assessment positively accepted in some nations and rejected in others?'' Educators find the issue crucial, for assessment must play an important role in a nation's education system. Critical implications of student assessment practices exist for each of the ten world class countries, for world class status must include an acceptable and reliable testing program. Implications for future testing practices in the United States follow.

National, State, or Local Tests

Which level of government should conduct student assessment? At the federal level, national leaders and politicians discuss national testing as a future possibility. At the state level, testing practice varies; and a simple, brief explanation escapes the researcher. Suffice it to say that some states develop a hands-off policy and leave testing to the local school district, while other states develop state tests. State tests that exist, however, tend to be minimum competency tests offering no data regarding maximum achievement. State educational systems also operate in a parochial manner, and each probably would not share or copy an exemplary testing program if one emerged in any single state. At the local level, the board of education usually knows little about testing, pays attention only to comparison tables, and offers little direction to administrators and teachers. American students probably test more often than students in any other country, but the tests often seem superficial, and teachers and students often ignore results.

As stated earlier in the chapter, national testing is the world class standard for educational assessment. If the United States desires world class status, educational leaders must get serious about the development of national curriculum and national testing. Fifty different educational systems will never do better than produce a patchwork system of testing that prevents national comparison of student achievement or a school's national or international performance (*National Tests: What Other Countries Expect Their Students to Know,* 1991).

The Scope of National Testing

Assuming that a national test in the United States leads to world class status for American schools, a second implication, the scope of testing, requires examination. As previously mentioned, Britain, with national tests at four levels, experienced a testing boycott in 1993. Educators must learn from negative British experiences and avoid too much testing. If educators must avoid too much testing, how much testing is too much? France eliminated national testing at the primary level and turned evaluation of the primary experience over to the local school. Boyd (1993) suggests that teachers test national curriculum in Scotland at a natural time during the child's learning experience. That natural time occurs when the child appears to have mastered the attainment task. Countries that rarely question national testing, such as Japan, Korea, and Taiwan, successfully administer national tests to determine first, high school placement and second, higher education placement. The individual school tests all students at the conclusion of the primary years and all students attending the academic secondary school during the final year. The United States should test all students at the end of the elementary experience and all students at the conclusion of mandatory school attendance. Teacher-made tests should be used at all other levels.

Writing National Tests

Politicians ignore educators when they plan for national goals and curriculum. In 1990, state governors developed the goals for American education without inviting a public school educator. How sad and how wasteful! Most educators adopted the goals because of political expedience, but lack of teacher ownership dooms most of the goals to the shredder. The same educators who develop a national curriculum must develop national tests; otherwise, alignment will not occur. Political leaders must recruit the most capable of the profession for the task; and educators should receive time to research curriculum, research testing, and communicate with other classroom teachers. Extra-legal interest groups, including those in the business sector, should play only a consultant role in the decision-making process. Otherwise, legislators, business leaders, and members of special interest groups should remain public policymakers and not educational experts dictating curriculum and testing.

Tests should reflect curriculum taught in the classroom. Currently, both the SAT and ACT avoid testing for factual knowledge taught in the classroom, and the most widely used norm-referenced tests in the United States divorce themselves from classroom knowledge. How can educators in this country make students believe that hard work in school matters, when classroom subject matter remains untested on the most high-stakes tests (*National Tests: What Other Countries Expect Their Students to Know*, 1991)?

Also foolish is the practice of not making teachers and students aware of simulated test content and test structure. Testing is not some mysterious adventure that a student must undertake without a road map. In addition, testmakers should understand that the world class standard for test construction is essay testing. Every country conducting national testing, with the exception of Japan makes extensive use of written and oral essay tests.

Using the Results of National Tests

The *purpose* of testing is perhaps the most important implication of educational testing. Otherwise, we cannot answer the question, "How should educators, parents, and others use test results?" Using test scores to compare schools partially caused the boycott of Stage Three testing in Britain. Unfortunately, all ten world class countries make group test results public; but fortunately, individual student scores remain confidential. New Zealand publishes only the names of those students who pass.

France and Germany publish pass and fail rates for each high school; and in Japan, Korea, and Taiwan, test results determine the reputation of the school and perhaps the teacher. Using tests to compare teachers is ill-advised. English (1993) conducted research on curriculum alignment and testing and concludes that socioeconomic status determines 60 percent of a student's test score. Also, since learning is a cumulative activity, measuring a student's progress and attributing the results to the current teacher is unfair. Using tests to compare schools is also ill-advised. Each student's home environment differs, affecting the student's achievement. Comparing schools and teachers based on test results is counterproductive, and educational policymakers should drop the practice.

How should persons use test results? Individual test results should establish learning objectives for a student, and group test results should establish criteria to evaluate the effectiveness of curriculum and teaching methodology. Educators should use test results to make decisions about a student's future in a nondiscriminatory way. Parents and teachers should use test results as a motivational tool, encouraging students to work hard and do their best. Testing should provide a significant challenge for students that has real meaning for future success in life.

AFTERTHOUGHT

Each nation attempts to define what students should know. A majority of the world class nations define this knowledge through the use of national goals, national curriculum, and national testing. Nations use test results to help determine a student's future schooling. The most successful national testing programs do not attempt to test knowledge at several levels, but instead, focus on one or two levels. The United States appears to test more frequently but places less emphasis on test results. Essay testing is the international norm, and some countries feel that multiple choice testing is too simple even at first grade.

REFERENCES

Assessment, Recording and Reporting: Third Year, 1991–92. 1993. A Report from the Office of Her Majesty's Chief Inspector of Schools, London: Office for Standards in Education.

Boyd, B. 1993. Interview (June 18).

The Daily Telegraph. 1993. London, England, (June 10):18.

Education in Britain. 1991. United Kingdom: Produced for the Foreign and Commonwealth Office by the Central Office of Education.

Education in Canada. 1989. Ottawa, Canada: External Communications Division, External Affairs and International Trade Canada.

Education in Korea, 1991 – 92. 1992. Seoul, Korea: National Institute of Educational Research and Training, Ministry of Education.

Education in New Zealand. 1991. Wellington, New Zealand: Ministry of Education.

Education Statistics of New Zealand. 1991. Wellington, New Zealand: Research and Statistics Division, Ministry of Education.

8 Education. 1991. New Zealand: Ministry of Education, New Zealand Council for Educational Research.

English, F. 1993. Ainsley Lecture in School Administration. Western Carolina University, Cullowhee, North Carolina.

Holmes, B., ed. 1983. *International Handbook of Education Systems. Vol. 3.* New York: John Wiley and Sons.

Kim, H.-T. 1992. Interview (October 14).

Kurian, G. T., ed. 1988. *World Education Encyclopedia. Vol. 3.* New York: Facts on File Publications.

Liao, C.-H. 1992. Interview (October 21).

McAdams, R. P. 1993. *Lessons from Abroad: How Other Countries Educate Their Children.* Lancaster, Pennsylvania: Technomic Publishing Company, Inc.

National Tests: What Other Countries Expect Their Students to Know. 1991. Washington, D.C.: National Endowment for the Humanities.

New Zealand Official 1990 Yearbook Extracts. 1990. Washington, D.C.: Education Monograph provided by the New Zealand Embassy.

9 Education. 1990. New Zealand, taken from the *New Zealand 1990 Yearbook.*

Pierre, B. and S. Auvillain, eds. 1991. *Organisation of the French Educational System Leading to the French Baccalaureat.* Washington, D.C.: Embassy of France Cultural Service, Office of Education.

Simmer, S. and D. Simmer. 1990. *Facts and Figures on the Education and Culture System in Israel.* Jerusalem: Publications Department, Ministry of Education and Culture.

The Times. 1993. London, England, (June 10):17.

Chapter 10

DEFINING A WORLD CLASS STANDARD FOR SCHOOL GOVERNANCE

Persons in control of schools determine what gets taught, who teaches, and how the outcomes of education are assessed. All nations studied had national control of education, large regional districts, and local control. The locus of power could be centralized at one level or could exist in a relative balance between levels. The most central questions about governance are, "Who funds education and who establishes the curriculum?" Most commonly, funding and curricula are controlled nationally in the world class nations. The local school head governs at the local level. The local school head is appropriately called "head teacher" because the head teacher is not trained and not expected to fulfill many management functions such as teacher selection, observation and evaluation. In many nations, autonomous experts called "inspectors" evaluate the school, staff, and the quality of outcomes. The role of parent in terms of governance varies by nation. The role of private schools is investigated.

PERCEPTION: RANKING THE UNITED STATES ON SCHOOL GOVERNANCE

On question eleven, more than one-third of the respondents ranked the United States in the bottom two categories (see Table 10.1). Over 60 percent of the respondents chose either the bottom third and last place ranking, and that is where the United States actually ranks. Nineteen percent ranked the United States either first or in the top third, and another 19 percent ranked the United States in the middle third. The responses indicate confusion about the use of national goals in the United States.

TABLE 10.1.

Rank United States schools as they compare to the following nine national school systems: Canada France Germany Britain New Zealand Taiwan Israel South Korea Japan	First	Top Third	Middle Third	Bottom Third	Last
		(Percentage of Total Responding)			
11. Greatest use of national goals for education? (*n* = 179)	6	13	19	35	27
12. Highest percent students in private schools? (*n* = 179)	9	24	34	27	6

When ranking the United States in percentage of students in private schools, question twelve, there was almost even distribution between the top, middle, and bottom third. These responses indicate no defined expectation among the respondents about the percentage of students attending private schools in America or the world.

REALITY: WORLD CLASS STANDARDS FOR SCHOOL GOVERNANCE

All nations studied had a department in the national government responsible for education. There is great variance, however, in the role and authority of that agency. Those nations with clearly mandated responsibilities at the national level have the greatest control of education. In all the world class nations, some form of local control exists. Following is a synopsis of national and local control of education in five of the countries.

School Governance in Korea

The Republic of Korea specifically outlines the purpose, organization, and structure of Korean education in the Education Law of 1949:

All citizens have the right to receive an education according to his ability;

all children should receive at least an elementary education and such education as may be prescribed by law; the state is responsible for promoting lifelong education; and basic matters related to the management of systems of school education and lifelong education, financing of schools, and the status of teachers are prescribed by law. (*Education in Korea, 1991−92,* 1992, pp. 49−50)

Article 81 of the Education Law stipulates that the following schools will exist: kindergartens, primary schools, middle schools, high schools, and both colleges and universities. It also establishes teachers' colleges, colleges of education, junior colleges, and specialty schools. Further, the law establishes the school year, the minimum number of days for education, and the organization of the academic calendar. It sets goals and objectives for each school level, establishes the basic curriculum, and establishes an education decree that prescribes the textbooks the teachers use. The law assures standardization of educational opportunity and quality through a curriculum framework that is re-assessed every seven to ten years. Between the establishment of the Republic of Korea in 1948 and the year 1985, the government reformed the curriculum five times. The 1985 curriculum reflected then-current concerns about education: (1) emphasis on improving basic learning abilities, (2) integration of the information oriented industry, and (3) relevance. The renovated curriculum is to produce a society epitomized by (1) health, (2) self-directed improvement, (3) creativity, and (4) moral consciousness (*Education in Korea, 1991−92,* 1992).

In the Republic of Korea, control of the curriculum is deliberate, planned in two year cycles starting with the lowest grades, and then implemented over two years. The Ministry of Education carefully controls textbooks, recognizing three types of books: (1) those authored by the Ministry of Education, (2) those inspected and approved by the Ministry, and (3) those accepted by the Ministry for use in Korean schools. The government sets standards for facilities and teachers. Most Asian countries respect teachers highly and regard them as very professional. In Korea, the Ministry actively discourages parent involvement in their children's education, perhaps because of the Korean penchant for bribing civil servants.

In May 1957, the Korean government endorsed a "Children's Charter" that outlines the rights of children. The charter is rare among nations and is reproduced in Table 10.2.

TABLE 10.2 *The Children's Charter (May 5, 1957)*.

In as much as children are new citizens who shall determine the future of the nation, their minds and bodies shall be treasured. All efforts should be made to see to it that children grow with justice, beauty and courage.

1. Children should be valued as human beings and raised properly as members of society.
2. Children should be born healthy and educated with genuine affection at home and in society.
3. Children should be provided with proper facilities and an environment in which they can study and play as they please.
4. Children should not be burdened with excessive study or other duties.
5. Children should be rescued first in time of danger.
6. Children should not be made the object of exploitation under any circumstances.
7. Hungry children must be fed, sick children treated, physically and mentally handicapped children assisted, delinquent children reformed, and orphans and juvenile vagrants cared for.
8. Children should be brought up to love nature, the arts and sciences. They should develop an inquisitive nature and moral character.
9. Children should be brought up as good citizens to contribute to the freedom and peace of mankind and to the development of culture.

Note: From *Education in Korea, 1991 – 1992* (1992).

School Governance in Japan

Like Korea, the Japanese use a highly centralized system. The Ministry of Education, Science, and Culture, or *Monbusho,* makes all major decisions. The Minister of Education holds a powerful position that is among the most influential in the government. Since the end of the United States occupation in the 1950s, the *Monbusho* started exercising strict control of education. The forty-seven prefecture schools report to a five-member, appointed school board. This board selects the prefecture's superintendent, whose duty is to carry out the dictates of the *Monbusho.* These dictates stem from broad authority over finances, teacher testing and certification, hiring, retention or dismissal, pay of teachers, and educational improvement. The *Monbusho* also establishes the curriculum, sets priorities for education, including the time devoted to the teaching of each subject, and determines acceptable textbooks. Within each prefecture is a maze of municipal and area school boards that carry out the directives of the *Monbusho.* One member of the board is the local area superintendent.

The Japanese system promises equal educational opportunity for all students by providing a national curriculum, nationally accepted textbooks, and national guidelines for teaching. Part of the authority of the *Monbusho* comes from the funds (approximately 50 percent) provided for each prefecture. Additional funds go to those areas that do not have sufficient local resources to match the national average.

The conclusion of compulsory attendance ends free education for all Japanese citizens. There are not enough upper secondary school classes to meet demand, causing a rise in private school offerings beyond the school-leaving age. The commonly used cram school or *juku* is funded solely by parents.

School Governance in Germany

Schools in Europe follow a different and somewhat more democratic pattern. Instead of autocratically overseeing all major decisions in education, there is more local control. In Germany the system used in the former ''East'' was much more autocratic than the system in the former ''West.'' The West German system is now found in all sixteen states or *Länder.* West Germany has experienced little change, but East Germany had to adjust to a system they had been taught throughout the Cold War was responsible for the ''failure'' of the West.

The German education system is philosophically directed by a national education committee comprised of the education ministers from each *Länder.* The national body is largely symbolic, setting goals and directions, but having little budget or discretionary power. The real control of education surfaces when students enter into higher education and the trades. In order to score well on the competitive examinations, there must be alignment among the curricula taught in each *Länder,* and the examinations and the national committee provide this.

The cooperation among *Länder* results in a federal system. There is a national salary schedule for teachers modified to reflect differences in the cost of living in various parts of Germany. Each *Länder* has a common school calendar, a uniform organization of German schools, and agreement on a basic curriculum and student assessment program. Each *Länder* sets its own curriculum framework, adopts textbooks, and publishes teacher guides for the course of study. McAdams (1993) reported, ''German parents and laymen prefer to leave education to the educators, and do not directly involve themselves in school affairs except in extreme circumstances'' (p. 123).

School Governance in Britain

The British system has been in a state of flux since the Reform Act of 1988. Great Britain had a system not unlike that of the United States, only more historically shackled. The system changed from the local education authority, which had almost total control over teacher hiring and retention, curriculum, and testing, to a national curriculum and testing, parental choice in selecting schools, and local governance of individual schools. The new British system is a unique blend of local control and a nationalized system. Students elect a "Head Boy" and "Head Girl" to organize and represent the student body. The national curriculum and highly structured testing that open or close educational opportunities beyond the school-leaving age provide the federal government with a form of checks and balances with the local governing body.

Scotland is closely aligned with the education system in England and Wales, although it is a bit more conservative. Scottish citizens appear to have greater faith in schools than do their English counterparts. Only one school in Scotland opted for the most independent form of school governance possible under the reform act, while nearly 5 percent of the schools in England and Wales requested it.

Part of the school reform movement in Scotland was the development of a "Parent's Charter" or "Citizen's Charter" that should interest American educators. This introduction by Prime Minister John Major introduces the charter in the foreword of *The Parents' Charter in Scotland* (1992):

> The Citizen's Charter is about giving more power to the citizen. But citizenship is about our responsibilities—as parents, for example, or as neighbors—as well as our entitlements. The Citizen's Charter is . . . a testament of our belief in people's right to be informed and choose for themselves. (p. iii)

Unlike the English charter, the Scottish charter details parent's rights and responsibilities. The charter is organized around four basic themes: (1) a program to improve the quality of Scottish education, (2) parental choice of schools when possible, (3) parents' rights to know service standards and to remedy service that is unacceptable, and (4) the expectation of value given for tax money paid. The charter guarantees parents information about their child's educational progress and provides comparative information about area schools. Both kinds of information are important to parents, who can opt to send the child to another school. The Secretary of State for Scotland, Ian Lang, explained,

> As parents you have the primary responsibility for your children's education. You have a right to the best possible education for them, and to have your views known and taken into account. When you send your child to school you are a partner with the school and the education authority. This partnership must be a strong one, founded on close collaboration and mutual support. (*The Parents' Charter in Scotland,* 1992, p. iv)

Parental choice established competition between schools to attract the best students, so schools published test scores and college admission successes. Marketing education in a free enterprise environment was feasible during a time of greatly declining school enrollments (25 percent of the school population was lost during the decade of the 1980s) that caused massive school closings. Survival of the fittest determined which schools should be left open.

The Parents' Charter came from three reforms spanning a decade: (1) in 1981 the government legalized choice; (2) in 1988 it enabled school boards for all of the 2,300 schools in Scotland to have parents become actively involved in the governance of their schools; and (3) in 1991 the government issued the Parents' Charter. The charter outlines both *rights* and *responsibilities* (see Table 10.3).

The Parents' Charter also includes:

- a full explanation of what schools must publish, including standardized examination results, budgets, etc.
- a report about the school against which an individual student's progress can be judged
- an explanation of the Government's Assisted Places Scheme that allows parents, based on income, to expect government support for private education

It explains the special education available to those in need. It further: (1) explains the auditing process (see School Inspectors below), (2) offers guarantees about the quality of teaching, and (3) explains how the school is to be governed and what parents can do if things go wrong. The Scottish Office supplements the charter with a number of parent

TABLE 10.3 The Parents' Charter—your rights and responsibilities.

Your Rights	Your Responsibilites
A free school place for your child	To provide education for your child
A choice of school for your child within the limits of availability	To ensure that your child attends school regularly
To obtain information about your child's progress	To take an active interest in your child's education—for example, by encouraging learning at home and
To appeal if things go wrong	talking to the school about any
To vote and stand in school board elections	problems or difficulties your child may have
Receive information from the school board about its activities	To attend parents' meetings called by the school
Receive help with assessment or special education needs that your child may have	To participate in voluntary activities supporting the school
Explore the possibility of self-governing status for your child's school	To support the work of the school board and consider standing as a board member
Depending on income, an assisted place for your child at an independent school	

Note: From *The Parents' Charter in Scotland* (1992, p. 3).

guides that include (1) explanations about the Assisted Places Scheme, (2) how to choose a school—details about curriculum and assessment, and (3) details about self-governing schools. Additionally, information exists about selecting an independent school and a list of booklets available at HMSO bookshops. The booklet list includes: (1) a parents' guide to educational law, (2) a publication on "Keeping Parents Posted," (3) a parents' guide to special education, and (4) a publication on how to promote home-school partnerships and an active school board (*The Parents' Charter in Scotland,* 1992, p. iv).

School Governance in New Zealand

The government of New Zealand also has a system of national education governance that relies on local schools for implementation of the government's directives. In 1987 the government reviewed the administration of public education in New Zealand, resulting in a report, "Administering for Excellence." It endorsed the concept of choice and two themes addressed in American schools: cultural sensitivity and equity. After an extensive survey, the government issued a report entitled "Tomorrow's Schools: The Reform of Educational Administration in New Zealand." As a result of the report, the Ministry established a board of trustees in each school and decentralized authority. Each school was responsible for creating a Charter of Governance. The charter allowed groups of at least twenty-one parents to secede and establish their own school as long as it met national guidelines. The government went to a block grant concept, with the local school being responsible for achieving the objectives set in the charter. A separate report looked beyond the school-leaving age, recommending that there be greater nonpublic involvement and nonfunding of programs (*New Zealand Official 1990 Yearbook Extracts,* 1990).

The Ministry of Education plays an active role in New Zealand schools despite decentralization. It establishes national curriculum guidelines and objectives, approves all school charters, collects and distributes statistics about schools, and oversees private education. To assist in decentralizing, the national ministry was downsized; and eleven districts were established with fourteen education service centers to promote access to Ministry services. The government also established a Parent Advisory Council as an independent investigation agency with statutory authority to inspect when parents complain that their child's needs are not being met by the school. It also assists groups that want to establish another school or to educate their children at home.

A board of trustees governs schools. The board includes parents elected by parents of the school and includes the school principal, a staff member, and older students when appropriate. The scheme is similar to that in use in Great Britain.

 The world class standard of school governance varies from West to East but commonly relies on a strong national government to set guidelines about (1) what is taught, (2) how results are assessed, and (3) how to set basic standards for the nation's schools. The United States is far from meeting this standard, and the standard may not even be desired by American educators.

An Education Review Office is maintained by the Ministry of Education to review individual schools and to monitor their effectiveness for the ministry (*New Zealand Official 1990 Yearbook Extracts*, 1990).

SCHOOL INSPECTORS

Another means of controlling educational quality and outcomes is through the use of school inspectors who are somewhat similar to district supervisors in the United States. The title *school inspector* is common to many of the nations studied including England, New Zealand, Republic of Korea, and Germany. The term *inspectors* may not be well received by American ears where it is often linked to a Sherlock Homes image, but it is a common part of public education in many parts of the world. The term does not have to be negative. For example, when the authors interviewed Peter Malcolm, principal of Otumoetai College (high school) in Tauranga, New Zealand, he was asked why such a small nation was the wellspring of so many educational ideas (whole-language and reading recovery instruction among others). His reply was, "Oh, the inspectors. They bring a variety of good ideas to us" (Malcolm, 1993).

A good example of the inspectors' role is found in Britain where inspectors organize under Her Majesty's Chief Inspector for Schools. The inspectorate (HMI) provides an independent audit of schools based on a clearly understood series of standards. The British Office for Education draws inspectors from the ranks of mid-career teachers with excellent teaching records. On a rotating basis, inspectors review all schools, including private schools during an intense week of inspection. Each inspector is involved in approximately two dozen such visits each year. The inspectors spend their days in the schools and their evenings in meetings where they assess what they have observed. The procedure is not unlike many accreditation reviews in the United States. McAdams (1993) reports, "These HMI evaluations represent the only type of close supervision that is recognized as valuable and valid by the teaching profession" (p. 155). Chapter 12 includes a detailed explanation of British inspectors. However, following are lists of primary and secondary school outcomes or findings resulting from an inspection visit to schools. The list [taken from *Standards and Quality in Scottish Schools, 1991–1992* (1992)] intends to help the reader understand the usefulness of inspection to school governance.

Sample Primary Assessments and Findings

(*1*) HMI found the following good features of assessment: appropriate emphasis on continuous assessment of classwork, regular correction of written work, good feedback to pupils, full knowledge of pupils' needs and abilities, and maintaining folios of work.

(*2*) HMI noted the following issues relating to writing: insufficient time and opportunity given to writing in a variety of contexts and for a range of purposes and too few opportunities for pupils to write or draw their own ideas, interests, and experiences.

(*3*) HMI found that a good ethos is associated with a sense of identity and pride in the school, a welcoming environment, high pupil and teacher expectations, strong and purposeful leadership, positive attitudes toward pupils, recognition of the motivating effect of praise, and a concern to work with parents and the wider community.

(*4*) HMI found that links between homework and achievement are strongest when the school has a clear rationale for homework, the task is appropriate to pupils' abilities, the task is linked to ongoing classwork, there is recognition and reward for work done, there is some degree of parental involvement, and there is guidance and support.

(*5*) HMI found the following strengths in school policy and procedures in learning support: early identification of needs, class teachers and specialists working together to agree on programs, use of appropriate methods and resources, careful monitoring and recording of progress, regular exchanges of information with parents, and appropriate in-service training and staff development.

(*6*) HMI found the following weaknesses in school policy and procedures in learning support: support in English language and mathematics only; inadequate collaboration between class teachers and specialists; inadequate matching of pace, resources, or tasks to perceived needs; and inappropriate withdrawal of pupils for mainstream activities.

(*7*) HMI found that the most successful links with school boards arose when members took an interest in the work of the school, curriculum development, standards of attainment, the quality of available resources, and matters of health and safety.

(8) Where HMI found constraints on accommodation, the most frequent references were to water leaks, inadequate storage, safe vehicle access and parking facilities, poor maintenance of play surfaces, and facilities for indoor physical education in small schools.

(9) Commendable school aims included fulfilling the intellectual and social potential of each child; stressing the development of literacy; numeracy; aesthetic awareness; curiosity; knowledge and under-standing of the wider environment; developing positive attitudes to self, others, and to the local and global environment; developing personal religious beliefs and understandings and indicating moral values; developing a sense of community.

Sample Secondary School Assessments and Findings

(1) National advice on the curriculum identifies eight curricular "modes," each of which comprises a related group of subjects, for example, language and communication—that includes English, modern foreign languages, etc; social and environmental studies—that includes history, geography, modern studies, etc. Individual courses are rated from very good to unsatisfactory.

(2) Inspectors found that factors present when standards were good included parental encouragement, high teacher expectations, brisk pace of lessons, challenging tasks, and tasks matched to capabilities.

(3) HMI found the following strengths in learning and teaching: clearly understood objectives, clear presentation and demonstration of teaching points, effective use of praise, well-selected and supported range of tasks, and skilled selection and use of resources.

(4) HMI found the following weaknesses in learning and teaching: lack of structure in lessons, unimaginative homework assignments, in-consistent teacher expectations, low productivity in self-paced work, poorly managed class discussions, and insufficient recogni-tion of pupils' achievements.

(5) HMI found weaknesses in meeting pupils' needs: uniform pace for all pupils, able pupils "avoiding" more challenging work, in mixed ability groups slower learners left behind, and a limited range of quality courses at S5/S6.

(6) HMI found the following features of good provision in learning support: well established school policy, strong support from senior

management, all teachers sharing responsibility, effective procedures for identifying needs, effective links with primary schools, effective links with guidance and teaching staff, effective links with home, and well-maintained records.

(7) HMI found the following defects in provision for learning support: lack of recognized school policy, poor communication, large caseloads, inappropriate balance between consultancy and cooperation, high staff turnover, poor diagnosis of need, poor record keeping, and absence of support for able students.

The work of the inspectors is largely guided by the twelve ethos or indicators of an effective school. The American reader will be familiar with much of the effective schools research that precipitated these indicators. Peter Mortimer in *12000 Hours* found that the emerging effective schools research in the United States was equally applicable in Great Britain. The following are the twelve ethos indicators from *Standards and Quality in Scottish Schools, 1991 – 92* (1992):

- pupil morale
- teacher morale
- teacher's job satisfaction
- the physical environment
- the learning context
- teacher-pupil relationships
- equality and justice
- extracurricular activities
- school leadership
- discipline
- information to parents
- parent-teacher consultation

The reports from the inspectors are useful to school heads and governing boards because they provide the comparative basis to judge the effectiveness of the school and to determine where new in-service training or leadership is needed. The value of the inspector's work is dependent on the inspector's ability to focus on the right indicators, however. If accurate, the inspectors can provide information about best practices and most effective programs among schools, fulfilling the role of a good supervisor. If local educators view the role as "snoopervision," the value of school inspection is lost.

SCHOOL PRINCIPALS OR HEADS

All of the nations studied had a leader appointed to direct a school. In the United States, Canada, and New Zealand this person is called the principal, a term that arose from multi-classroom schools where the leader was the *principal teacher*. The term *head teacher* reflects the role of school leader who is more of a comrade than the American counterpart. This difference reflects the different roles of labor/management in the United States versus the teaching principal who spans the gap from classroom teacher, administrator, and member of the school board in Great Britain. The role of the building administrator is the key to comparisons of leadership among the nations. Hurley's study of American teachers' expectations of their principal concluded that they should be disciplinarians first and instructional leaders second. He also concluded that teachers' expectations shape their administrator's behavior, forcing them into managerial roles rather than instructional roles (Hurley, 1992).

In Great Britain, head teachers historically have not been specially trained in school management and administration. Those rising to the headship are dedicated, well respected teachers who literally head the teachers in the school. Department heads expect the head teacher to consult about budget and time allocations and to manage school discipline. British heads do not observe in classrooms or evaluate teachers other than first-year novice teachers. Following the 1988 Reform Act, however, the head teacher was to observe teachers once every two years. At this writing, the Ministry for Education was struggling to accomplish the two-year evaluation.

The local education agency (LEA) provides expertise for the head, and inspectors report their findings to the head who then shares the results with both staff and the governing body. Deputy heads, pastoral care (guidance) staff, and department heads supplement the building administration in large schools. British heads are not selected by their teachers or the governing body; rather, the LEA selects them from those who apply for the position.

With the advent of school choice and self-governance, the lack of training of the heads became a major problem. Several heads of self-governing schools reportedly hired a bursar or finance officer as their first action. The authors interviewed several head teachers from grant-maintained schools. All added a bursar as a result of "G-M" status. The federal government provided 15% greater funding for G-M schools, but this advantage was largely lost due to the added expense of the bursar. At the same time, the British tabloids were reporting abuses by Heads in an HMI Audit Commission report. Billions of pounds were reportedly misspent. The report cited family favoritism, excessive spending, etc.

The reform movement in Great Britain is catching up with the head teacher. With greater responsibility and power comes the need for better preparation of heads. The Education Management Information Exchange of the National Foundation for Educational Research in England and Wales published a report titled *Preparation, Induction and Support for Newly Appointed Head Teachers and Deputy Heads* (Baker, 1992) that reported the need to provide training for head teachers before they assumed the role. In the report, Baker (1992) concludes:

> Overall, it is clear from this small study that authorities are increasingly recognizing the need for, and importance of, providing management support, training and development for senior managers. What is being done, however, is done against a background of budget cuts and increasing uncertainty about the future of LEAs. . . . There will possibly be a greater emphasis in the future on a "competence-based approach" to senior school management development. There may also be a requirement, as is currently found in a number of other countries, for prospective head teachers to have acquired a qualification in educational management and administration. (p. 39)

The situation in Germany is similar, with head teachers requiring no special training or skills. Appointment is for life. Once selected, there is some training in school management for the head teacher. Like his/her British counterpart, the head teacher has little to do with teacher evaluation or selection of teachers, but the head teacher is responsible for implementing the curriculum, maintaining discipline, and allocating resources. Many head teachers continue to teach on a part-time basis. The administrative role of teacher evaluation and tenure is given to the regional education authority, but it is not unusual for teachers to have five or more years lapse between formal evaluations of their teaching (McAdams, 1993).

The principalship in Japan reflects the culture's veneration of great experience. Principals are drawn from those teachers with twenty-five or more years of experience, following long and deliberate preparation for this leadership role. McAdams (1993) reports,

These individuals often leave their families behind while posted in the less desirable locations. Eventually they are appointed a principal, having demonstrated the qualities valued in every Japanese organization: ability, self-sacrifice, and dedicated patience. (p. 217)

There is no special certification program or degree requirement for principals, but a training program and competitive examination must be completed prior to obtaining such a position. Because teachers in Japan are normally respected professionals, the principal in Japan does not directly supervise by classroom observation and control of practice, as occurs in the United States. Rather, the Japanese principal guides the teacher, protects the school from external pressures, and works collaboratively with teachers. The district superintendent's staff supports the principal by providing experts in curriculum and pedagogy and the staff supervision. Just as Japanese teachers expect to be transferred within the municipality or prefecture, the principal is normally transferred every four years, allowing the centralized authority of the prefecture to be maintained. The principal in Japan, however, exists in a respected and honored role (Ishizaka, circa 1990).

> The world class standard for school leader training is established by the United States and Canada who require specific credentials. All school leaders have prior training in school leadership and have earned their graduate degree.

Canada and the United States establish the world class standard for school administrators, with certification and graduate school training required of school administrators. While the American principal is no longer the principal teacher of a bygone era, the specialty training in management, administration, and instructional supervision appears to be superior to the limited training of the head teacher. The Canadian concept varies by province as it varies in the United States by state, but Canadian principals appear to be a bit closer to the head teacher model than is found in most United States schools. Canadian principals may be more likely to teach a class than is common in the United States.

PRIVATE SCHOOLS

All nations in the study have private schools, and the authors regard the frequency and percentage of the school population attending private schools as a measure of the population's affinity for public schools. Figure 10.1 shows the distribution of private schools in three age ranges for nine countries in the study.

By far the highest percentage of students in private schools is found at the pre-primary level, reflecting a governmental and cultural feeling that the role of the parent is greatest at that age range. New Zealand, with the highest percentage of private school enrollment, often has two-year-old students in preschool programs. This fact may account, to some extent, for New Zealand's high literacy rate. Because compulsory attendance laws cover the primary age group, the percentage of students in private schools is lowest for this group, with the sole exception of France. Private cram schools or other supplementary schools are not included in these figures. Once compulsory attendance ends, the percentage of students in private schools begins to increase. The increases in Japan and the Republic of Korea result from parents trying to circumvent the rigorous entrance examinations required by the star schools.

The world class standard for percentage of students in private schools is 45 percent at the pre-primary age range, 5 percent during the primary years, and 14 percent during the secondary years. The United States percentage is below the world class standard for both pre-primary and secondary school but above it at the primary school level.

IMPLICATIONS

Just as the nations of the world vary about the concept of school and its role in society, so they vary on the issue of control or governance of schools. Persons who control schools control the future of a society, so

Nation	Pre-primary	Primary	Secondary
Canada	4	4	6
France	12	15	21
Germany	66	2	8
Britain	7	5	9
New Zealand	99	2	5
Israel	17	n/a	n/a
Japan	77	1	14
Republic of Korea	60	1	41
United States	36	11	8
Average	45	5	14

Note: From *World Education Report* (1991).

Figure 10.1 *Percentage of students in private schools at three levels.*

issues of school governance are hotly contested when raised. In reviewing the ten nations in this study, the cultural values of each nation can clearly be identified in their system of school control. School administrators are clearly important in each nation.

National Goverance

There appears to be a philosophical/cultural difference between the eastern Pacific Rim nations and the European-based nations (including New Zealand) when it comes to school governance. The government dictates educational standards more often in the nations of the eastern Pacific Rim than in the European-based nations. The United States and Canada are even less inclined to allow federal control. The British, who have individual school governments and a national curriculum and testing, appear to have split the difference between local and federal control. Given that the United States is moving, albeit slowly, toward national standards for education (see Chapter 8), the authors recommend a study of the British system (see Chapter 12). The majority of nations in the study can articulate what it means to be "an educated national," while the United States cannot agree on what it means to be an educated American. That is a serious weakness in our system. National control of curriculum and testing is world class and must be adopted by the United States if world class standards are to prevail.

Inspection and School Improvement

One important variable among the nations involves school reform and improvement. Many nations use inspectors in that role, while the United States uses instructional supervisors and regional accrediting agencies for much the same purpose. The United States, particularly during the present time of downsizing central offices, is at risk of losing the value of school supervision as the basis of school improvement. The time and energy formerly used for classroom visitations, improvement conferences, and support for new ways of teaching is now used for accountability and reporting instead. The accountability movement came from mistrust of schools and teachers and must not be confused with school improvement. Probably American teachers spend great quantities of time trying to meet accountability standards rather than working on more effective teaching.

The use of outside experts who monitor schools is foreign to American education but is worth examining. Individual school governments, particularly in large urban school districts where board of education members are total strangers, are also worth considering.

School administrators should consider the development of children's and parents' charters. The authors presented the Parents' Charter from Scotland because it listed both rights *and* responsibilities. If a charter is not directly tied to the mission of the school and does not encompass the school's vision, then it belongs in the dust bin with school philosophies that are words on paper rather than a reality. In developing charters, school personnel must realize the limits of their responsibilities, just as children and parents need to realize the existence of *their responsibilities.*

Local Governance

The United States and Canada set the world class standard for local school administration because their administrators are specifically trained and certified for their roles as managers of the schools. Yet the authors were struck with the quality of administrators met during their study of schools in Great Britain. The very skills that allow teachers to become head teachers in some systems are the same innate characteristics that allow some principals to succeed while other graduates of the same training program are unsuccessful. In the United States, school leaders must avoid choosing principals on a political basis. Selecting head teachers makes more sense. We must look for the brightest and best educators and train them to be instructional leaders.

The American board of education is a local governing body that has become a dinosaur. Chalker (1992) proposes a future orientation for the American board of education:

> At the local level, the traditional board of education should be restructured as education enters the twenty-first century. Whether appointed or elected, the board should be advisory and should be composed of teachers, administrators, parents, community leaders, and university educators. Once useful in a less complex society, the current elected lay board of education is becoming a liability. Too often, politics dominate the local board, and individual board members are not student oriented. Today's superintendent spends far too much time caring for board members who often have little impact on the instructional success of the school. (p. 7)

The restructured board should have much of the authority usurped today by state governments. Legislated learning has been unsuccessful over the past decade, and research exists showing more student achievement when schools are free from bureaucratic control (Chubb and Moe, 1990). Site-based management is an idea whose time has come.

No one would buy something expensive if the same quality were available for free. That holds true in education as well. Yet parents in the United States elect to pay for primary education at a rate more than double that of the world class standard, so school personnel have work to do. The forces propelling Kentucky's reform movement, voucher systems, and educational bankruptcy feed at the same trough of malcontent, also indicating the importance of the tasks ahead for school leaders. The solution to this malcontent is an enhanced local partnership between school and home under national leadership.

AFTERTHOUGHT

(*1*) The United States needs a national education authority that defines the term *educated American*. National curriculum is needed.

(2) With the United States slowly developing national standards for education, decentralized authority at the local school may be the best way to implement those standards. School boards, however, need to be restructured or replaced as the local governing authority.

(*3*) In the rush toward accountability and the downsizing of the economy, the United States might forget school improvement; and school improvement is the ongoing school reform of greatest value.

(*4*) The rights and responsibilities of children, parents, and schools need to be defined and provided for. That is the basis on which school governance should rest.

REFERENCES

Baker, L. 1992. *Preparation, Induction and Support for Newly Appointed Head-Teachers and Deputy Heads.* Slough, England: National Foundation for Educational Research in England and Wales.

Chalker, D. 1992. "Refocusing School Leadership for the 21st Century Across the Board," *The Education Digest,* (58)3:4−8 (Condensed from *Thresholds in Education,* 18:26−30).

Chubb, J. E. and T. M. Moe. 1990. *Politics, Markets, and America's Schools.* Washington, D.C.: The Brookings Institute.

Education in Korea, 1991−1992. 1992. Seoul, Korea: Ministry of Education.

Hurley, J. C. 1993. "The Organizational Socialization of Rural High School Principals: Teacher Influences," *Journal of Research in Rural Education,* (8)2:20−31.

Ishizaka, K. Circa 1990. *School Education in Japan.* Tokyo: International Society for Education Information.

Malcolm, P. 1993. Interview (June 18).

McAdams, R. P. 1993. *Lessons from Abroad: How Other Countries Educate Their Children.* Lancaster, Pennsylvania: Technomic Publishing Company, Inc.

Monbusho. Circa 1992. Monograph by the Ministry of Education, Science and Culture distributed by the Consulate of Japan, Atlanta Office.

New Zealand Official 1990 Yearbook Extracts. 1990. New Zealand: Ministry of Education.

The Parents' Charter in Scotland. 1992. Edinburgh, Scotland: The Scottish Office of Education.

Standards and Quality in Scottish Schools, 1991−1992. 1992. Edinburgh, Scotland: The Scottish Office of Education.

World Education Report. 1991. Paris, France: United Nations Educational, Scientific and Cultural Organization.

SUGGESTED READING

Farkas, S. and J. Johnson. 1993. *Divided within, Besieged without: The Politics of Education in Four American School Districts.* A report from the Public Agenda Foundation Prepared for the Charles F. Kettering Foundation, New York: The Public Agenda Foundation.

CHAPTER 11

DEFINING A WORLD CLASS EDUCATION STANDARD FOR PARENTS, HOME, AND COMMUNITY

Each new generation renews hope that new leadership will change the world and improve life for all mankind. Every nation in the world places faith in the educational system to assure the development of these new leaders. Before school, however, comes the home. The home environment prepares a child for school, and the parent is the child's first teacher. The time from birth to age five, say child development experts, is crucial to the proper development of a human being. Chapter 11 presents data covering six components of parental, home, and community influence that affect a child's early development and later the child's education.

(1) The literacy rate of each world class country, 1991
(2) Parent involvement in the school life of children
(3) The number of television sets per 1,000 inhabitants in each world class country, 1988
(4) The number of newspapers per 1,000 inhabitants in each world class country, 1988
(5) The suicide rate of males and females: (1) ages five to fourteen and (2) ages fifteen to twenty-four, 1986
(6) The divorce rate per 1,000 population, 1988

PERCEPTION: RANKING THE UNITED STATES ON THE QUALITY OF PARENT, HOME, AND COMMUNITY INVOLVEMENT IN THE EDUCATIONAL PROCESS

The questionnaire includes five questions related to parenting, the home, and community (see Table 11.1).

The respondents varied their reaction to question thirteen. First, each

185

TABLE 11.1.

Rank United States schools as they compare to the following nine national school systems: Canada France Germany Britain New Zealand Taiwan Israel South Korea Japan	First	Top Third	Middle Third	Bottom Third	Last
		(Percentage of Total Responding)			
13. Highest literacy rate? (*n* = 178)	5.6	18.5	38.2	28.1	9.6
14. Most home involvement in schools? (*n* = 174)	1.7	9.0	25.3	51.0	13.0
15. Greatest use of private "cram" schools to prepare students for standardized tests? (*n* = 173)	13.3	17.0	14.5	28.0	27.2
16. Highest rate of suicide among school age youth? (*n* = 173)	8.7	22.0	31.0	32.0	6.3
17. Greatest percent of students with divorced parents? (*n* = 175)	47.0	42.0	7.0	2.3	1.7

determined the rank of the United States when compared to the other world class countries on the subject of literacy. Thirty-eight percent of the respondents placed the United States in the middle third category, and responses on both sides of the middle were fairly well balanced. Otherwise, responses converge on the middle category.

If educators perceive the educational system as average in the basic goal of developing a literate society, the perception serves as a wake up call. Literacy in the United States should be world class. Indeed, the perception is close to reality and that intensifies the alarm.

Question fourteen asks, "How would you rank home involvement in United States schools with home involvement in the other nine comparison countries?" Nearly 90 percent of the sample group responded either in the middle third category or lower third category. The response is not surprising, since school administrators often complain about the lack of parental interest in a child's education.

Question fifteen asks the responding administrators to rank the United States on the use of so-called "cram schools" to supplement a child's education. The question surfaces because the Pacific Rim countries have near mandatory cram school attendance. Thirteen percent placed the United States first in the use of cram schools. Approximately one-third of the responses are in the first place category and/or the top third category, a surprising response to a country where cram schools are virtually nonexistent. More realistic are the 50 percent of responses in the lower third category or the last place category.

"Do school age youth in the United States have a high suicide rate when compared to school age youth in the other nine world class countries?" asked question sixteen. Responses spread evenly over the five categories. Perceptions obviously vary regarding teenage suicide in the United States. The American media report suicide regularly, but the public perceives suicide as a more common practice in countries like Japan where pressure to achieve is fierce. The data in Figure 11.4 will interest educators who perceive teenage suicide to be a foreign problem.

Question seventeen asked the respondents to indicate the status of divorced parents in the United States, as compared to the other world class countries. Forty-seven percent awarded first place to the United States, and another 42 percent placed the United States in the top third. Perception and reality are close on the issue of divorce in the United States. People perceive the rate to be high, and the rate is high. Ask any school administrator about the incidence of divorced parents having children in the school, and they will verify the perception. The data in Figure 11.3 support the perception that the United States is world class in number of divorces.

REALITY: THE WORLD CLASS STANDARD FOR PARENT, HOME, AND COMMUNITY INVOLVEMENT IN THE EDUCATION PROCESS

The early chapters of this book that speak to educational issues often refer to parent, home, and community influence as important ingredients in enhancing school achievement. Every nation studied recognizes the importance of the parent and home environment in a child's life. The big question is, "Why then are parental involvement in school and a child's home stability perceived to be less than world class in American society?" This chapter features five statistical studies and one narrative in an attempt to answer the question. The narrative subject is parental involvement in education, and each statistical study results in a world class standard. The data have meaning only if one accepts the hypothesis that a positive parental influence, a stable and caring home environment, and a supportive community determines success in school. The authors believe strongly that this hypothesis is reality.

The Literacy Rate of Adults in the Ten World Class Countries

Assume for purposes of this study that adult literacy reflects the value placed on education in a given home. Assume that literate parents value learning at least enough to value school completion. Assume that the more literate a society, the more successful the school system serving that society. The assumptions are defensible and once accepted, make literacy a fair measure of parental and home influence on a child's education. *Literate parents want literate children!*

Figure 11.1 shows the 1991 percent of literate adults in each of the world class nations. Britain reports 100 percent literacy, and the other European countries, France and Germany, report a 99 percent literacy rate. Each country has an established and polished school system. In each of the three countries, literacy is the mission of each primary school, and the completion rate at the primary level is near perfect.

Israel appears at the opposite extreme, showing a literacy rate of 90 percent. Israel continues to struggle with a dual education system where

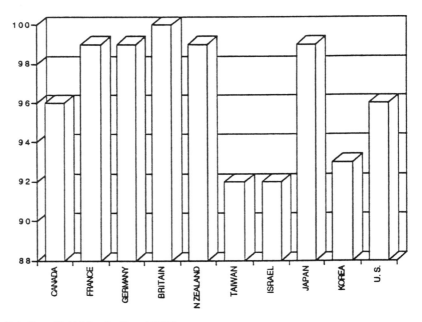

Note: From *World Education Report* (1991).

Figure 11.1 *The literacy rates of the ten world class countries, 1991.*

Hebrew schools show much higher attendance and completion rates than do Arab schools (Simmer and Simmer, 1990). A high rate of illiteracy exists in Taiwan and Korea also, but recent education reforms should improve the literacy rate. Japan is a model for other emerging nations like Taiwan and Korea, for Japan has reached 99 percent literacy.

 The world class standard for adult literacy is the mean average for the ten nations of 97 percent. The United States, with a literacy rate of 96 percent is a percentage below the world class standard.

The United States and Canada must find a way to reach the world class literacy standard, for both countries have the resources necessary to accomplish the task.

Parent Involvement

The idea of parental involvement in schooling is difficult to quantify and place on a table. Because of the importance of parental involvement in education, research and wisdom of practice form the basis for this narrative presentation on the subject. Parental involvement in schooling has a powerful influence on a child's education and is, perhaps, the most important educational input addressed in this study of world class education.

Parental involvement in education involves two processes with similarities and important differences. First, parental involvement is the process of the parent and the school interacting. Examples of this interaction are parental membership in the PTA, a parental visit to open house, and parental and educator participation in a parent and teacher conference. When the parent and teacher participate together in school events, the child receives a message that school is important and worthy of adult time. When the parent fails to participate, educators feel that an optimum learning environment does not exist. Educators often complain that only parents of successful students participate in school activities, while parents of unsuccessful students stay away. Too often, this is true.

In the world class countries, this first type of parental involvement varies in application. In France, parental involvement at school is possible but not actively encouraged. French education is extremely traditional, and tradition places responsibility for learning inside the school building. Korean parents have a keen interest in school success, but Korean educators discourage parental involvement in school, often so that parents will not bribe the teacher in return for better grades (Hur, 1992).

Like the United States, Britain, Germany, New Zealand, and Canada encourage parental involvement at school. Israel reports a lack of parental involvement; but recent reforms encourage involvement, particularly through scheduled meetings between the parent and teacher (Karyan, 1992).

 Britain's Parents' Charter is the world class standard for involvement between parent and school.

The Parents' Charter, a part of the British Reform Act of 1988, establishes rights for parents of school age youngsters and activities that make the parent an active partner in a child's education. The charter provides five key documents for parents (*Education in Britain*, 1991):

- an annual report on the child's progress
- performance tables with comparative information on all area schools
- a summary of the most recent inspection report covering the child's school
- an action plan addressing weaknesses reported in the school inspection
- an annual report from the school's governors that includes test results, truancy figures, school-leavers' destinations, budget information, and election procedures for parent-governors

The Scottish Office revised the charter to include parental responsibilities. The complete charter is offered in Chapter 10.

Parental involvement follows a second process perhaps more crucial to world class education than the first process. This second process defines the parents' interaction with the child at home starting in the formative preschool years and continuing through the schooling experience. It includes the parents' attitude about the child as a student and the interaction brought about by the attitude. In the preschool years, preparation of the child for school directs the quality of the interaction between parent and child. During the school years, positive parent and child interaction continues to encourage and support achievement in school.

At this point, the term *parent and child interaction* requires definition. The authors call it the establishment of an "education ethic." Establishing an education ethic involves ten important activities required of all parents and significant adults in the child's life:

- maintaining high expectations for a child in school
- disciplining the child so that the child can accept discipline in the school
- creating a love of learning by showing a child the wonders of life and the child's environment
- creating a love of reading by reading to the child and modeling the importance of self-reading
- establishing education as a prerequisite for success in life
- teaching the child that success results from hard work
- developing a physically healthy child
- creating an environment for the child free from violence, unhealthy conflict, and drugs
- teaching the child that teachers must be respected
- teaching the child that effort, not ability, is the key to success

How does America fare in establishing the education ethic? McAdams (1993) recognizes the importance of social and cultural contexts that influence the school, with the most important being the attitude that society perpetuates toward the rearing and education of children. In recent decades, reports McAdams, the capacity of the American family to provide for the material, moral, and social welfare of children has diminished. Too many American parents pass harmful messages about education to their children. Adults often prepare children for school with warnings that school is boring and teachers are mean. Parents ask children to report attempts by school officials to discipline the child. Parents often verbally abuse teachers and administrators, and the threat of a lawsuit is all too familiar to school officials. Adults also portray summer vacation as a welcome escape from school. Truthfully, educators need summer vacation to escape from the negative messages delivered by students from parents.

Canada experiences many of the same problems as the United States. The Chamber of Resources in Alberta, Canada, looked for prime contributors to Alberta's perceived academic failure. The resulting study found parental attitudes to be key. Many parents in Alberta encourage students to hold part-time jobs, even at the expense of studies. Parents actually discourage homework as an undesirable encroachment on a child's time. Parents feel that their children are only young once and should have the freedom to pursue their own interests (*International Comparisons in Education,* n.d., copyright © Alberta Chamber of Resources). The study could easily describe the values of many American parents.

Students participating in the IAEP assessment (Lapointe et al., 1992) responded to questions about home characteristics. The results confirm the notion that parental involvement can have an important impact on a child's school success regardless of the family's social or economic status. When asked if they thought their parents wanted them to do well in mathematics, almost all students in each population gave positive responses. Agreement ranged from 97 percent in Israel (Hebrew schools) to 79 percent in Portugal.

Regardless of the country studied, children who report to school disciplined and motivated to learn achieve successfully. The Asian countries most clearly model the "education ethic." Stevenson and Lee (1990) conducted a classic study to determine the reasons for the high academic achievement of Chinese and Japanese children compared to American children. First and fifth graders in Japan, Taiwan, and the United States took tests measuring achievement in reading and mathematics. American students did poorly in mathematics compared to students in Taiwan and Japan. American students did better in reading, but a disproportionate number of American children were classified as poor readers.

Stevenson and Lee (1990) discovered reasons for the superior achievement of Asian students after interviewing the children, their mothers, teachers, and principals. The reasons fit the definition of the "education ethic" proposed by the authors. The following selection from an abstract of the study conducted by Stevenson and Lee is so important that it should become common knowledge for all educators and parents of school age children:

Background information about the children's everyday lives revealed much greater attention to academic activities among Chinese and Japanese than among American children. Members of the three cultures differed significantly in terms of parents' interest in their child's academic achievement, involvement of the family in the child's education, standards and expectations of parents concerning their child's academic achievement, and parents' and children's beliefs about the relative influence of effort and ability on academic achievement. Whereas children's academic achievement does not appear to be a central concern of American mothers, Chinese and Japanese mothers viewed this as their child's most important pursuit. Once the child entered elementary school, Chinese and Japanese families mobilized themselves to assist the child and to provide an environment conducive to achievement. American mothers appeared to be less interested in their child's academic achievement than in the child's general cognitive development; they attempted to provide experiences that fostered cognitive growth rather than academic excellence. Chinese and Japanese mothers held higher standards for their children's achievement than American mothers and gave more realistic evaluations of their child's academic, cognitive, and personality characteristics. American mothers overestimated their child's abilities and expressed greater satisfaction with their child's accomplishments than the Chinese and Japanese mothers. In describing bases of a child's achievement, Chinese and Japanese mothers stressed the importance of hard work to a greater degree than American mothers, and American mothers gave greater emphasis to innate ability than did Chinese and Japanese mothers. (pp. v, vi)

Data collected a few years ago about Indo-Chinese boat people who came to the United States mired in poverty with little or no knowledge of the English language support the idea of an Asian education ethic. The Indo-Chinese students enrolled in American schools and quickly achieved at the top of the class. Primarily, investigators found home environment responsible for the students' rapid success. Each evening, parents and children gathered to complete homework. Learning for all members of the family was first priority and nothing interfered. The values of each family included a firmly entrenched education ethic.

Mothers appear to be particularly significant in establishing the "education ethic." In Japan, the "dragon mother" gets intensely involved in the child's education. The mother observes the child in school and may even attend school for the child if illness prevents the child's attendance (Katsula, 1992). This practice will probably fade as more mothers work in Japan, but an intense interest in the child's education is entrenched in the Japanese culture. Stevenson and Lee (1990) found Chinese and Japanese mothers not excessively demanding persons holding unrealistic aspirations for their children. While the mothers watch diligently over the student's progress, they display a realistic appraisal of their children's abilities and accomplishments. They believe in hard work. American mothers, on the other hand, seem to be too positive about their child's performance and may provide little incentive for their children to strive for higher levels of achievement.

> The world class standard for establishing an "education ethic" belongs to the Asian countries. Parents in Japan, Taiwan, and Korea perpetuate a culture that stresses hard work, high expectations, high parent involvement, and an emphasis on student achievement. American parents usually do not express the same values with any degree of intensity.

Rosemond (1993), a family psychologist also writing a syndicated newspaper column, provides an excellent summary for this dissertation on parenting. Rosemond reports the activities of two different families visiting the zoo. Family number one—husband, wife, and three children—reported pandemonium, with children running in all directions, yelling, and demanding every trinket on sale. The father reported that the family did not have a good time; and in fact, the husband and wife became angry at each other because of the children's poor behavior.

Family number one spied family number two at the zoo. Family number two consisted of an Asian mother and three children similar in age to the children in family number one. Children in the Asian family were well behaved, calm, quiet, and rarely required direction. The American father, who experienced much difficulty with his own children, admired the behavior of the Asian children. Rosemond suggests that Asian parents are generally appalled at the behavior of American children. Asian parents do not tolerate misbehavior in the home or in school. American parents would do well to stop and fix a situation that desperately needs fixing.

Television Sets and Daily Newspapers in the World Class Countries

Figure 11.2 presents data showing the number of television sets in each world class country and the number of newspapers in each country.

For purposes of developing an education ethic, television watching carries a negative connotation and newspaper reading a positive connotation. Countries with large numbers of television sets and fewer newspapers have citizens who watch rather than read. In countries where people develop the habit of watching rather than reading, education suffers.

In terms of number of television sets and newspapers and their effect on education, significant patterns or trends don't exist. A few observations are in order, however. Germany, Japan, and Israel are near or above the mean or world class standard in both categories. Persons in the three countries appear media-conscious and able to afford both larger numbers of television sets and newspapers. France, New Zealand, Taiwan, and Korea are below the world class standard in both categories. Presumably, the four countries do not covet or cannot afford either media in large numbers.

Country	Television Sets	Country	Newspapers
United States	812	Germany	585
Germany	759	Japan	569
Japan	709	Britain	396
Israel	592	Israel	357
Canada	586	New Zealand	328
Britain	435	United States	255
France	399	Canada	225
New Zealand	372	France	214
Taiwan[2]	312	Taiwan	202
Korea	204	Korea	24
Mean	473	Mean	334

[1]Note: From *World Education Report* (1991)
[2]Note: From *The World Almanac and Book of Facts* (1992).

Figure 11.2 The number of television sets and newspapers per 1,000 inhabitants in the ten world class countries, 1988.[1]

The United States occupies the more meaningful position in Figure 11.2. The United States is first in television set ownership with 812 per 1,000 population. The figure by the mid-1990s could be approaching one per person. At the same time, the United States is sixth in newspapers printed, with 255 per 1,000 population, so publishers print about one newspaper for every four persons. The data beg the following question, "Has watching become more popular than reading in the United States?" The question is without an answer in this book, but data in Chapter 9 covering world class students, suggest that students in the United States watch more television than students in most other nations. Data in Figure 11.2 support the data in Chapter 9 and suggest that American parents make more television sets available to students than are made available to students in any other world class country.

Divorce in the World Class Countries

The divorce rate is certainly a meaningful measure of the home environment influence on student success. Figure 11.3 shows the 1988 divorce rate for all of the world class countries except Taiwan. The

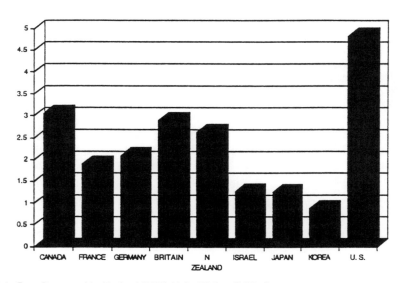

Note: From *Demographics Yearbook* (1990), United Nations Publication.

Figure 11.3 The divorce rate per 1,000 population in nine of the world class countries, 1988.

divorce rate for the United States, 4.83 per 1,000 population, is the highest of the countries.

The countries culturally closest to the United States—Britain, Canada, and New Zealand—show divorce rates above the world class standard. All three, however, are well below the rate for the United States. Israel, Japan, and Korea have the smallest rate of divorce. In all three countries, cultural and religious mores appear to keep the family together.

McAdams (1993) reports a census study in 1991, showing that 26 percent of American children lived in single-parent families, usually with the mother. Many single parents are excellent caregivers and do their best to support the child in school. Single parents must work, however, leaving limited time for the child; and simple arithmetic tells that two parents can double the amount of time spent encouraging a child to succeed in school.

 The world class standard for divorce in the world class countries is 2.3 divorces per 1,000 population. The rate in the United States is more than double the world class standard.

Ask teachers and/or administrators about divorce, and they will quickly reveal the number of children in their school living in single-parent homes. Children from broken homes carry difficulties to school. Even before the divorce, children of divorced parents often experience the trauma of an unhappy home; and following the divorce, the child must adjust to a new home with only one adult present. Visitations when the parent is not in the home are often difficult. The child's relationship to grandparents and other significant relatives changes. Through all of this trauma, school work suffers. In the best single-parent homes, children experience trouble with adjustments brought to the home by divorce. Figure 11.3 clearly indicates that the United States leads the other nations in the creation of this school problem.

Suicide Rates for School Age Youth

Americans often ask, ''Doesn't suicide often result from the pressure to achieve expected of the school age youth in many foreign countries?''

The answer is apparently no. Students from the world class countries interviewed during the research process responded positively about their school experiences. Students acknowledged high parental and school expectations but felt that the expectations motivated them to achieve and that achievement itself was rewarding. Suicide was not considered a problem.

Figure 11.4 and Figure 11.5 show the suicide rates for eight of the world class countries. Figure 11.4 presents data for primary youth from age five to age fourteen, and Figure 11.5 presents data for young adults from age fifteen to age twenty-four. A disadvantage of the study is that the young adult group also includes a sizable population no longer in school. The data also report suicide rates for males and females in each age group. Figure 11.4 and Figure 11.5 present data in rank order with the greatest rate of suicide first.

 The world class standard for incidence of suicide among the school age population is (1) .7 per 1,000 population of males, ages five to fourteen; (2) .3 per 1,000 population of females, ages five to fourteen; (3) 17.1 per 1,000 population of males, ages fifteen to twenty-four; and (4) 5.3 per 1,000 population of females, ages fifteen to twenty-four. The United States exceeds the world class standard in all categories.

Canada and the United States, countries accused of harboring lax education standards, lead the countries in incidence of male suicide. Both countries are also above the mean rate for incidence of female suicide. Japan, where Americans perceive pressure to achieve on tests as unreasonable, shows a rate below the mean in all categories except for females, ages fifteen to twenty-four.

In Korea, a country not cited in Figure 11.4 or Figure 11.5, suicide is an unfaithful act and a disgrace to the family. Duck Haeng Hur (1992) reports the Korean suicide youth rate as half of the rate in Japan.

Suicide rates do not appear related to school pressures. Although pressure to achieve in school might be a contributing factor to a person's decision to commit suicide, data do not support a direct relationship.

Country	Males, Ages Five to Fourteen	Country	Females, Ages Five to Fourteen
Canada	1.1	New Zealand	.8
United States	1.1	Canada	.3
France	.9	United States	.3
Germany	.9	France	.2
New Zealand	.7	Germany	.2
Japan	.6	Japan	.2
Britain	.2	Britain	.1
Israel	.2	Israel	n/a
Mean	.7	Mean	.3

Note: Extracted, by permission, from *World Health Statistics Annual* (1988).

Figure 11.4 *1986 suicide rates for eight countries with world class education standards. Rates are per 1,000 population for males and females ages five to fourteen.*

IMPLICATIONS

The overwhelming single implication of the data presented in Chapter 11 is that schools mirror the cultural expectations of parents and other significant adults engaged in child rearing practices. United States citizens have schools that reflect their values and practices. Stated another way, people in the United States have the schools that they desire

Country	Males, Ages Fifteen to Twenty-Four	Country	Females, Ages Fifteen to Twenty-Four
Canada	26.9	New Zealand	8.0
United States	25.5	Japan	6.5
New Zealand	22.9	Canada	5.9
Germany	17.6	United States	5.9
France	16.0	France	4.6
Japan	11.6	Germany	4.5
Britain	9.9	Israel	4.5
Israel	6.6	Britain	2.3
Mean	17.1	Mean	5.3

Note: Extracted, by permission, from *World Health Statistics Annual* (1988).

Figure 11.5 *1986 suicide rates for eight countries with world class education standards. Rates are per 1,000 population for males and females ages fifteen to twenty-four.*

and perhaps even deserve. Restructuring of schools alone, advocated by many politicians and interest groups, will not bring world class education to the United States. The United States must examine and restructure cultural expectations as well.

Following are implications for each input standard presented in Chapter 11.

Literacy

Literacy rates must improve in the United States. Other countries studied expect students to possess basic literacy by the completion of primary school. Educators in the United States must study these successful literacy programs in world class countries and adjust curricula. Too many American youth pass through elementary school without the basic tools necessary to survive in today's world.

Questionable practices exist in American elementary schools, such as tracking and labeling excessive numbers of students as learning disabled. Many educators establish low student expectations early in the student's school life, and too many students work down to the expectations. On the other hand, teachers cannot reasonably improve literacy until children enter school ready to learn. The key to improving literacy seems to be a combination of changes improving the way parents and schools approach the reluctant learner.

United States educators make admirable efforts to teach *adults* basic literacy, but more improvement is still possible. Britain, with 100 percent literacy, provides a model, The Adult Literacy and Basic Skills Unit, that provides after-school instruction for illiterate adults (*Education in Britain,* 1991).

Parental and Home Influences

Parental influence and home environment raise the most important implications of the research conducted on world class education. For decades, research has been available that explains how parents can help their child achieve in school. Read carefully the four following known ingredients about student achievement. Educators must publish them over and over for parents.

(*1*) Parents must teach children that school is essential for future success.

(2) Parents must become vital partners in each child's schooling.

(*3*) Parents must support and respect teachers and administrators and pass these values to their children.

(*4*) Parents must teach children that school requires hard work and that ability alone will not equal success.

Why aren't parents preparing children for school using the above suggestions? Many dysfunctional American homes contain troubled parents, and school success is the last thing on the home agenda. Child abuse exists beyond comprehension in many American homes and will not go away overnight. Divorce rates will not decrease overnight either, although rates did decrease slightly in recent years. Parenting practices will also not improve overnight. Parenting is at a crisis stage in many American homes, and the results are children creating a crisis in school. America must immediately make the improvement of family life a priority if America's schools are to become world class. Until children go to school disciplined and ready to learn, educators cannot be miracle workers. Schools cannot successfully be restructured until society is restructured. The message is clear but often ignored by critics of schooling in America, who call for world class schools rather than a world class society. Educators tolerate these critics too much and should rise up in indignant protest.

Cram Schools

Hopefully, cram schools will not become popular in the American educational system. Many American educational leaders question why the Asian countries need cram schools when their schools are superior. Resources in the United States should concentrate on the public school system, not a system of private schools that can easily become elitist.

Consumption of Television Sets and Newspapers

The United States is the world class leader in number of television sets per inhabitant. This statistic, along with the data showing that American students are world class leaders in television watching, disturbs educators. Television interferes with school achievement. The number of television receivers in use is a clear indication that school age children possess a television set. Parents *can* control the use of television and first should start by removing the television set from the child's room. Second, parents should leave the family television dark until all school work is complete. New Zealand places a tax on every television in use, but this practice is apparently being abandoned; and it is unlikely that such a tax would be acceptable in the United States. Parents simply must act to limit television watching.

The low incidence of newspapers in the United States is a puzzle. The implication, however, is that citizens are watchers rather than readers. Educators do report that students in school are not avid newspaper readers. Research documents the importance of reading at home. Reading newspapers is a piece of that activity, so parents—read to your kids: read newspapers, read books, read mail, read anything, but read.

Divorced Parents

Divorce in the United States is world class. The effect on children's school work is less than world class. The school work of children whose parents are in the process of divorce often suffers, as does the child's social adjustment. Many students act out their frustrations with a broken home, disrupting their own learning as well as the learning of fellow students. The problems inherent in divorce are a social problem, probably beyond the scope of the local school. True, schools continue to address marriage and family issues in the curriculum and provide counseling services; but educators can't reach into the home and prevent a split family. Again, critics of schooling in the United States ignore an important social issue beyond the control of the local school.

Research in this chapter does not address the issue of unwed mothers, but like children from split homes, children of unwed mothers often experience problems in school. Does the American public really expect world class schools? If so, the public should start by commending educators for coping well with the problems of children from split and single-parent homes. Children do learn in school in spite of the burden placed on them at home. The public should then take a long look at the home environment of many American youth and prepare for a giant restructuring of society, along with the proposed restructuring of schools.

School Age Suicide

Suicide is painful at any age, but school age suicide has horrible implications for a society. At issue in this study is the effect that pressure to achieve has on suicide. The data do not support the widely held perception that high expectations for school age youths lead to suicide. Parents and educators must understand that high expectations for youth are not harmful. In fact, students from other cultures even consider high expectations helpful. Suicide is not an excuse an educator can use to explain the lack of expectations prevalent in many schools.

Summary

A successful world class student comes from a world class home, where world class parents live. The authors questioned three successful students from Denefields School, Tilehurst, Reading, England, about the cause of their success in school. Their comments provide closure for the ideas presented in this chapter about family and home. Karly Champion (1993), tenth level student at Denefields School said, "My mom and dad expect success. Mom and dad encourage me. They don't really get on me, but they know my ability. If you can't do the work, they help you. I wouldn't work as hard if not for them. I can cope with pressure, but sometimes it gets you down." Graeme Dornan (1993), tenth level student at Denefields School stated, "People with high ability can become successful. You've got to believe in your capability. A lot is left up to you. You have to set yourself goals. Mine is to work as hard as I can. I am anxious to learn. I have good relationships with teachers." Nicolai Dobby (1993), at the A level and a student at Denefields School said, "I have parents who push me very hard. They want me to do well. I enjoy school. I have always enjoyed school. I have always liked it, since I was little."

Moms and dads and a good home environment cause world class students. World class students cause world class schools. An "education ethic" is needed in the United States. This country is a great nation

Worksheet
How does your educational agency compare to the world class standard for parental involvement and home environment?

Literacy Rate

97%

_____   _____   _____
(World class standard)   (Your agency)   (Deviation)

Parental Involvement

Involved parents with
high expectations

_____   _____   _____
(World class standard)   (Your agency)   (Deviation)

Number of Television Sets and Newspapers per 1,000 Population

473 Television sets
334 Newspapers

_____   _____   _____
(World class standard)   (Your agency)   (Deviation)

Suicide Rate per 1,000 Population

Ages 5 – 14—.7 Males
Ages 5 – 14—.3 Females
Ages 15 – 24—17.1 Males
Ages 15 – 24— 5.3 Males

_____   _____   _____
(World class standard)   (Your agency)   (Deviation)

Divorce Rate per 1,000 Population

2.3

_____   _____   _____
(World class standard)   (Your agency)   (Deviation)

capable of establishing such an ethic if leaders will just stop bashing education and look at the total ingredients of world class schools.

AFTERTHOUGHTS

Meaningful change in the outcomes of education in the United States requires fundamental change in the way parents and teachers unite to instill an "education ethic" in each student. It is not one individual issue such as money, class size, teacher preparation, or governance that will establish world class schools in the United States. It is a matter of societal change. Society must change values about education if American schools are to achieve world class status.

REFERENCES

Champion, K. 1993. Interview (June 17).

Demographics Yearbook. 1990. New York: Department of Economics and Social Affairs Statistical Office, United Nations Publication.

Dobby, N. 1993. Interview (June 17).

Dornan, G. 1993. Interview (June 17).

Education in Britain. 1991. United Kingdom: Produced for the Foreign and Commonwealth Office by the Central Office of Information.

Hur, D. H. 1992. Interview (December 2).

International Comparisons in Education—Curriculum, Values, and Lessons. n.d. Alberta, Canada: Alberta Chamber of Resources.

Karyan, S. 1992. Interview (October 23).

Lapointe, A. E., N. A. Mead and J. M. Askew. 1992. *Learning Mathematics.* Princeton, New Jersey: International Assessment of Educational Progress, Educational Testing.

McAdams, R. P. 1993. *Lessons from Abroad: How Other Countries Educate Their Children.* Lancaster: Technomic Publishing Company.

Rosemond, J. 1993. "Asian Parents Have Different Set of Assumptions on Child-Rearing," *Asheville Citizen-Time,* (June 24):2C.

Simmer, S. and D. Simmer, eds. 1990. *Facts and Figures on the Education and Culture System in Israel.* Jerusalem: Ministry of Education and Culture.

Stevenson, H. and S. Lee. 1990. *Contexts of Achievement: A Study of American, Chinese, and Japanese Children.* Monographs of the Society for Research in Child Development, Vol. 55, Nos. 1–2. Chicago: University of Chicago Press.

The World Almanac and Book of Facts. 1992. New York: World Almanac.

World Education Report. 1991. Paris, France: United Nations Educational, Scientific, and Cultural Organization.

World Health Statistics Annual. 1988. Geneva, Switzerland: World Health Organization.

Ykari, S. 1992. Interview (December 2).

Chapter 12

A GLIMPSE OF THE FUTURE: EDUCATION IN GREAT BRITAIN

Educators remember the 1980s for the implementation of worldwide school reform. Many nations exchanged effective school practices. After studying world class education standards, the authors looked in the direction American education appears to be headed to find another nation experienced in making similar changes. Great Britain was an obvious choice. Below are major issues already confronted by Britain that American educators will confront by the end of the decade:

(1) The establishment of national goals in education assuring that students in the United States have a similar knowledge base

(2) The creation of a national accountability and mandatory national testing of the nation's education goals

(3) The creation of national certification standards for teachers with an attempt to equate higher pay with the certification; this will parallel a "downsizing" of district educational authorities

(4) The further enhancement of local school governance and site-based management of schools

(5) The continuing effort to establish schools of choice for parents and a school voucher system

(6) The realization that the United States will become a cultural polyglot with polarization of the population forming at the ends and a decreasing middle to bridge the gap

(7) The need to answer questions about "states' rights" versus the national need for an educated work force

Great Britain appears to have confronted these issues most successfully. The authors studied their experience and offer the reader a "Glimpse of the Future" for American schools.

REALITY: REFORMING A WORLD CLASS
SCHOOL SYSTEM

Many classrooms all over America display a poster that says: "None of us is as smart as all of us!" The British have already dealt with many of the issues with which Americans are just starting to come to grips. Americans can gain from others who had learned the price and the rewards of undertaking major reform.

An editorial in the Raleigh, North Carolina, *News and Observer* (June 15, 1993) appeared under the title: "National Standards vs. School Equality" by John Leo. It said in part:

> The heart of President Clinton's Goals 2000: Educate America Act was a council that would set up voluntary, national standards on what students should know and be able to do. Other modern industrial nations already do this. . . . But the emphasis now is on "opportunity to learn" standards that are supposed to spell out what schools must make available to students. This might include smaller classes, competent teachers, and up-to-date textbooks. . . . How was this committee able to change the subject so quickly and divert attention away from curriculum standards? . . . As Albert Shanker, president of the American Federation of Teachers, says: "We don't abolish medical school exams because not everyone has had the opportunity for top-notch pre-med education. Nor do we say that tests for airline pilots shouldn't count because not everyone has the opportunity to do well on them. . . ." Reformers like the National Governor's Association focus on standards, excellence, measuring job skills and preparing the work force for international competition. The most powerful wing of the educational establishment focuses on social equality and student cooperation. . . . Republicans fear that voluntary "opportunity to learn" standards will become compulsory. Diane Ravitch, an assistant secretary of education in the Bush administration, writes: "You do not have to be a seer to predict that the new standards would permit federal regulation of curricula, textbooks, facilities and instructional materials. . . . Secretary of Education Richard Riley received a letter from Governor Carroll Campbell of South Carolina who wrote that the revised bill "comes dangerously close to derailing our hard-won emphasis on student achievement . . . too much effort has been invested in much-needed school reform for it to be wasted now."

It all sounds familiar. British tabloids were replete with references to the controversial Education Reform Act of 1988 which replaced their ancient system of local school control. There was obvious mistrust of federal dominance of historically local issues. The government's intent had been to develop a simple statement about what British schoolchildren should learn and then to assess their mastery of it. It sounded simple enough. The reform was fourfold: develop a national curriculum, and accountability by national testing, while assuring local governance, and parental choice. This was a radical departure for Great Britain. An approximate parallel might be the health care reform issue currently being debated in the United States.

Left unanswered was the issue of who developed both the curriculum and the tests. By the time the education establishment had "improved" the idea, an unwieldy, time-consuming process resulted. Several Heads reported arguments about using the word "test" because some educators didn't like the idea of the government "testing" children. So they used the euphemism "standard assessment of tasks" instead.

American educators can learn a great deal from this effort to restructure education in Great Britain. The mere fact there were problems and criticism of this initiative doesn't mean it was all bad. Part of the controversy was humankind's natural reaction to change. The parallel with Leo's editorial is the ability to look back at the British experiment, while Leo was looking forward to America's reform.

One lesson from this comparative education study is that a world class standard shared by all ten countries is the proclivity to complain about public education and the "next generation." Within that context, there will always be those who will decry progressive methods and new concepts.

At this writing, national testing of fourteen-year-old students had become so controversial that many teachers in England and Wales were boycotting the tests. Besides the length of time devoted to giving the tests, the educational establishment was fundamentally opposed to testing and thought it unfair to less able children. The result was the creation of games and activities for seven-year-old students with which teachers were supposed to assess. This required several weeks of assessing rather than teaching.

On the issue of federal regulation versus local control of schools, the result was a compromise that included some of both. The standards and tests were to be mandatory with test results reported on school-by-school comparative "league tables." At this writing, head teachers threatened to boycott the tests by not reporting results.

As in Britain, systemic school reform will inherently be gut-wrenching and polarizing in any nation because of the importance attached to educating the next generation. The fact that major problems surfaced when implementing the reforms should not be construed to mean the reforms were a bad idea. They were not.

THE ENGLISH EDUCATION SYSTEM PRIOR TO REFORM

Obviously the school systems of Great Britain are deeply steeped in history. There is not a single British school system, but rather different systems in England, Wales, Scotland, and Northern Ireland. Each has an education agency that oversees schools. The agencies in England and Scotland participated in the study. Time did not permit travel to Wales and Northern Ireland. The Scots enjoy a rich history of differing markedly from their British cousins over the issue of public education, among other things.

Both school systems have a tradition of decentralization and independence from the influence of national government. Before the 1870s elementary schools in England and Scotland were primarily private or church-related. In Scotland, citizens expected churches to provide a school in each parish; but there was no means of enforcement. During the 1870s the government attempted the establishment of universal education for children below age thirteen. Compulsory education was established in the 1880s. Elected school boards formed to fill gaps between areas served by free church schools by establishing elementary schools. Secondary schools grew slowly without state encouragement. In England they tended to be private, gaining the name ''public school'' if they offered boarding facilities. In Scotland, there was adherence to the concept of providing a grammar school in each ''burgh'' or principal city. By the turn of the century, both private and public systems were not sufficient to meet increasing demand for secondary education.

In 1902 England revamped its system of government by increasing the authority of county governments and assigning them responsibility for maintaining the schools. The purpose of this activity was abolishment of the earlier patchwork of church schools and school boards. The growing gap between private ''public'' schools and state grammar schools was to be settled by developing county secondary schools. While the idea of two different philosophies coalescing sounded good, the compromise left an interesting anomaly—the complete lack of a prescribed school curriculum. The Scots, delayed by World War I, made a similar move in 1918; but control of the curriculum was given to the Scottish Education Office. Scotland has traditionally watched the British struggle with the reform and then acted. That tradition continues.

Britain joined many of the world's developed countries in conducting massive realignment of education following World War II. In 1944 the ongoing struggle between church schools and school board schools was theoretically settled. Publicly maintained schools of two types were recognized: (1) voluntarily aided schools where religious instruction could be denominational and (2) voluntarily controlled schools that taught religion based on rules designed for state schools. In voluntarily aided schools, the church maintained ownership of the school, maintained the plant, and contributed to new buildings. The local government provided the operating costs of the school and all salaries in both types of school. In 1947 the government extended compulsory education to age fifteen and abolished school fees, including those for books and other materials. By this time competitive tests for admission to grammar schools had already come into use, meaning that LEAs (local education authorities) had to decide whether to open their grammar schools to all students as comprehensive schools or allow them to select students based on academic achievement test scores. The latter move was more popular during the post-war period. To compensate for the higher standards, leaders suggested technical schools for the less academically proficient but seldom built them. So children at age eleven were under great pressure to gain admission to secondary schools and pass the test called "eleven plus."

During the 1960s, teachers who had no curriculum but were forced to teach test objectives criticized the "eleven plus" structure. Parents became critical when they saw the strain in their children's eyes. In 1965 the Labour Party asked LEAs to submit proposals for restructuring secondary schools as comprehensive schools. With few parameters available, the result was the implementation of a smorgasbord of possibilities. Also in the mid-1960s, the British were still trying to integrate the private public schools with the growing number of state secondary schools. The most common solution was for educators to provide schools for students age eleven to eighteen, with the school-leaving age established at age fifteen. As of age twelve, most students were "streamed" or grouped homogeneously for the remainder of their school years. The number of students staying beyond the school-leaving age increased significantly during the 1960s.

Curriculum remained an issue. The primary schools had no official control over the curriculum, but the pressure for examination performance at the secondary level affected the primary teacher and student. Secondary schools were increasingly accountable to national examination systems. Naturally, Scotland had a different examination system which was newer than the English system. In the English system there were eight examination boards, seven of which were controlled by universities. Students between the ages of fifteen and sixteen who wished to earn a general certificate of education (GCE) would ''stand'' a standardized examination. The government created a second examination for advanced students between the ages of seventeen and nineteen. Since the tests were subject oriented, students elected majors in the areas of the examinations they would stand. Students had to pass three examinations at the first level and a minimum of two at the more advanced level to obtain admission to British universities.

In 1965 the Ministry expanded the format of the second examination to give more of Britain's students the opportunity for further education. The examination came under the control of local secondary teachers who administered the test. More curriculum areas were added for the top half of the students not taking GCEs – a design that helped nearly 40 percent of the students nationally.

Predictably, Scotland did things a little differently. All testing remained under the control of the Scottish Education Department, and students could take the equivalent of advanced GCEs at a younger age so they could enter the university system earlier.

By the 1980s, the school systems of Great Britain had evolved into a system that was more decentralized but still controlled somewhat by a centralized education department. A group called ''Her Majesty's Inspectors'' theoretically oversaw the quality of the schools. The primary source of school funding came from the central government in the form of general grants to supplement county coffers. The Ministry made some attempt to equalize funding between wealthy, ''leafy suburb'' districts and those of more Spartan means. Governance of the schools was a county responsibility, with an appointed education committee reporting to the local government authorities rather than to parents or the community. This resulted from the tradition that parents and students were not expected to be involved in school governance. Parent-teacher organizations were rare.

Local authority grew under the model, whereby the *head teacher* (school administrator) was free to establish curriculum and the teachers were free to determine teaching methods and time on task issues. Teacher unions became quite strong, and negotiations with them included not only salaries but working conditions. Unions negotiated with officials at the national level (Parker and Parker, 1991).

With the national government providing the majority of funding for education, it seemed amazing that, with one exception, no real form of national accountability existed. Her Majesty's Inspectors (HMI) were established in both the English and Scottish school systems. The purpose of the inspectorate was to periodically perform a multi-member site evaluation in all schools in Great Britain. The HMIs would suddenly arrive at a school and intensely involve themselves in classes and the school routine for nearly a week. They prepared a report of their findings and forwarded the report to the head teacher and the central government. All schools, including private ones, were subject to these reviews. While they sound abrupt and formal, McAdams noted, ''These HMI evaluations represent the only type of close supervision that is recognized as valuable and valid by the teaching profession'' (McAdams, 1993, p. 155).

Obviously, the need existed for codifying the curriculum and improving instruction in the schools. Teachers could not be mandated or paid to attend staff development activities. During the 1980s, reform loomed over a struggling system that faced two new challenges. First, the influx of non-English-born immigrants became a flood that caused the schools to meet a new set of needs. Second, the baby boom days of the 1960s became baby bust days, resulting in as much as a 25 percent reduction in pupil enrollments and massive school closings (Carim, 1993).

The government was at a crossroads. Since 1976 some politicians called for entry into the ''secret garden'' containing the content teachers actually teach. Questions were raised about teaching methods and there was a demand for teaching a set core curriculum. The National Union of Teachers (literally, NUT) became predictably defiant of any person questioning their integrity (Lightfoot et al., 1993). Camps formed between those concerned about input equity or giving all students the same opportunities to learn and those concerned with output accountability such as comparative test results. Other issues such as parents' rights and freedom of choice arose. Based on a declining school population, could schools compete with each other so only the most productive would survive? All of these problems created a situation that resulted in the 1988 Education Act that included several novel approaches to problems familiar to many Americans. Implementing the Act has proven frustrating, exhilarating, liberating and confining, and certainly controversial. However, Americans can learn much from the effort.

REALITY: FOUR THEMES OF BRITISH EDUCATION REFORM[1]

National Curriculum

The Education Reform Act of 1988 introduced national curriculum to Britain. The Department for Education appointed working parties composed of teachers and interested citizens to produce curriculum in ten distinct subject areas (Singh, 1993). All public and private schools in England and Wales must use national curriculum for students aged five through sixteen. The core subjects are English, mathematics, and science; and teachers must emphasize the three subjects. Foundation subjects are technology, history, geography, music, art, physical education, and a modern foreign language; and these receive less emphasis. Key delivery stages have been established as follows:

- Key Stage 1 — up to age seven (infants)
- Key Stage 2 — seven to eleven (juniors)
- Key Stage 3 — eleven to fourteen (pre-GCSE)
- Key Stage 4 — fourteen to sixteen (preparation for GCSE)

All students in the first two key stages study the core subjects plus

[1]The authors obtained much of the information for this section during a visit to England and Scotland in June 1993. The authors gratefully acknowledge the efforts of the trip organizers, Gillian Cooper, British Consulate, Atlanta; Susan Fasken, Overseas Visitors Section, Information Department, London; and Robin Miller, Scottish Office Information Directorate. The authors gratefully acknowledge the contribution of educators visited in the following centers of learning — English schools: Rush Common Primary, Fitz Harrys Secondary, Denefields School; Scottish schools: Balerno Community High School, Currie Hill Primary School, Jordanhill School; national education departments: Department for Education, England; Scottish Office, Education Department; research organizations and universities: National Foundation for Educational Research; Educational Management Information Exchange; Reading University, Faculty of Education and Community Studies; Morray House Teacher Training College; University of Strathclyde, Jordanhill College.

technology, history, geography, music, art, and physical education. All subjects remain in Key Stage 3, and teachers add modern language. The Department for Education requires religious education, but it is not part of the national curriculum. Local schools determine the amount and type of religious instruction; and if parents do not approve, they may request removal of their student from the program. Key Stage 4 students, aged fourteen to sixteen, concentrate on a maximum of three subjects (*Education in Britain,* 1991). These students, called Form Six students, prepare for the university or a few specialize in vocational programs.

Attainment targets exist for each national curriculum subject. For example, speaking, listening, reading, spelling, and handwriting are English targets. Each attainment target has ten levels of accomplishment. One year is the expected time for attainment of each level (Singh, 1993). Teachers do not seem unnecessarily concerned, however, if students do not reach the attainment level.

National curriculum serves only as a guideline for schools in Scotland but Scottish educators apparently follow it closely. The ten subject areas are virtually the same at the secondary level as they appear in England and Wales, and all ten are part of a major curriculum development program recently completed for students in the five to fourteen age range.

The national curriculum results from years of national frustration caused by a lack of student accomplishment. Reacting to the frustration, the Department for Education developed national targets after consultation with the National Curriculum Council, but little time was available for piloting or implementing the targets by key stage. National curriculum became law in 1988. Implementation began in 1991; and two years later, ten subject areas are in place. Perhaps the swift implementation was a blessing, for major curriculum change is usually a slow process that becomes unnecessarily bogged down in bureaucracy.

The National Department for Education believes that national curriculum will establish high common standards for all students in England and Wales. Educators interviewed in the field also generally supported national curriculum. Allan (1993) claims:

> National Curriculum has no opposition. It is superb. It has taken the best classroom practice and used it. It is flexible and teachers can expand it. Time is the major problem.

McCutcheon (1993), Oxfordshire Educational Authority, said that teachers and parents accept national curriculum because it has helped equality. Problems, said McCutcheon, were as follows:

(1) Implementation was too quick.

(2) Change caused teachers to start over.

(3) Central direction was lacking.

(4) Curriculum developers did not consult teachers.

He stated that the National Curriculum was here to stay.

Other than minor distractions mentioned above, a few complaints emerged. Some teachers interviewed expressed discomfort with the national curriculum, calling it confining and saying that it prevented teachers from going off on their own (Dunsdon, 1993; Franchi, 1993). Such complaints seem mild considering that the government thrust rapid change upon teachers.

Scottish educators say there is ''no problem'' with the national curriculum as long as it remains a national guideline. Administrators thought teachers in schools were using the curriculum (Bedborough, 1993; McGlynn, 1993).

In summary, national curriculum in Britain appears to be functional considering such rapid implementation. The curriculum document contains broad targets for each level that seem to give clear common objectives to all teachers and students. The document is concise compared to the volumes of curriculum documents produced by many of the fifty states. Social science curriculum in North Carolina, for example, covers over 1,700 pages.

National curriculum gives clear direction to parents, who can better understand their child's studies. National curriculum in Britain should make schools more accountable and the targets seem easily measured. Easy, however, does not define British national testing developed concurrently with national curriculum in order to assess student progress in each curriculum area.

National Testing

National testing has traveled a rough road in Britain. At the conclusion of each of the first three key stages, the Department for Education decided to test children in England and Wales for achievement of the attainment targets using both teacher assessments and "standard assessment tasks" (SATs). At the end of Key Stage 4, teachers administer the GCSE to help determine entrance to Form Six study that prepares students for higher education. The higher education entrance exam, administered at the conclusion of Form Six, is the General Certificate of Education (GCE), Advanced (A) level (*Education in Britain,* 1991).

In principle, assessment in Scotland is similar to assessment in England and Wales, but minor differences exist. The ages when students take the tests differ, and the uses made of the results have a different focus. Other differences appear in the narrative that follows. Also, Chapter 9 contains details about British testing not covered in this chapter.

Many British administrators, teachers, and parents voice opposition to the tests. Teachers piloted the tests at the conclusion of Key Stage 1 in 1991 with some complaints but few disruptions. But, in 1993, teachers boycotted the Key Stage 3 tests for fourteen-year-old students. In Scotland, parents apparently asked teachers not to administer the tests. What happened to a process held in such high esteem by the Department for Education? Several reasons surface that have serious implications for American authorities responsible for developing national tests. Following are implications derived from discussions with British educators, parents, and students.

Test Development

Authorities recognize test development as a problem in England and Wales. First, the creation of a separate committee to develop national testing was flawed. Following the reform act in 1988, one group, the National Curriculum Council, assumed responsibility for developing national curriculum; and a second group, the School Examinations and Assessment Council assumed responsibility for testing the curriculum. British leaders learned that curriculum and testing must be the responsibility of the same authority. Curriculum cannot align with test questions unless the same persons complete both processes. A single body, the School Curriculum and Assessment Authority, will replace the two separate councils in 1993 (*Choice and Diversity: A New Framework for Schools,* 1992; Singh, 1993).

Second, teachers claimed little involvement in the construction of the SATs. Opposition to the tests peaked over flaws in the English test for fourteen-year-old students—specifically over testing of information on Shakespeare. Teachers called the questions inappropriate. Teachers also question whether multiple question tests are an appropriate way of testing verbal facility. Pearson (1993) stated, ''Teachers are not against the test but are against the rush in implementation; the tests were not constructed right.'' The lesson seems clear. Teachers who deliver the curriculum must construct the tests that measure the curriculum. Administrators must allocate adequate time for accurate construction of test questions, for accuracy involves obtaining input from teachers and carefully incorporating the input into the test questions.

Time for Administering Tests

The time necessary to administer all tests is a serious problem in the minds of British educators and parents. Teachers interviewed said quite frankly that the tests take too much time to administer (Dunsdon, 1993; Allan, 1993; Pearson, 1993). The School Examination Assessment Council recommended that the SATs be administered over a three-week period, but British educators estimate that the tests take up to five weeks to administer. A requirement that children read aloud, respond verbally to thought questions, and perform manipulative tasks required considerable time per student (Madaus and Kellaghan, 1993). Teachers have to grade the examinations—a process that is also time consuming. SATs also disrupt the school day in various other ways because of space requirements, rescheduling of classes, and reassignment of teachers.

Testing in the various states today is also time consuming, and teachers and parents raise similar complaints. Persons responsible for the development of national tests in the United States must remain conscious of time constraints.

Purpose of Testing

Teachers and parents question the purpose of the national testing program. National officials in England and Wales established the following objectives for national assessment:

- Testing should give schools and parents a benchmark against which to judge the progress of pupils both individually and collectively.

- Parents can hold schools accountable for performance, using published results of tests.
- Parents can use published test results to exercise choice in choosing the right school for their student (*Choice and Diversity: A New Framework for Schools,* 1992).

Pressure of accountability is an overriding goal of all three objectives.

Scottish officials use assessment results more exclusively to provide diagnostic and formative information exclusively for the use of teachers. Teachers can choose whether or not to share the information with parents (Madaus and Kellaghan, 1993).

Allan (1993) felt that the test results offered nothing new to teachers. Dunsdon (1993) questioned the use of test results by parents, because parents lack sufficient information about test results to make decisions about their children's future. McCutcheon (1993) felt that nobody thinks the current testing program is a good idea and that the practice of comparing schools on the basis of test results is biased.

Most criticism focuses on the testing program at Levels 1, 2, and 3. However, teachers have used the GCSE, the Level 4 test, for a longer period of time; and the test receives higher marks from parents. Students do not seem concerned about the purpose of the tests and seem to take them in stride. British educators accept the use of the GCSE to measure student accomplishment at the end of compulsory education, but question national testing at the conclusion of the earlier key stages.

The British experience in using test results to compare schools raises a world class question. Why must the leadership of any country insist that test results be used to compare schools? Researchers claim that societal factors account for over half of a child's test score, so citizens compare schools based on an uneven playing field. Why is that factor so hard for the educational leadership to understand? The British experience offers America a choice: adopt the testing objectives mentioned above for schools in England and Wales or adopt the testing practices for test usage in Scotland. The authors suggest the latter.

Value of Testing

The early experience of the British assessment program raises the question of value. The Department for Education and the Welsh Office claim that testing has increased student motivation, helped teachers by highlighting serious gaps in achievement, and improved the pass rate on the GCSE (*Choice and Diversity: A New Framework for Schools,* 1992). Bedborough (1993) states that the Scottish tests provide a yardstick for learning and a link to national curriculum. As noted above, other educators question the value of the testing program.

Many parents and teachers claim the disadvantages of testing diminish any perceived or actual value. Some teachers feel that the tests have offered no new knowledge about student learning. Parents pleased with their schools question the need for new testing information. The Department for Education has not clearly established the need for the national testing program. Obviously, persons who will shape the future of national testing in the United States should start the process with an analysis of value. How will persons use the test results? How will the media report the results? Test results used to improve student learning have value. But educators must justify using test results to compare schools, or the British experience serves no useful purpose for the United States.

Local Control of Schools

The following dialogue on local control outlines the British idea of site-based management, an idea developed beyond the imagination of educators in other countries. The grant-maintained movement removes power from the state government and the local education authority and places that power in the lap of the school community. The British experience with local control provides other countries with a wealth of information regarding site-based management, never before addressed in the international arena. The Department for Education claims that the effort is at the heart of the government's new education policies; and the department clearly hopes that, over time, all schools will become grant maintained (*Grant Maintained Schools: Questions Parents Ask,* 1992).

The Education Act of 1988 introduced the idea of grant-maintained schools (GM schools). GM schools are completely self-governing. The Department for Education sends funds directly to the school, and the school staff allocates the funds where the governing body deems appropriate. A grant-maintained school is an individual school, not a school system as exists in the United States. The autonomous leaders of the GM school determine all personnel needs, educational needs, student needs, and needs of the physical plant.

How does a school become grant-maintained? The governing body (board of governors) of a school initiates a resolution requesting a ballot of parents on the issue of GM status. Twenty percent of the parents can also petition the governors to consider GM status. Parents vote on the proposal, and if a majority prefers GM status, the governors submit a proposal to the Secretary of State. The Secretary decides each proposal on its merits (*School Governors: How to Become a Grant-Maintained School*, 1991). By June 1993, the Department for Education approved 492 schools in England for GM status and one school in Scotland. Parents must officially request GM status; but unofficially, the school staff led by the head teacher is quite influential in the process. Parents who request GM status without the approval of the school staff would surely meet with opposition in the implementation stage. Obviously, schools in Scotland have not embraced the concept. Resistance to English politics and pride in the traditional Scottish educational system are reasons for individual schools not favoring GM status. School boards in Scotland traditionally have assumed little control compared to governing boards in England and Wales, and Scottish school boards seem content to leave school governance in the hands of the professionals.

How does GM status change the governance of the school? Who runs the school under GM status, and who loses control? When a school successfully seeks GM status, the local education authority loses control and no longer governs the school. The governors gain the control formerly held by the LEA and have complete responsibility for every aspect of the school. The national government remains responsible for national curriculum and national assessment, however. The governors control the budget, teaching conditions, salaries, who will mow the lawn, and what uniforms the students will wear – the governors make all decisions. Since GM status releases the school from control of the county LEA, the governors need only use the services of the LEA as a voluntary contracted service. Funding comes directly to the GM school from the central government in each British Dominion. In England and Wales, a new funding formula gives each GM school the usual Annual Maintenance Grant based on enrollment, plus a percentage to replace the costs of services previously supplied by the LEA. The additional funding varies from 7 percent to 33 percent of the Annual Maintenance Grant and currently averages 15 percent (*Grant-Maintained Schools: 1993–94 Funding Worksheet*, 1993; Allan, 1993).

Grant-maintained schools also receive a number of Special Purpose Grants (SPGS) usually used to pay for the additional office staff needed to administer the additional responsibilities of grant status and to provide funds for staff development, insurance, and additional equipment. The most common addition to the administrative staff is a bursar who complements the head teacher by assuming fiscal responsibility and handling bidding procedures and contractual arrangements (*Grant-Maintained Schools: 1989–92,* 1993). Additional funding is clearly a major reason why local schools have chosen GM status. The head teacher and building teachers talk positively about the improvements made to the school and the presence of additional equipment.

Most grant-maintained schools employ extra teachers. Governors use extra funds to reduce class size and hire additional specialists to broaden the curriculum. Almost all grant-maintained schools increased the number of nonteaching staff, an addition that has relieved teachers of many routine tasks. Grant-maintained status protects the teacher's salary scale at its present level and guarantees teachers all advantages earned before GM status. Teacher duties and work rules continue when schools receive GM status, but the GM board of governors may apply to the Secretary of State for permission to bring in its own pay scale and conditions of employment (*Grant-Maintained Schools: Questions Staff Ask,* 1992). One GM board of governors initiated this action, in effect negating the negotiated agreement with the union. Usually, however, governing boards appear eager to maintain positive relations with the unions, and the government does not expect widespread permission to negate union contracts. Teachers appear to have mixed reactions to GM status, enjoying the additional staffing and equipment but missing the access to LEA support services (*Grant-Maintained Schools: 1989–92,* 1993). If and when more governing bodies negate old policies and rules and replace them with a new governing structure, the change will test the teachers' acceptance of grant status.

Understanding the governance of GM schools equates to understanding the board of governors. In England, each individual school must have a board of governors. In Scotland, the Department for Education named the governing body a school board; but the department only suggests formation of the board. Approximately 25 percent of the schools still have not formed a school board. Observers said that Prime Minister Margaret Thatcher was startled to learn in 1988 that Scottish schools had no governing body similar to the English board of governors (McGlynn, 1993).

In all British countries, the membership of the school governing body differs from the board of education in the United States. Figure 12.1 shows a comparison of the English board of governors and the American board of education.

English governing boards have much to offer American educational leaders. Consider the following advantages: (1) the board in England includes the head teacher and at least two elected teachers; (2) only parents elect governors rather than all registered voters. This condition places the schools in the hands of those persons most interested in education; (3) elected board members appoint additional members to the body who have a sincere interest in education and who have expertise in running the school. The membership of the board of governors is broad-based and more suited to assume the responsibilities of GM status.

Comparison	English Board of Governors	American School Board
Jursidiction	Single-school	District of one or many schools
Number and method of selection	(5) Parents elected by parents (1) Head teacher (2) Teachers elected by teachers (11) First governors appointed by elected board. Two must be parents, and others usually represent business interests. (2) Nonvoting students, usually Head Boy and Head Girl (optional and usually secondary)	(Usually five to nine registered voters) Elected by registered voters or, less often, appointed by other governing body.
Authority	Govern under the direction of the local education authority or if grant maintained, have complete authority	Govern as directed by the state legislature. Powers vary according to the state philosophy.

Figure 12.1 A comparison of the English board of governors and the American board of education.

The governors have overall responsibility for every GM school including complete control of the budget. The main player in the movement to GM status, however, is the head teacher. The head is similar to the American principal, assuming responsibility for instructional leadership, student conduct, and school management. These responsibilities increase under GM status (*Grant-Maintained Schools: Questions Parents Ask,* 1992). The head teacher has no formal administrative training at the university, and schools require no license to hold the position. Governors appoint head teachers using such criteria as teaching success and proven leadership ability in the school or a neighboring school. Head teachers used to be part-time teachers, but increased responsibility changed the position to full time in larger schools.

In Scotland, the head teacher is not a member of the school board but plays the most influential role in the life of the Board. The head teacher's influence expresses itself in approval or disapproval of board action and high profile activity while the board is at work (MacBeath et al., 1992).

Boyd (1993), Assistant Director of the Quality in Education Centre, University of Strathclyde, Scotland, has assumed responsibility for training head teachers and school board members. Staff at the Quality in Education Centre wrote a dozen training manuals available to head teachers and board of education members covering the skills required of an instructional leader. Observers of British schools suggest that formal training can benefit head teachers and governors in England and Wales.

LEA schools, or schools that have not selected GM status, look suspiciously at the GM school's practice of admitting students. Parents choose their student's school in Britain, creating the possibility of selective admission. Armed with additional funds, the GM school seems to be in a position to attract additional students and, therefore, be more selective. The Department for Education provides a safeguard against selective admission by GM schools. The governing body of each prospective GM school seeks the Secretary of State's approval of a policy developed to admit students. The policy must maintain the previous character of the school, and selective enrollment, therefore, is not acceptable. A GM school, for example, cannot discriminate against pupils with special educational needs (*Grant-Maintained Schools: Questions Parents Ask,* 1992). Although the school is an exception because of its previous history as a university demonstration school, Jordanhill School, the only GM school in Scotland, has a waiting list that requires a parent to request enrollment at the time the child is born (Bedborough, 1993). Because of the suspicion of selective enrollment in GM schools, the national government intends to continue monitoring enrollment policies. It seems to many, however, that GM schools might just work if they are more popular with parents.

Grant-maintained schools are new on the British scene. The Secretary of State approved only 2 percent or about 500 GM schools in England, and only one GM school exists in Scotland. The English Department for Education proclaims that all schools will become grant-maintained, while the Scottish Office encourages but does not require the practice. What is the track record of GM schools after the first two years of existence? Slater and Griffiths (1993), Department of Education staff persons responsible for selling LEA schools on the advantages of GM status, cite the following advantages of GM schools:

(*1*) Each school has control of the entire budget and flexibility in spending.
(*2*) GM status creates a feeling of community in the GM school.
(*3*) Parents are more involved in schools, including the selection of textbooks.
(*4*) GM status has created a new enthusiasm for change.

Parents, governors, head teachers, and teachers in schools that have chosen GM status generally favor the change. The most common advantage of GM status cited by educators is increased funding used to repair buildings, purchase equipment, and add staff. In spite of skepticism from personnel in LEA schools, people in GM schools trust the government to continue additional funding.

Another side of the coin exists, however. LEA schools not yet choosing GM status claim loyalty to the local education authority and the services offered by the authority. J. Fisher (1993), head teacher at Rush Common Primary, feels that GM status will force the local school to assume custodial responsibilities and that instruction will suffer. McCutcheon (1993) labels the grant-maintained initiative a failure and thinks that most schools applying for GM status are at risk. J. Griffiths (1993), an information specialist for schools in England and Wales, studied the early movement of schools to GM status and states that fewer schools than the government had anticipated are opting out of LEA control. D. Fisher (1993, pp. 2−3), Education Management Information Exchange, lists the following major concerns with GM schools to date:

(*1*) The disparities between capital allocations available to GM and LEA schools

(*2*) The inability to sensibly rationalize school places if opting-out were to allow manifestly underscribed schools to escape closure

(*3*) The need to agree with GM schools admission arrangements that harmonize with those of the LEA, of which at least give no particular advantage to any group of parents

(*4*) The difficulties for an LEA of maintaining cost-effective professional support services for their remaining schools as opting-out grows

(*5*) The level of annual maintenance grant paid to GM schools

(*6*) The establishment of sound business arrangements between an LEA and GM schools in buying and selling services

Grant-maintained schools are in the early stages of development, and change in the quality of teaching and student learning is not yet evident. Slater (1993), Department for Education, stated that in England ''nothing significant in test score improvement shows over the others.'' School officials use additional GM funds, to some extent, to improve the quality of the educational experience; so Her Majesty's Inspectors anticipate improvement (*The Implementation of Local Management of Schools*, 1992).

Add politics to the concerns about the future of GM schools. The Education Reform Act of 1988 reflects the education agenda of the Conservative Party. GM schools, therefore, will remain on the accepted agenda as long as that party remains in power. It is certain, however, that the initiative will vanish if the Labour Party gains power. The reluctance of Scottish officials to embrace GM status is certainly because the Scottish representatives to Parliament are members of the Labour Party. The push to establish GM schools in England and Wales reflects the party's wish to firmly entrench GM schools in the educational culture, so that the opposition cannot remove them.

Change brings controversy, so the struggle over school governance in Britain is predictable. Regardless of the outcome, the GM initiative has already produced advantages for all schools. Because of the GM movement, the local education authority gave all constituent schools more control over their budget. The local education authority now delineates services more clearly and markets the services so that GM schools can purchase them. This practice makes all schools more aware of the scope of the LEA. Finally, the GM movement provides practical information on the idea of site-based management. Educational leaders throughout the world often discuss the idea, but seldom try to implement local school management on a large scale. Britain is trying.

Accountability

Accountability is the last of five great themes describing Britain's educational policy for the 1990s. This section breaks accountability down into two initiatives. First, British school leaders expect accountability to develop through the implementation of parental choice; and second, leaders initiated a school inspection plan to insure accountability.

Parental Choice

Parental choice has been a part of the British educational picture since 1980. Choice has three correlates for parents.

Successful choice depends on the idea that parents know their children best and can best choose the school that fits their needs. Schools must admit pupils up to the limits of their physical capacity; and if school officials deny admission, a local appeal committee hears the complaint of the aggrieved parents. Parents also remain free to choose between state and private education (*Choice and Diversity: A New Framework for Schools,* 1991).

Choice forced schools to make public their philosophy, goals, and objectives. Schools developed colorful brochures and opened doors to parents for visits. The state promised parents tables showing the test results of all schools, but the controversy surrounding the tests and the fairness of this practice makes the future of this initiative doubtful. Attendance data are available to parents, and the governing board delivers the results of the school inspection report at a public meeting.

School personnel seem to take choice in stride. Since the national government allocates school budgets based on pupil enrollment, parental choice influences individual schools—the more pupils, the larger the budget. Schools are also more receptive to the ideas and wishes of parents, since policy encourages openness. McGlynn (1993) stated that "education is a secret garden, and we are attempting to open up the garden."

Choice is the privilege of parents serving on the school's governing body. Parents elect parents who choose to run for the board of governors; and once elected, governors appoint additional parents to the governing body. Only parents can run for office, and only parents vote for elected officials. The governing body has legal authority to make all local decisions for the school they represent, and indications point to a serious effort by parents to be good governors. Even in Scotland, where boards of education are a new addition to the educational governance, school board members express satisfaction with their new role and an appreciation for the opportunity to serve (MacBeath et al., 1992).

Parents exemplify the idea of choice when they exercise the right to choose GM status for their child's school. Parents virtually own grant-maintained schools, and the board of governors govern them. Appointed members to the board of governors usually have expertise in school matters and can offer such services as legal advice, law enforcement services, construction and maintenance advice, and child welfare information.

Inspection of Schools

The purpose of school inspection in England and Wales follows:

> The purpose of inspection is to identify strengths and weaknesses in schools in order that they may improve the quality of education offered and raise the standards achieved by their pupils. Particular attention is to be paid to pupils' standards of achievement that are better or worse in a subject than the average for their age group, and to the reasons for such differences. (*Framework for the Inspection of Schools,* 1993, p. 4)

In 1993, The Department for Education in London advertised for applications to be a school inspector. Those who apply need not be educators, but they do need a background in program evaluation and an ability to get along with people. The salary is substantial and training is provided. Educational leaders in both England and Scotland take inspection seriously. The government charges Her Majesty's Inspectors with the responsibility to review schools and report on the quality of education offered, the use of resources, and the spiritual, moral, social, and cultural development of pupils in the school (*Framework for the Inspection of Schools,* 1993). Inspectors establish clear standards for schools and make them available in printed form. The process of inspection differs somewhat in England and Scotland, however.

In England, Her Majesty's Inspectors enter a school for a week, inspect all aspects of the school operation, and then report to the board of governors and parents. Indicators guide the inspection, including indicators pertaining to school data and indicators requiring the judgment of the Inspectors. Inspectors visit classes and sample lesson plans (*Framework for the Inspection of Schools,* 1993).

Inspectors that encounter a school considered at risk or likely to fail report the school to the Department for Education. The department notifies the head teacher and governors of deficiencies and the need for improvement. Eventually, improvement is necessary or the Department for Education can disband the school. In Scotland, Her Majesty's Inspectors adopted procedures of the Southern Association, an accrediting agency in the United States. Each Scottish school must develop a school improvement plan before Her Majesty's Inspectors arrive on the scene. The school improvement plan forms the basis for inspection, and Inspectors hold local educators responsible for the implementation of the plan. The Scottish Education Office wishes inspection to be non-threatening and the responsibility of the local unit. American influence on Scottish inspection poses an interesting scenario.

Government leaders considered school inspection shameful until 1989 when an audit of inspection procedures brought impetus to a new system of inspection. A new and powerful Chief Inspector of Schools subjects all schools to regular and rigorous inspection.

IMPLICATIONS

The four themes driving British education reform have implications for educational reform in the United States, for each British reform theme is currently a theme in the restructuring efforts of schools in the United States. In order of their British presentation, the implications are as follows.

National Curriculum

Theme number one, national curriculum, appears to have reached a level of acceptance in Britain in four years. Educational leaders in the United States should pursue national curriculum quickly and decisively. Educators should write curriculum after consultation with business leaders and parents if the public expects teachers to accept national curriculum. Curricula developers should develop macro objectives rather than micro objectives so that the curriculum is concise yet broad enough to allow local adaptation. Suggestions for implementing the curriculum should accompany the objectives as well as opportunities for staff orientation and staff development. While federal officials can only suggest the use of national curriculum in the fifty states, incentives can make implementation desirable. As much as possible in a democratic country, the process should remain free of political entanglements and prohibit interference from special interest groups, who have a track record of interfering with curriculum development. The federal government should legally protect curriculum development from these forces if possible. Curriculum development and implementation must be a nonnegotiable item for teacher unions. Teachers and administrators cannot negotiate learning, for learning requires a cooperative effort among teachers, administrators, and parents; and negotiations cause adversarial relations among these groups.

National Testing

Theme number two, national testing, has met with obstacles in Britain that the United States can avoid. In the United States, the same group of educators that design the curriculum should develop the tests that measure the curriculum. Each subject area test should align with curriculum objectives, so teachers are clear about the test content. Tests should not be secret documents that surprise teachers and students and encourage a certain percentage of failure. National tests should test achievement and progress on the national curriculum. Educators should use test results to evaluate the effectiveness of the instructional program and the achievement of individual students.

Test preparation in the United States must avoid the past practice of testing too often and testing for the wrong purpose. Teachers should administer tests at a natural time in the learning experience of the child—when the child completes the experience tested. Testing twice during the student's school progress matches the world class standard for national testing. The testing sequence could include one test scheduled at the conclusion of the fifth or sixth grade and a second test scheduled at the conclusion of the tenth grade. This sequence does not provide a national test to determine admission to higher education. The SAT and ACT presently serve the educational establishment and can continue to help sort students for higher education. School leaders should delay the administration until grade twelve, however. At all other times, teachers should be able to test national curriculum at the point where it is most natural and least stressful.

Finally, politicians should avoid using test results to compare schools and to compare teachers. Newspapers should not publish test results, and only educators should make comparisons. The media need not publish test results, and only educators should receive comparison data. The public should hold school administrators accountable for test results in their own system, and accountability should mean correcting situations where test results indicate poor teaching and stunted student learning.

Local Control

Theme three involves the movement toward local control of schools, or *site-based management,* as educators have coined the movement in the United States. American educators and legislators talk about the importance of site-based management as opposed to the legislated learning of the 1980s and early 1990s, but little action results from the dialogue. Talk is cheap, and the educational establishment must take leadership in the promotion of site-based management of schools. School leaders have little to lose. Local management in the United States means transmitting power to the local school system, not to each individual school as is the case in Britain. But the local school district must delegate the new power to each individual school, or the movement bears little fruit. Local superintendents need only look to the British model to understand that the superintendency is not absolutely necessary for a school to operate. Granted some states are closer to site-based management than others, but all states should follow this practice.

State legislators must remove responsibility for budgeting, instruction, personnel, and building and grounds from the state house and place responsibility with the LEA. In turn, the LEA should pass appropriate power to the building. Since the board of education is also political, power should transfer only after the law requires local school boards to be more broad-based in membership. Local boards must disband, and new boards must be created that include administrators, teachers, parents, and perhaps students.

Site-based management can only be successful if local educators can assume responsibility for leadership. Britain did not provide the opportunity for head teachers to assume their new role; and the United States must make that provision for superintendents, principals, and teachers. Site-based management can be successful if the nation commits to its use and prepares its educational leaders to assume responsibility for educating America's youth.

Accountability

The final British reform theme is accountability. The other three themes are ineffective if a country does not build accountability into educational restructuring. Choice is an intricate part of British accountability and appears to have little opposition. Since parental choice is an established part of the political agenda in the United States, the practice should continue here as well. Those who structure accountability should not allow the voucher system that accompanies choice, for vouchers benefit school systems that are fortunate enough to have excellent resources and/or private schools that are exempt from the bureaucracy of legislated learning. Politicians who espouse the voucher system seem intent on destroying a public school system that has served America well. The system may need fixing, but it does not deserve the rhetoric that accompanies the promotion of vouchers. Perhaps when government leaders can provide equal funding for schools and equal access to those schools, the leaders can resurrect the voucher system; but in the meantime, they should drop the issue.

The state of Michigan, during the summer of 1993, outlawed the property tax as a method of financing schools. The legislature has yet to choose a replacement for the tax. Michigan legislators have a chance to seriously reform educational finance and equalize funding. The initiative bears watching.

Americans should look closely at the British inspection system. The recent commitment to quality inspection has produced procedures that are thorough and clearly articulated to public school educators. Each state should adopt such a commitment and a procedure to actualize that commitment. Too many schools exist in the United States that do not produce a high level of student achievement, and too many administrators and teachers fail to provide quality instruction. Each state should identify these slackers and replace them with quality schools and educators. This will be difficult to accomplish, however, until all schools operate on a level playing field. The outcome of accountability is schools equal in terms of resources and accessibility.

AFTERTHOUGHT

British educational reform offers Americans a glimpse of the future. The themes of British reform are the same themes that have become a major ingredient of the American reform movement. Britain is trying new approaches to education, and the United States is not far behind. The United States must learn from those who precede us.

REFERENCES

Allan, J. 1993. Interview (June 11).

Allan, T. 1993. Interview (June 17).

Bedborough, B. 1993. Interview (June 18).

Boyd, B. 1993. Interview (June 18).

Carim, E. 1993. Interview (June 21).

Choice and Diversity: A New Framework for Schools. 1992. Presented to Parliament by the Secretaries of State for Education in England and Wales by Command of Her Majesty. London: Department for Education and the Welsh Office.

Dunsdon, C. 1993. Interview (June 14).

Education in Britain. 1991. United Kingdom: Produced for the Foreign and Commonwealth Office by the Central Office of Information. Upton Park, Slough, Berkshire: National Foundation for Educational Research in England and Wales.

Fisher, J. 1993. Interview (June 14).

Framework for the Inspection of Schools. 1993. Issued by Her Majesty's Chief Inspector of Schools in England. London: Office for Standards in Education. Reprinted by permission of the Office for Standards in Education.

Franchi, N. 1993. Interview (June 15).

Grant-Maintained Schools, 1989 – 92. 1993. A Report from the Office of Her Majesty's Chief Inspector of Schools. London: Office for Standards in Education. Material reproduced by permission of the Controller of Her Britannic Majesty's Stationery Office.

Grant-Maintained Schools, 1993 – 94 Funding Worksheet. 1993. London: Department for Education.

Grant-Maintained Schools: Questions Parents Ask. 1992. London: Department for Education.

Grant-Maintained Schools: Questions Staff Ask. 1992. London: Department for Education.

Griffiths, B. and K. Slater. 1993. Interview (June 11).

Griffiths, J. 1993. Interview (June 21).

The Implementation of Local Management of Schools: A Report by H.M. Inspectorate, 1989–92. 1992. London: Department for Education Information Branch. Material reproduced by permission of the Controller of Her Britannic Majesty's Stationery Office.

MacBeath, J., E. McCaig and B. Thompson. 1992. *Making School Boards Work.* A Study of School Boards Commissioned by the Scottish Office and Carried Out by the MVA Consultancy and the Quality in Education Centre. University of Strathclyde Centre, Jordanhill Campus, Southbrae Drive, Glasgow G131.

Madaus, G. and Kellaghan. 1993. "The British Experience with Authentic Testing," *Phi Delta Kappan,* pp. 458–469.

McAdams, R. P. 1993. *Lessons from Abroad: How Other Countries Educate Their Children.* Lancaster, Pennsylvania: Technomic Publishing Company, Inc.

McCutcheon, B. 1993. Interview (June 14).

McGlynn, A. 1993. Interview (June 18).

Parker, F. and B. Parker. 1991. *Education in England and Wales.* New York: Garland Publishing, Incorporated.

Pearson, J. 1993. Interview (June 15).

School Governors: How to Become a Grant-Maintained School. 1991. London: Department of Education and Science.

Singh, J. 1993. Interview (June 11).

Chapter 13

AN AMERICAN BLUEPRINT FOR WORLD CLASS SCHOOLS

A blueprint is a detailed plan for achieving some large undertaking. Developing American world class schools is certainly such a large undertaking. The authors draw on research presented in previous chapters, to present a blueprint for achieving world class American Schools.

World Class Standards
American Schools

United States citizens talk about world class schools but fail to define world class. If the definition is to be first in all categories, American citizens must ask, "Do Americans really *want* to be first in *all* categories of world class schooling?" The authors think not. World class means a longer school year, more demands on students, more homework, national curriculum and testing, and other conditions often rejected by educators and parents. If being first is not the goal, should not America's schools at least meet the world class standards developed in the preceding chapters? This suggestion appears more practical. Americans should make decisions about changing their schools deliberately, with one eye on world class standards and one eye on practicality.

Following are suggestions for building world class American schools in the form of input standards. Together, the suggestions form a blueprint for establishing world class education in America's schools. The reader can accept or reject each suggestion based on its practicality. If Americans are not ready to accept world class standards, however, Americans should not use the term loosely.

BLUEPRINT FOR WORLD CLASS FINANCING OF AMERICA'S SCHOOLS

1. The federal government must fund programs at the preschool level, continue to fund compensatory education and special education, and initiate funding to support the improvement of urban education.

Preschool education for children and parents must increase in the United States if education is to become world class. France is the world class model. Children must report to school ready to learn. Compensatory education is also a necessity in the United States, for too many children fall behind and never catch up. Hopefully the preschool initiative will reduce the need for compensatory education; but until that happens, improved literacy requires federal funding.

Special education funding must continue, but the federal government must rethink the Education for All Handicapped Act. Since the introduction of the act, educators have certified too many students as handicapped, creating a huge per-pupil expenditure that drains the education coffers. Educators should also resolve the problem of integrating special education students into regular classrooms because the argument reflects poorly on the educational system.

Urban or inner-city education requires federal intervention if the country expects progress. The problem is too big for the states.

Federal funding should return to the pre-Reagan level of 9 percent. If politicians must cut funding to maintain the 9 percent federal funding level, grant programs that fund innovative practices must go. The contribution of innovative programs remains questionable, for education still looks very much like it did fifty years ago.

2. The United States at all levels should maintain the 1988 level of educational spending, which is about 6.8 percent of GNP.

The current level of spending is well above the world class standard, but spending must remain above the standard to meet the cultural demands of education in the United States.

The demands placed on America's schools and the public's reluctance to change those demands make education in the United States more costly than it is in other nations. American citizens demand a broad curriculum, a broad extracurricular program, and extensive student services. Most important, Americans must pay more because of the presence of disruptive students and the goal of keeping students in school at any cost.

3. State legislators must immediately address inequities in funding for education so that pupils have equal access to educational dollars.

Why does a nation as great as the United States permit a broad range of per-pupil expenditure? Overall, per-pupil funding in the United States is world class, but the differences from local district to local district are intolerable. School leaders in under-funded districts must sue to gain equality in one state after another. It is a sad commentary for a democratic society when citizens must sue their own lawmakers to achieve equality. Failure of any state to equalize funding should result in federal intervention as a corrective measure, much as the federal government intervened to insure integration of schools.

4. The property tax is no longer a fair and equitable means of financing education, and the states must limit the use of property taxes to support schools.

Sound economic theory and practice should dictate school financing. A summit of state educational leaders and economists should gather to develop a blueprint for financing education. The blueprint should relieve educators from the responsibility of requesting yearly increases in local property tax. Michigan recently outlawed property tax as a means of funding education, and other states should watch the results.

BLUEPRINT FOR ESTABLISHING WORLD CLASS AMERICAN TIME ON TASK

1. The school year is too short. A minimum student school year should be 200 days. The school year for teachers should be at least 220 days.

This is a change that many Americans simply do not want. But the amount of time provided for learning must increase if the United States is to compete with the learning outcomes of students in other nations. The salary of teachers must be increased as the school year lengthens, and this change should be phased in at a rate of five days per year over a four-year period. Saturday classes will not work in the United States.

2. The length of the instructional day should be increased by assigning homework to lengthen the amount of learning time in the student's day.

A longer day in school is not needed. In fact the United States is so obsessed with learning time that even small children have little time to enjoy themselves or their school. The eastern Pacific Rim countries count an "hour" of instruction as forty-five to fifty minutes for early childhood instruction. They also have festival and other "play days" in their school year, which leaves time for enjoyment along with time to prepare for the next standardized test.

School systems that opt for greater use of homework as part of the teaching-learning continuum should have a well-understood board of education policy on minimum amounts of homework per night. It would be best to inform parents through a homework guide that there will always be a minimum amount of reading homework each night. There should be a clear understanding that parents have responsibility to help their children learn.

Staff development for teachers in the use, purpose, and effect of homework should precede the increase in homework. Carefully designed, schoolwide strategies for assigning homework should be designed so that teachers don't gang up with too many assignments in one night.

3. The number of hours of instruction in a school year should be carefully studied.

Perhaps a better approach to immediately expanding the instructional year would be to study the experiment with year-round schools. Having nine- or ten-week quarters in the school year with extra time for remediation and enrichment makes more sense than the lengthy summer break American schools now offer. The amount of learning loss, particularly among students from less affluent homes, means that precious learning time is squandered on reteaching forgotten skills.

4. The years covered by compulsory attendance should be expanded into earlier years, and the year when compulsory education ends should be reviewed.

Most American schools show nearly 100 percent enrollment in kindergarten before compulsory attendance takes effect. All students at age five should be in compulsory school programs, perhaps for a shorter school day than others. Education before age five is also world class and should be provided in the United States.

There needs to be an examination of why age sixteen is so important.

At one time, compulsory attendance and child labor laws end and driving begins. So, too, does the idea of working to support a car begin, making the car more important than school. The right to drive and the right to leave school shouldn't occur on the same day.

BLUEPRINT FOR ESTABLISHING WORLD CLASS AMERICAN CLASS SIZE

1. Each state should establish an average class size figure based on the world class standard. The world class standard for thirteen-year-old students is twenty-nine. An option is the establishment of the following pupil-teacher ratio: primary—twenty-two to one—and secondary—sixteen to one. The pupil-teacher ratio, however, includes all educators in the district and all students.

Providing a class size small enough to raise student achievement is beyond the financial capacity of the United States. Besides, students achieve well in countries with class sizes much larger than in the United States. The Asian countries provide the world class standard. Before class size can be increased to levels found in the Asian countries, however, cultural expectations for United States students must change.

2. Since the world class standard for average class size is larger than current average class size in American schools, class size may increase. However, educational decision makers should only use funds saved by increasing class size to release teachers from such mundane duties such as lunch duty and bus duty.

United States teachers spend more time on nonclassroom supervision than teachers in most world class countries. Each state legislator should study the teacher's day in the European countries and establish professional standards for their teachers. American teachers waste time eating lunch with students, guarding restrooms, and walking the halls. No other occupation requires employees to perform such demeaning tasks. American teachers need more planning time.

BLUEPRINT FOR ESTABLISHING WORLD CLASS AMERICAN TEACHERS

1. The United States needs to continue its efforts to increase the years of preparation required for teacher certification.

The United States is world class in teacher preparation, but other nations are closing the gap. The United States should consider and fund a five-year preparation program for teachers.

In recommending this step, the authors specifically do not recommend higher pay for upper secondary teachers than for elementary teachers. However, higher pay for greater preparation needs to be provided. Using scholarships and pay incentives is appropriate.

The United States currently sets the world class standard for preparation of school administrators. Many countries still lack such a program.

2. *The pay of American educators needs to be increased.*

This is the most predictable item on the blueprint! One way to do this effectively would be to increase the span from starting teachers' pay to career veterans' pay. The enormous salary differentials between affluent and poor school systems need to be eradicated.

Attempts to reward effective teachers need to be expanded. There is no question that some teachers deserve more than others based on educational output. One way to increase salaries for the most effective teachers is to establish a higher level of certification that, like a driver's license, needs to be proficiency-proven after a set period of time. Merit pay is suspect as a means of increasing teacher output.

3. *National standards of teacher certification need to be established.*

This effort is already well under way. It simply should not be illegal to smuggle a teacher across state lines. This effort should be combined with the attempt to establish a national curriculum and a national school system. Just as there should be a national definition of what it means to be an educated American, so should there be a single definition of what it means to be a licensed teacher.

This will be a difficult process, and those who undertake it are well advised to keep the standards simple enough to be obtainable. Likewise, any cost associated with national teacher certification needs to paid by the LEA, not by the teacher.

BLUEPRINT FOR ESTABLISHING WORLD CLASS AMERICAN STUDENT BEHAVIOR

1. *Homework is world class, and teachers must be required to include meaningful homework assignments in lesson plans.*

The homework debate must end, for homework is world class. Appropriate homework should start at the beginning of the elementary experience and increase in intensity throughout the elementary and secondary experience. The standard for secondary students should be approximately two hours per day. Homework guidelines should become part of the professional knowledge base for teachers. Teacher training institutes can instill a homework ethic in prospective teachers, and local schools can follow with required homework policy.

2. Students must limit television watching.

The world class standard suggests the following: (1) remove the television set from the student's room, (2) restrict television watching to time remaining after the completion of homework, (3) allow students to select only one hour of prime time television during the school week. Students can and do control their own television habits in other world class countries. Canada can serve as a model.

3. The United States must increase school completion significantly to equal the world class standard.

Society must establish school completion as the number one priority in a child's life. The goal must be the creation of students intent on finishing school. Adults in society can help by establishing the following world class activities:

(*1*) Adults should stop the negative talk about school and start talking positively about the importance of school. Positive talk and follow-up praise for a student's accomplishments will maintain a positive school outlook.

(*2*) Teachers and parents should teach students to set goals that insist on the completion of schooling and should reject goals that involve early school leaving.

(*3*) Significant adults should remove activities that seduce students away from school and destroy interest in school.

Adults should demand that legislators raise the driving age to seventeen or eighteen, and that school leaders discourage driving to school. Restrict work hours for students until age eighteen, rather than sixteen. Most world class countries have these restrictions. The behavior of many adults makes school-leaving seem cool for students rather than a disaster.

4. Give school officials the right and responsibility to remove disruptive students from America's classrooms.

The behavior of many American students is disgraceful and wastes the time of teachers and students prepared to learn. Violence is too common in school, and conditions often reduce educators to the role of policemen. Educational leaders should send disruptive students home until the behavior changes or to alternative schools where trained experts can change behavior. America will soon have excessive space in military installations, so why not use the space and military personnel for alternative experiences for disruptive youth? The idea might sound drastic; but American students, as a whole, are far below the world class standard for student behavior, and drastic changes are necessary.

BLUEPRINT FOR ESTABLISHING WORLD CLASS AMERICAN CURRICULUM

1. The United States needs a national curriculum framework that is flexible enough to meet local education needs yet specific enough to create common skill development for all American school children.

This recommendation falls in the category of easier said than done. The substantial work by many professional organizations in education started the effort to develop a subject-specific national curriculum. To develop a national curriculum, there must be one national education authority that stipulates the curriculum framework and defines the relative balance of content areas within the curriculum framework. The work of the various professional education associations should be used when appropriate.

When agencies develop the national curriculum, there should be four guiding principles:

(*1*) The national curriculum framework should be simple and written void of educational jargon. It should be a document parents and business leaders can read and understand.

(*2*) The same group that develops the national curriculum framework should use the concept developed by the National Assessment of Educational Progress and write an aligned set of tests designed to assess the mastery of the national curriculum framework. Examples of student mastery should be included in the framework so that parents and teachers can commonly discuss the progress of a specific student.

(*3*) The national curriculum framework should be designed for no more than three-quarters of the time allotted for teaching. The use of the remaining time should be determined by the local education authority in order to meet the particular needs of local students.

(4) The inevitable questions about educational access should be eliminated from the discussions about the national curriculum framework. Such questions need separate answers.

2. The curriculum should include ethics and moral education.

This is not a call for religious education, given the mosaic of religious beliefs held by constituent groups in America. There appears to be a common misconception among many American educators that the United States Supreme Court's prohibition against teaching religion means that simple principles like right and wrong, love of country, and opposition to violence can't be taught. They can and should be, even though this will be a controversial area.

3. The curriculum designed for students exceeding the compulsory attendance years should be carefully studied. The comprehensive high school may not provide the best design in all settings. Those students who fail to master appropriate school-leaving skills should be required to stay in school part-time until they master the skills defined for exit. These students should be compelled to attend school until they reach age eighteen.

Special purpose schools such as vocational education schools for selected vocations should be designed and built in conjunction with community/junior colleges. This would ease the transfer into these colleges and greatly increase the use of expensive equipment used in classes like high-tech auto mechanics. Other schools developed somewhat like magnet schools might be academically specialized. This could facilitate a choice system. Transportation to these schools should be the responsibility of the student, except for those who are financially limited. For this group, a travel voucher could be explored.

For students who fail to meet school-leaving standards, the diploma could be withheld. Extended child labor laws should restrict the amount of work these students are allowed to do until they either pass a school-leaving examination or reach age eighteen.

BLUEPRINT FOR ESTABLISHING WORLD CLASS AMERICAN STUDENT ASSESSMENT

1. National testing should be developed and required of all students at two levels of schooling: (1) at the completion of the elementary years at about age twelve, and (2) at the completion of mandatory schooling at age sixteen.

National testing logically follows the implementation of a national curriculum. Assigning test development to the same group preparing national curriculum will help align tests with national curriculum objectives. The best and brightest of the teaching profession should prepare national tests, with business leaders and politicians playing only a consultative role. Local teachers should score the tests. Educators should use the results of the elementary test to assess student achievement and guide placement in the secondary experience. Educators should use results of the secondary test to assess student achievement and guide placement in vocational programs or college preparatory programs. Both programs should offer intensive and meaningful instruction that national tests measure.

American educational decision makers must be careful not to establish testing at too many levels or age groups. Successful world class nations test only at two or three levels. The English testing initiative offers a meaningful lesson to Americans—don't overtest. Germany seems to have the best model for the United States. The American public has a fixation on testing, to the point where testing lacks meaning and the confidence of educators. America needs realistic student assessment.

2. Once Americans implement national testing at the two levels mentioned above, a future goal of American education should be the development of a national test administered to students completing the twelfth grade college preparatory program. Until designees develop the new national test, the SAT or the ACT can continue as tests determining entrance to higher education.

Excellent models for the higher education entrance exam include the French *baccalaureat,* German *Abitur,* and the English GCE A level test. The test should measure subject matter taught in the school. The test should be available to all American students desiring further education, but a passing mark should be a requirement for university admission. Students who do not receive a passing grade can retake the exam at a later date or enroll in a two-year college.

3. All tests, other than national achievement tests, should be the responsibility of the local school.

Teachers can test student progress on national curriculum at a more natural time when the student is ready. This seems particularly appropriate at the elementary level. Teachers must learn how to develop world class tests and proper use of testing results. Locally prepared test results should be used to assess student achievement, diagnose problems, and provide remediation or enrichment indicated by the test results. Educational decision makers should resolve the controversy created by the use of test results to evaluate teaching. Student achievement should provide one measure of a teacher's effectiveness, but administrators and teachers familiar with the teacher and the teacher's students should make the judgment. Test results of local tests and national tests should remain privileged information available only to professional school officials. The media need not receive test scores. Parents should have access to their student's results and receive a fair assessment of the student's ability and progress as compared to other students.

4. Local tests and national tests should extend beyond multiple choice testing as much as possible. Almost every world class country requires essay testing, demonstrations, and oral examinations.

Time is a consideration when considering the format of tests. Educators object to tests that require large blocks of time and take time away from instruction. Educational leaders must find an acceptable practice. Teachers can often assess student achievement by having students demonstrate competence or orally recite information. The public, however, must trust this assessment and not insist on a score simply because they received a score during their schooling.

Other countries successfully use essay testing. French teachers use essay tests early in the school experience and continue essay testing through the *baccalaureat* level. American teachers should examine the French experience.

Tests should not be secret documents with content unknown by teachers and students. Both parties should be familiar with test content and have the experience of practice on simulated questions.

The testing program proposed can be a serious tool to motivate American students. Similar programs in other nations successfully motivate students to achieve, and the idea that testing in other nations causes severe student stress is a myth. American students can cope with high expectations, as well as foreign students.

BLUEPRINT FOR ESTABLISHING WORLD CLASS AMERICAN EDUCATION GOVERNANCE

1. The United States cannot afford the fragmented, decentralized, and imbalanced governance that results from the nonstandardized school systems in the United States.

Educators must view their classes as containing the only next generation in America. There must be a single national education agency that sets standards, monitors equity, and reports the educational progress of the next generation. The incredible inequity that exists within the current American education system cannot be tolerated. To be effective, this agency should also assure a similar standard of funding for all schools.

2. The interests of local parents cannot be completely ignored in the name of national education standards.

Based on the needs of an individual school, school governance involving parents at the individual school needs to be increased. This should only occur when parents and the community at large assume responsibility for students and their learning outcomes. When involving parents in school governance, educators should also involve parents in the development of the school outcomes. Given the diverse nature of America's work force, the first step could involve educators going to the parents' workplace instead of always expecting parents to come to school.

3. Because the public must accept and support the graduates of private schools, there should be minimum standards set for private education that closely parallel the minimum standards set for public education.

The right of parents to elect private schools must be preserved, but not at the expense of providing an inferior education in the name of choice. The state should establish basic standards for teachers, curriculum, and testing for all schools. Many private schools easily exceed such standards, but those that fail to meet them should be closed.

BLUEPRINT FOR ESTABLISHING WORLD CLASS AMERICAN PARENTS, HOME ENVIRONMENT, AND COMMUNITIES

1. The United States Department of Education should target the world class standard of 97 percent literacy for citizens in the United States.

World Class countries charge the primary school with the objective of literacy. The European countries are near the 100 percent mark for adult literacy, and the United States is well below the European standard. A goal of the American elementary school should be the improvement of literacy to the 97 percent level. Students possessing the ability to attain literacy should remain at the elementary level until basically literate; but until this level of literacy becomes reality, adult literacy programs must continue.

2. Quality parenting should become a priority of the federal, state, and local government in the United States.

Parents are the child's first teachers, and their success usually determines the success of the child in school. In every country where children report to school ready to learn, schooling is successful. The United States has a more troubled family environment than that encountered in other world class countries. The American divorce rate is much higher, the incidence of unwed mothers is disturbing, and child abuse is alarming. The nation must cope with these social problems that threaten the future of the nation's most valuable resource — its children.

Citizens cannot blame schools for the deplorable conditions existing in many homes and the excess baggage children bring to school. Schools, in fact, do an admirable job with students bearing the scars of a hurtful home environment. Schools must be part of the solution, but social agencies, churches, business establishments, and other public institutions must assume more responsibility for the solution. Parenting skills should really be taught well before marriage or the child-bearing years, and parenting instruction must include activities that prepare a child for school. Parents and other significant adults must teach children to value school, teachers, and the joy of learning. Adults must teach students to set goals and work hard toward the accomplishment of those goals. Most of all, parents must instill discipline in the child's daily routine, since discipline is a prerequisite for successful learning.

Restructuring schools will not produce World Class American Schools unless citizens agree to restructure society.

3. Local school districts should develop a parents' charter that clearly indicates the responsibility of the school to parents and the responsibility of the parents to the school.

The British "Parents' Charter," modified in England and Scotland presents a good model for the implementation of this suggestion. The American version should follow the Scottish model, however, and include the parents' responsibility to the school.

4. Parents should turn off the television set and turn children on to reading and learning about the world about them.

A world class recommendation dealing with television watching appears in the student section, but the parent must set the stage for insuring the success of the recommendation. Parents must turn off the television set at an early age and substitute reading activities and learning experiences. When the child starts school, the television should remain off until homework is complete. Parents should model activities other than television watching.

Viewers have documented excessive violence on television and the detrimental effect of violence on the values of youth. Too many children watch television without the guidance of the parent, and too many parents use the television to entertain the child. Limited television exposure will pay dividends in school achievement.

5. Society must look carefully at the social decay of family and community values and instill sanctions against antisocial behaviors.

There is no good method to legislate a return to productive family and community values, but national and local leaders should broadcast again and again the damaging effects of such lax values on children. The United States must face the fact that dysfunctional families deter the development of world class schools. Every other recommendation for world class status depends on the installation of sound, moral values in the lives of children. Do not always expect educators to be able to turn around students who lack a values structure. Educators accomplish a great deal with dysfunctional youth but need help. Americans must learn that the advertised failure of America's schools is, in reality, the failure of society to instill an education ethic in the lives of students.

6. While establishing world class education, Americans should establish high expectations for students.

Data do not support the idea that school pressure leads to depression and perhaps suicide among the student population. American students will adjust to high expectations, challenging curriculum, and tests that measure achievement. Students and school experts from the world class countries both refute the contention that foreign students are unhappy with the school environment. Students can thrive on achievement and the accomplishment of significant goals.

7. Educators must not let negative people stand in the way of quality education. Negative people in the United States love to bash education with a mind closed to reality. American educators should be proactive in labeling negative thinkers. Educators must emphasize the positive and ignore the negative minority.

The school leader's energies should focus on improved learning and growth—goals too important to let negative people stand in the way.

Negative thinking about schools comes from negative people. Educators must emphasize the positive in schools and bring positive people to the forefront where they will set the tone for the thinking majority (Chalker and Hurley, 1993).

EPILOGUE

America, like all nations, has an educational system controlled by cultural values and individual or group desires. Education serves American society well; but society is sometimes a fickle education partner, blaming educators for a variety of societal problems well beyond the control of the school. The authors propose, therefore, that Americans have an educational system that Americans seek and deserve. If Americans seek world class education, Americans must be willing and able to make changes that reflect world class education. If we are not able or willing to make those changes, we must make the best of what we have.

American citizens who call for world class schools must then provide the nurturing society required for world class status. In America, everything is possible. The country is a world leader—a condition made possible by the educational system. World class schools are possible if people look carefully at world class standards and adjust accordingly. A world class effort will produce world class schools.

REFERENCE

Chalker, D. and J. C. Hurley. 1993. "Beastly People," *Executive Educator,* 15(1): 24–26.

SUGGESTED READING

The National Council on Education Standards and Testing. 1992. *Raising Standards for American Education—A Report to Congress, the Secretary of Education, the National Education Goals Panel, and the American People.* Washington, D.C.: United States Government Printing Office.

Assessment, Recording and Reporting: Third Year, 1991—92. 1993. A Report from the Office of Her Majesty's Chief Inspector of Schools, London: Office for Standards in Education.

Baker, L. 1992. Preparation, Induction and Support for Newly Appointed Headteachers and Deputy Heads. Slough, England: National Foundation for Educational Research in England and Wales.

Butterfield, F. 1992. "Why They Excel," *Parade Magazine.*

Caplan, N., M. Choy and J. Whitmore. 1992. "Indo-Chinese Refugee Families and Academic Achievement," *Scientific American.*

Chalker, D. 1992. "Refocusing School Leadership for the 21st Century Across the Board," *The Education Digest,* 58(3):4—8 (Condensed from *Thresholds in Education,* 1992, pp. 26—30).

Chalker, D. and J. C. Hurley. 1993. "Beastly People," *Executive Educator,* 15(1):24—26.

Chapman, R. 1986. *New Dictionary of American Slang.* New York: Harper & Row, Publishers, p. 473.

Choice and Diversity: A New Framework for Schools. 1992. Presented to Parliament by the Secretaries of State for Education and Wales by Command of Her Majesty, London: Department for Education and the Welsh Office.

Chubb, J. E. and T. M. Moe. 1990. *Politics, Markets, and America's Schools.* Washington, D.C.: The Brookings Institute.

Demographics Yearbook. 1990. New York: Department of Economics and Social Affairs Statistical Office, United Nations.

Education in Britain. 1991. United Kingdom: Produced for the Foreign and Commonwealth Office by the Central Office of Information. Upton Park, Slough, Berkshire: National Foundation for Educational research in England and Wales.

Education in Canada. 1989. Ottawa, Canada: External Communications Division, External Affairs and International Trade Canada.

Education at a Glance. 1992. Paris, France: Organisation for Economic Cooperation and Development.

Education in Korea, 1991—92. 1992. Seoul, Korea: National Institute of Educational Research and Training, Ministry of Education.

Education in New Zealand. 1991. Wellington, New Zealand: Ministry of Education.

Education Statistics of New Zealand. 1991. Wellington, New Zealand: Research and Statistics Division, Ministry of Education.

English, F. 1993. Cullowhee, North Carolina: Ainsley Lecture in School Administration, Western Carolina University.

Epstein, I. 1985. *Taiwan.* New York: Facts on File Publications.

Fishman, S. 1993. "Germany: Education," *Encyclopedia Americana. Vol. 12,* Danbury, Connecticut: Grolier, Inc., pp. 621—625.

Framework for the Inspection of Schools. 1993. Issued by Her Majesty's Chief Inspector of Schools in England. London: Office for Standards in Education.

Franklin, S. H. 1985. "New Zealand," *Encyclopedia Americana. Vol. 20,* Danbury, Connecticut: Grolier Inc.

Grant-Maintained Schools, 1989—92. 1993. A Report from the Office of Her Majesty's Chief Inspector of Schools. London: Office for Standards in Education.

Grant-Maintained Schools, 1993—94 Funding Worksheet. 1993. London: Department for Education.

Grant-Maintained Schools: Questions Parents Ask. 1992. London: Department for Education.

Grant-Maintained Schools: Questions Staff Ask. 1992. London: Department for Education.

Her Majesty's Inspectorate. 1992. *Teaching and Learning in Japanese Elementary Schools.* Edinburgh: The Scottish Office, Education Department.

Herzog, M. J. 1993. "The Group," *Democracy and Education,* pp. 37—41.

Hess, R. D. and H. Azuma. 1991. "Cultural Support for Schooling. Contrasts between Japan and the United States," *Educational Researcher.*

Hirsch, C. R., ed. 1992. *Curriculum and Evaluation Standards for School Mathematics.* Reston, Virginia: National Council of Teachers of Mathematics.

Holmes, B., ed. 1983. *International Handbook of Education Systems. Vol. 3.* New York: John Wiley and Son.

Hurley, J. C. 1993. "The Organizational Socialization of Rural High School Principals: Teacher Influences," *Journal of Research in Rural Education,* 8(2):20—31.

The Implementation of Local Management of Schools: A Report by H.M. Inspectorate, 1989—92. 1992. London: Department for Education Information Branch.

International Comparisons in Education—Curriculum, Values, and Lessons. Circa 1992. Alberta, Canada: Alberta Chamber of Resources in Partnership with Alberta Department of Education.

Ishizaka, K. Circa 1990. *School Education in Japan.* Toyko: International Society for Educational Information, Inc., Reference Series 5.

Jaeger, R. M. 1992. "World Class Standards, Choice, and Privatization: Weak Measurement Serving Presumptive Policy," *Phi Delta Kappan,* 74(2):118—128.

Jonen, G. and H. Roche, eds. 1992. *The Educational System in the Federal Republic of Germany.* Bonn, Germany: Foreign Office of the Federal Republic of Germany.

Kim, J. E. 1985. *South Korea.* New York: Facts on File Publications.

Kozul, J. 1991. *Savage Inequalities: Children in America's Schools.* New York: Crown Publishers, Inc.

Kurian, G. T., ed. 1988. *World Education Encyclopedia. Vol. 3.* New York: Facts on File Publications.

Lamley, H. 1985. "Taiwan," *Encyclopedia Americana. Vol. 26,* Danbury, Connecticut: Grolier Inc.

Lapointe, A. E., J. M. Askew and N. A. Mead. 1992. *Learning Science.* Princeton, New Jersey: The International Assessment of Educational Progress, Educational Testing Service.

Lapointe, A. E., N. Mead and J. Askew. 1992. *Learning Mathematics.* Princeton, New Jersey: Educational Testing Service.

MacBeath, J., E. McCaig and B. Thompson. 1992. *Making School Boards Work.* A Study of School Boards Commissioned by the Scottish Office and Carried out by the MVA Consultancy and the Quality in Education Centre. Jordanhill: University of Strathclyde, Faculty of Education, Jordanhill Campus.

Madaus, G. and Kellaghan. 1993. ''The British Experience with Authentic Testing," *Phi Delta Kappan," pp. 458–469.*

McAdams, R. P. 1993. *Lessons from Abroad: How Other Countries Educate Their Children.* Lancaster, Pennsylvania: Technomic Publishing Company.

McLean, M. 1993. ''France: Education," *Encyclopedia Americana. Vol. 11,* New York: Grolier, Inc., pp. 702–705.

Monbusho. circa 1992. Atlanta, Georgia: Monograph by the Ministry of Education, Science and Culture, Consulate of Japan, Atlanta Office.

Monikes, W., ed. 1992. *Inter Nations Bonn.* Bonn, Germany: Inter Nationes, pp. 9–22.

Moody's International Manual. 1991. New York: Moody's Investors Service, Incorporated.

National Center of Education Statistics. 1992. Washington, D.C.: U.S. Government Printing Office.

National Tests: What Other Countries Expect Their Students to Know. 1991. Washington, D.C.: National Endowment for the Humanities.

NEA Mobilizes for Action: Advancing the National Education Agenda. 1991. Washington, D.C.: National Education Association.

Nelson, F. H. 1991. *International Comparison of Public Spending on Education.* Washington, D.C.: Research Department, American Federation of Teachers, AFL-CIO.

Nelson, F. and C. O'Brien. 1993. *How U.S. Teachers Measure up Internationally: A Comparative Study of Teacher Pay, Training, and Conditions of Service.* Washington, D.C.: Research Department, American Federation of Teachers, AFL-CIO.

Neuber, M., ed. 1991. *Inter Nationes Bonn.* Bonn, Germany: Inter Nationes Bonn.

New Zealand Official 1990 Yearbook Extracts. 1990. Washington, D.C.: Education Monograph Provided by the New Zealand Embassy.

North Carolina Statistical Profile. 1992. Raleigh: State of North Carolina.

An Outline of Revision of the Course of Study in Japan. 1992. Tokyo: Ministry of Education, Science and Culture.

The Parents' Charter in Scotland. 1992. Edinburgh, Scotland: The Scottish Office of Education.

Parker, F. and B. Parker. 1991. *Education in England and Wales.* New York: Garland Publishing, Incorporated.

Peterson, A. D. C. 1985. "Continuity and Change in British Education," *Encyclopedia Americana,* Danbury, Connecticut: Grolier, Inc.

Pierre, B. and S. Auvillain, eds. 1991. *Organisation of the French Educational System Leading to the French Baccalaureat.* Washington, D.C.: Embassy of France, Office of Education.

Pittman, R. B. 1993. "The 21st Century and Secondary At-Risk Students: What's Ahead for Teachers in Rural America," a paper presented at the *ACRES National Rural Education Symposium,* Savannah, Georgia.

Preparing for Our Future. 1992. Detroit, Michigan: National Board for Professional Teaching Standards, 1992 Annual Report.

Report on the Development of Education in the Federal Republic of Germany, 1990–1992. 1992. Report of the Federal Republic of Germany for the 43rd Session of the International Conference on Education, September 1992.

Rosemond, J. 1993. "Asian Parents Have Different Set of Assumptions on Child-Rearing," *Asheville Citizen-Times,* (June 24):2C.

Safran, N. 1985. "Israel," *Encyclopedia Americana. Vol. 15,* Danbury, Connecticut: Grolier Incorporated.

School Governors: How to Become a Grant-Maintained School. 1991. London: Department of Education and Science.

Shanker, A. 1993. "Coming to Terms on World-Class Standards," *Education Week.*

Shiina, M. and M. Chonan. 1991. Japan-U.S. Teacher Education Consortium. ERIC Document.

Shirato, I. 1985. "Education in Japan," *Encyclopedia Americana. Vol. 15,* Danbury, Connecticut: Grolier Inc.

Shuker, R. and R. Adams. 1985. *New Zealand.* New York: Facts on File Publications.

Simmer, S. and D. Simmer, eds. 1992. *Facts and Figures about Education & Culture in Israel.* Jerusalem, Israel: State of Israel Ministry of Education and Culture, Publications Department.

Sinclair, K. 1985. "Education and Cultural Life in New Zealand," *Encyclopedia Americana. Vol. 20,* Danbury, Connecticut: Grolier Inc.

Sprinzak, D., E. Bar and D. Levi-Mazloum. 1992. *Facts and Figures about Education and Culture in Israel.* Jerusalem: Ministry of Education and Culture.

Standards and Quality in Scottish Schools, 1991–1992. 1992. Edinburgh, Scotland: The Scottish Office of Education.

Stevenson, H. W. 1992. "Learning from Asian Schools," *Scientific American.*

Stevenson, H. and S. Lee. 1990. *Contexts of Achievement: A Study of American, Chinese, and Japanese Children.* Monographs of the Society for Research in Child Development, Vol. 55, Nos. 1–2, Chicago: University of Chicago Press.

Whitworth, F. E. 1993. "Canada: Education," *Encyclopedia Americana. Vol. 13,* New York: Grolier, Inc., pp. 402–406.

Will, G. F. 1993. "Parent-Pupil Ratio Is Key to Success," *Cleveland Plain Dealer,* (Sept. 12):3C.

The World Almanac and Book of Facts. 1992. New York: World Almanac.

World Education Report. 1991. Paris, France: United Nations Educational, Scientific, and Cultural Organization.

The World in Figures. 1988. Boston: Editorial Information Gathered by Economist, G.K. Hall, Inc.

World Health Statistics Annual. 1991. Geneva, Switzerland: World Health Organization. Zealand Council for Educational Research.

Donald M. Chalker is Associate Professor of Education, Department of Administration and Curriculum, College of Education and Psychology, Western Carolina University. In addition to teaching school leadership courses, he directs the Office of School Services and the Alliance of Business Leaders and Educators, the sponsor of the world class research reported in this book. Dr. Chalker previously served the public schools in Michigan and Ohio as a teacher, counselor, assistant principal, principal, assistant superintendent, and superintendent of schools. He holds a Bachelor's and Master's degree from Kent State University. Dr. Chalker received his doctorate from Wayne State University in 1981. He and his wife, Harriet, have four adult children and four grandchildren.

Richard M. Haynes is Associate Professor of Education, Department of Administration and Curriculum, College of Education and Psychology, Western Carolina University. He also serves as Director of Field Experience and directs a large FIPSE grant that involves university collaboration with the public schools. Dr. Haynes has written five books for young adult readers. He served as a supervisor of humanities and assistant superintendent in North Carolina and was an instructor at both the public school level and community college level in Florida. He received his doctorate from Duke University in 1978. Dr. Haynes and his wife, Dianne, have two daughters — one in high school and the other teaching in the public schools.

Both authors present their research on world class schools nationally. Interested parties can reach the authors at Western Carolina University, Cullowhee, North Carolina 28723 (Phone: 704-227-7415).